THE MEANING OF THE
SALZBURG FESTIVAL

THE MEANING OF THE

SALZBURG FESTIVAL

*Austria as Theater and
Ideology, 1890–1938*

Michael P. Steinberg

Cornell University Press

ITHACA AND LONDON

First published 1990 by Cornell University Press.

International Standard Book Number 0–8014–2362–7
Library of Congress Catalog Card Number 89–42881
Printed in the United States of America
Librarians: Library of Congress cataloging information
appears on the last page of the book.

♾ The paper used in this publication meets the minimum requirements of the American National Standard for Permanence of Paper for Printed Library Materials Z39.48–1984.

Contents

Illustrations

Preface

THIS book analyzes the place in Austrian cultural, intellectual, and political history of the Salzburg Festival, the month-long summer season of opera, theater, and concerts which was inaugurated in 1920 and continues to the present day. Founded only two years after the collapse of the Habsburg Empire, the festival originated not in luxury or in a spirit of pleasure and entertainment but in economic and cultural despair. Its purpose was the rediscovery and reconstitution of a transcendent Austrian cultural heritage which would help to bridge the gulf that separated the empire from the small Austrian republic. The construction of the festival amounted to the construction and assertion of an Austrian identity. The festival thus provides the historian with a paradigm for examining representational and ideological practices in Austria from the late imperial period through the end of the First Republic.

I am concerned here, then, with exploring the historical meaning of the festival. Readers who want a documentary history or a chronology of "who sang what when" can glean that information from Josef Kaut's *Salzburger Festspiele* and from Stephen Gallup's *History of the Salzburg Festival.*[1] This book takes seriously but analyzes criti-

---

1. Josef Kaut, *Die Salzburger Festspiele, 1920–1981* (Salzburg, 1982). This volume contains a concise documentary history, as well as a complete listing of all performances and performers from 1920 through 1980, compiled by Hans Jaklitsch, the director of the Salzburg Festival Archive (the *Festspielhausarchiv*). Stephen Gallup's *History of the Salzburg Festival* (London, 1987) is especially helpful for the post-1945 period, which is not my focus at all.

cally the claim of its founders that the festival provided a model of and for an Austrian national identity; its interpretive path enters that historical dimension where texts and contexts—formal constructions and social processes—converge. The festival was itself a formal construction achieved through a combination, literally, of texts (repertory), performed in a highly ritualized setting. Austrian identity was to be reconstituted through this representational project grounded in theater and ideology. For the Catholic baroque, theatrical artifice provided the language for the assertion that God's world theater (the *theatrum mundi*) revealed itself as comprehensible and controllable. This theatricality and the cosmology it serves have religious origins but secular ramifications, which become dominant in the modern period. In its religious incarnation, theater represents Austria, and Austria represents a divine order and mission. In its modern, secularized incarnation, theater represents Austria, and Austria is held to be an end in itself. Theatricality—a world-view attained through theatrical device—is thus the means toward a national cosmology. More specifically, it is the means through which a national cosmology can be asserted as a formal, cohesive, and absolute totality. Theatricality and totality thus determine the Salzburg Festival ideology. (I use the term *ideology* throughout the book in the narrow sense, in other words to denote a discourse of interests disguised—consciously or not—as a discourse of truth.) The Salzburg ideology and its image of an Austrian totality thus belied the true Austrian predicament, which was one of cultural fragmentation and dissolution. And at a closer look, the construction of the festival itself emerges as a conflicted and fragmented confrontation of the complicated and multifaceted aspects of the maelstrom known as fin-de-siècle Austrian culture.

Between 1890 and 1918, as Carl Schorske has shown, Austrian culture operated not as a coherent system but as a network of confrontations between programs of critical modernism and increasingly dominant forms of political, social, and cultural conservatism.[2] If in general the term *modernism* suggests the affirmation of the future while *conservatism* suggests the desire to reinstate a perceived idea of a more cohesive and secure past, then, more

2. Carl E. Schorske, *Fin-de-siècle Vienna: Politics and Culture* (New York, 1980).

specifically, the term *critical modernism* as it will be used in this book suggests that crucial to the internal development of many formal discourses (including atonal music and psychoanalysis) is a dimension that seeks to criticize and to change political, social, and cultural life. Furthermore, critical modernism posits no absolutes and hence sees no end to processes of social as well as formal change, criticism, and indeterminacy. Conservatism, which also seeks change, tends to do so in terms of a return to an image of absolute value and ultimate stasis.

After 1918 Austrian culture faced the challenge of reclassifying and returning meaning to categories of self-representation that had become meaningless with the fall of the empire: nation, language, religion, history. The conservatism of late Habsburg society, ever more militant as the task of self-definition and self-representation became more desperate, prevailed in the First Republic as well, and the surviving as well as the newly emergent intellectuals faced the choice between, on the one hand, critical modernism and its resulting isolation, and, on the other hand, the momentum of cultural and political reconstruction. The category of "Austria" implied a glorious past, and therefore reconstruction tended toward conservatism. For Hugo von Hofmannsthal, the principal spiritual and institutional founder of the Salzburg Festival, the path to political action and relevance became defined in terms of the conservative drive to reconstitute and render coherent a transcendent Austrian cultural identity and tradition.

Reality was to be reformulated through representation. The Salzburg Festival program (in both senses of the word) was to embody a cultural heritage that in turn would project a reconstituted Austrian totality. This totality, I will argue, was falsely constituted and ideologically determined. It is therefore the contention of this book that an understanding of the Salzburg Festival requires us to discover and to analyze—on the level of the festival itself as well as on the level of the "Austria" to which it refers—the connections between the manifest content of coherence and totality and the latent content of persisting cultural, intellectual, and political conflicts evident in Austria before and after 1918.

The terms *manifest* and *latent content* recall of course the categories of Freudian dream analysis. I choose them deliberately, for two reasons. The first is that the processes of meaning and meaning-making have to be carefully measured against, and often distin-guished and deciphered from, the intentions and interpretations of their own historical agents. If events and representations were self-explanatory, history would need to be nothing other than a journalism of the past. But the intentions and interpretations of historical actors do not necessarily operate with the same perspec-tive as that of the analytical historian. The existence of various levels of meaning implies the need for the analysis of depths, and it is here that principles of psychoanalysis and textual criticism have been of enormous help to cultural history. It follows that the reliabil-ity of such historiographical practice must be judged by how power-fully the patterns of meaning it uncovers generate in turn further historical discovery and understanding. The second reason for my invocation of Freud is my contention that his principles for the interpretation of dreams *are* in fact principles for a critique of ideol-ogy, in other words principles through which the ideological repre-sentation of personal or indeed of cultural experience as a totality can be broken and through which actual, multiple, and conflicting patterns of meaning can be discovered. Furthermore, it is in this essential critique of representation and totality that Freud can be said to address problems of fin-de-siècle Austria within the very categories of psychoanalytic discourse. The categories of manifest and latent content suggest dimensions of culture as well as of personality. If Vienna is in any real sense a city of dreams, it is so only in the Freudian sense: as a surface culture of ideologically determined manifest content under which lies its overdetermined, conflicted, and volatile latent reality.

This book combines intellectual and cultural history with textual analysis and the critique of ideology. The specific components of that ideology are theatricality and totality. These analytical intentions inform the book's organization and style as well as the scope of its temporal and spatial references. Because I argue that the very category of "Austria" is artificial and often deter-mined according to a totalizing ideology, I cannot formulate a narrative or a structural analysis that would presume some degree of essential coherence within the object of analysis. In other words, I see the very notion of a culture as a holistic system and hence the notion of a holistic cultural analysis as components themselves of the kind of cultural ideology that is to be criticized. Neither can I write an Austrian history that takes for granted temporal or spatial boundaries that themselves may be generated by a totalizing view of a historical epoch or national territory. Thus in both time and space this work has several levels of reference. Since I characterize the battle over Austrian identity as one fought between proponents of conservatism on one side and of critical modernism on the other, I have loosely framed my analysis according to the life-span of that battle: from (approximately) 1890, the start of the decade that saw the rise of Austrian modernism, to 1938, the year of the *Anschluss* with National Socialist Germany and hence the moment the question of the establishment and representation of Austrian identity loses all pertinence. The relevant festival dates stretch from the founding in 1920 to the season planned for 1944, canceled at the last moment on orders of Josef Goebbels. (The post-1945 festival operates, as does Austria, in a radically altered set of circumstances that is beyond the scope of the book.) But on both the modernist and the conservative sides, intellectual and cultural patterns emerge that have references to, for example, the 1860s (the "Ringstrasse period"), to the period of the German enlightenment, and to the periods of the Habsburg and Bourbon baroque. Similar ambiguities exist in space: Austrian history operates in constant reference to and in confrontation with greater German as well as other European contexts.

The Salzburg Festival ideology shares an agenda with much of the cultural ideology characteristic of Germany and Austria from the mid-nineteenth through the mid-twentieth century: the denial of ambiguity and diversity in the interest of homogeneity and totality. In its method as well as in its chapter divisions and organization this book strives to offset an account of an ideological process against analyses of the various underlying patterns and problematics of cultural identity and ambiguity with which it interacts. The introductory first chapter places this ideology within a broad nineteenth-century European historicist pattern built on references to baroque culture. "The ideology of the baroque" emerges as a discourse of reappropriation—the recapturing of a perceived golden age by means of the representational principles seen to be the products of that golden age: theatricality and totality. The second chapter presents the "manifest" festival discourse: the institutional, intellectual, and ideological process of festival and cultural planning.

The four central chapters attempt to uncover patterns and paradoxes of latent content, context, and meaning. Although baroque models of theater and culture enabled and shaped the Salzburg enterprise, the festival's purpose was also to rededicate Austria to the cosmopolitan principles of the German enlightenment. The festival ideology is thus determined by baroque and nationalist tendencies on one side, and by cosmopolitan and enlightenment claims on the other. Chapter 3 attempts to work through this paradox by taking both sides seriously and by arguing that early twentieth-century conservative readers of the German enlightenment and its heritage—including the Salzburg Festival founders and others—were to a great extent legitimate and responsible in holding enlightenment tenets to be compatible with their own nationalism. What they saw says something real about the German enlightenment; the frame of mind that they shared with their enlightenment models I have called "nationalist cosmopolitanism."

Because Chapter 3 makes it clear that the Salzburg ideology (despite its baroque, Catholic guise) draws heavily from broad German traditions, Chapter 4 looks at the question of Austria and Germany with respect to party politics between 1918 and 1938. The chapter argues that language-based cultural nationalism rather than religion-based particularism dominated Austrian political ideology in the period. A sense of Austrianness composed of a baroque outlook and enlightenment tenets generated a nationalism that proved internally compatible with the greater German nationalism that was declared its antagonist.

Chapter 5 weaves these issues into the paradigmatic intellectual biography of Hugo von Hofmannsthal. Literary, textual analysis here becomes the most convincing way to show the delicate balance of paradoxes: nationalism and cosmopolitanism, German identity and Austrian, conservatism and modernism, Catholicity and Jewishness. The chapter argues that the increasing rigidity of Hofmannsthal's late work emerges from a desire to repress ambiguity and to create a controlled allegorical universe that would reinforce an increasingly fixed political ideology.

Hofmannsthal's distant Jewish lineage and the surprising manner in which that lineage provoked anti-Semitic attacks on the Salzburg Festival occasion the discussion in Chapter 6 of the final and perhaps the most difficult of the cultural paradoxes I address: "The Catholic Culture of the Austrian Jews." Here I try to chart the points of convergence and friction between, on the one side, modernism and conservatism in Austria, and, on the other, Jewish identity, assimilation, and resistance with respect to the dominant Catholic culture.

Chapter 7 closes the narrative of the festival begun in Chapter 2. To that chapter's discussion of models and plans, this chapter responds with an account of realization and reception. More important, it looks at milestones in the festival's history from 1920 to 1943 through the refractions created by the central four chapters.

This is intellectual history in a loose sense as well as in a strict sense: in a loose sense because in addition to analyzing formal bodies of thought it analyzes visual and musical representations, ritual behavior, political process, and institutional history. This breadth of scope makes me comfortable in defining intellectual history as the history of meaning. But this is also intellectual history in a strict sense, because it holds textual analysis and textual models of analysis to be the most productive at the same time as it holds that the centrality of politics must become more vital, not less, as commitment to textual analysis deepens. If textual analysis and models of textuality provide for the historian, as for the critic, the richest modes through which to problematize and to understand the object-world, the legitimacy of such understanding must be grounded in a fundamental sense of that object-world's politicality. To put it another way, the history of meaning must also be the history of meaning-making, in other words the history of conscious and unconscious strategies of ideology, contestation, and resistance which compete for representation and control of meaning, and hence of reality and experience. Thus, power and contingency constantly inform and offset structure and representation.

•

The information and interpretation that form this book accumulated with the help of much good advice. But "guter Rat ist teuer," and I therefore acknowledge first my debts to the Deutscher Akademischer Austauschdienst for a grant that enabled initial research in Frankfurt, Marbach, Salzburg, and Vienna in 1983 and to the National Endowment for the Humanities for a summer stipend that supported final research in 1987. Among the many people who helped me in these four places I would like to single out Dr. Rudolf Hirsch of the Hugo von Hofmannsthal Gesellschaft, Frankfurt; Dr. Werner Volke of the Deutsches Literaturarchiv, Marbach; Professors Fritz Fellner and Ernst Hanisch of the University of Salzburg; Mr. Hans Jaklitsch of the Festspielhausarchiv, Salzburg; Dr. Heinz Lunzer of the Dokumentationsstelle für neuere österreichische Literatur, Vienna; Dr. Otto Biba of the Musikverein archive, Vienna; and Dr. Jarmila Weissenböck of the Theatersammlung (Österreichische Nationalbibliothek), Vienna.

To teachers, colleagues, and friends I extend gratitude that is both general and focused on specific issues. Carl Schorske introduced me to Austrian politics and culture and to intellectual history; he remains a teacher, critic, and exemplar of the principle that penetration, more than coverage, must be the hallmark of intellectual history. My own practice of intellectual history owes much to him, as it does to Leonard Krieger, to Harry Harootunian, and to Dominick LaCapra. I am grateful also to John Boyer and to Stephen Toulmin; to Wendy Doniger O'Flaherty's sense of how myths operate in modern imaginative contexts (opera in particular); and to David Grene's understanding of theatricality as a historical principle. The late Arnaldo Momigliano will always remain for me an inspirational presence, not only for his unapproachable historical mastery but also for his embodiment of the intellectuality, engagement, and integrity of a vanishing European generation.

These scholars have all read, criticized, and strengthened this book at one or more of its formative stages, as have Arno J. Mayer, Leon Botstein, Isabel Hull, Daniel Herwitz, Daniel Borus, John Ackerman, and Peter Agree. I have addressed many of the texts and problems under consideration here in courses and have often benefited from the critical responses of dedicated students. Finally,

I had the opportunity in the late summer of 1987 to join Carl Schorske, Leon Botstein, and Peter Haiko on the faculty of a two-week session of the Salzburg Seminar, held in Max Reinhardt's Schloss Leopoldskron, on the subject of fin-de-siècle Vienna—a serendipity that speaks for itself.

The manuscript was revised and prepared for publication during three rewarding years of teaching at Colgate University. Among many dear colleagues there I would like to single out Curtis Hinsley, chair of the history department for two of those years and a constant source of scholarly, professional, and personal encouragement. I am grateful as well to the Colgate Research Council and to Bruce Wanamaker for his invaluable editorial assistance.

Much of Chapter 6 appeared as portions of an article called "Jewish Identity and Intellectuality in Fin-de-siècle Austria: Suggestions for a Historical Discourse," published in *New German Critique*, no. 43 (Winter 1988). I am grateful to the editors for the permission to use this material here. My thanks go also to Marion Hanscom and the Max Reinhardt Archive of the State University of New York at Binghamton for help in my search for photographs. Kay Scheuer, senior manuscript editor, and the entire staff of Cornell University Press have made the process of publication a pleasure for me.

This book is dedicated to Carol Warshawsky. In the spirit of its argument, I will refrain from baroque embellishment. In that same spirit, however, I will invoke a principle dear to many Austrian thinkers, among them Hofmannsthal's Composer in *Ariadne auf Naxos*: "Es gibt manches auf der Welt, das lässt sich nicht sagen!" This tenet connects the book's dedication to many of its scholarly concerns. I hope that the following pages will show it to have generated as much sensitivity as anxiety.

MICHAEL P. STEINBERG

Hamilton, New York

CHAPTER 1

The Ideology of the Baroque, 1860–1938

I

IN 1947, Hermann Broch agreed to write a brief essay on the prose writings of Hugo von Hofmannsthal, a project that soon expanded beyond his intentions to become a massive appraisal of European culture between 1860 and 1920.[1] As a novelist turned historian/cultural critic, a Jew converted to Catholicism, and an Austrian in American exile, Broch found himself in an equivocal position in regard to Hofmannsthal—both sympathetic and distant. Hofmannsthal was the Austrian par excellence, but perhaps he was so precisely because he embodied the cultural and intellectual ambivalence of the Catholic of Jewish extraction, of the cultural and social reconstructionist who had started as an aesthete imprisoned in decorative form, in, to use Broch's term, a culture of decorativity.[2] The category of Austrianness thus emerged for Broch as a principle of nonidentity. The ambivalent figure of Hofmannsthal and Broch's equivocal relationship to him together formed the initial paradigm for a historical and critical investigation in which the delicate relationship between historian and historical object persisted, but in which the historical object expanded from the life of

1. Hermann Broch, *Hugo von Hofmannsthal and His Time: The European Imagination, 1860–1920* (Chicago, 1984).
2. Broch, p. 1ff.

1

Hofmannsthal to become the life of the late Habsburg Empire, and, ultimately, the culture of the European fin-de-siècle, with that term bearing the apocalyptic tone typically imparted by an Austrian vantage point. If the career of Hofmannsthal seemed to unfold according to a pattern of solipsistic aestheticism followed by modernist revolt followed in turn by a reconstituted and now politicized aestheticism, the critical appraisal of European culture between 1860 and 1920 also focused on the battle between persistence of old forms of thought and art and all forms of critical modernism.

Traditionalism remained culturally dominant, however, and Broch thus began his study with a condemnation of Austrian historicist architecture for its embodiment of the "non-style" of late-nineteenth-century culture.[3] Ringstrasse Vienna had offered all varieties of "neo-" architecture: a neo-Gothic town hall to express the rebirth of the autonomous medieval city, a neo-Renaissance university, a neoclassical Parliament, a neo-Palladian opera house and a neobaroque court theater. In both the biography of Hofmannsthal and the concentric history of Austria, the neobaroque carries most weight, because the historical models to which it alludes are the most nationalistically defined, politically and culturally. The neobaroque, or what I call the ideology of the baroque, becomes the Austrian historicist-conservative phenomenon par excellence, identified by an Austrian (Broch) with relation to the experience of a compatriot (Hofmannsthal). But in Broch's European analysis it expands into a critical principle through which expressions of conservative ideology can be identified in various, related European contexts.

The neobaroque is a late-nineteenth-century cultural style, sometimes materially manifest, as in architecture, sometimes manifest through behavior and gesture, as in the performance style associated with the Burgtheater or indeed the style of social intercourse modeled on court behavior. Its goal is to reconstitute and represent the present, in this case the late nineteenth century, in the image of a golden past. It is, thus, in Eric Hobsbawm's formulation, an "invented tradition," in other words, "a set of practices, normally

---

3. See Broch, chap. 1, "Art and Its Non-Style at the End of the Nineteenth Century."

governed by overtly or tacitly accepted rules and of a ritual or symbolic nature, which seek to inculcate certain values and norms of behavior by repetition, which automatically implies continuity with the past. In fact, where possible, they normally attempt to establish continuity with a suitable historic past. . . . However, insofar as there is such reference to a historic past, the peculiarity of 'invented' traditions is that the continuity with it is largely factitious."[4]

In this context the term *baroque* emerges not as a periodizing label and not only as an artistic or architectural style but as a cosmological claim representing theological, cultural, and political principles of the Counterreformation. The very claim that the hierarchic chain of being uniting the Catholic world and God could be represented was itself a Catholic principle rejected by Protestantism (and in turn reaffirmed in the rejection of the Reformation). The baroque thus combines a system of representation with the confidence in the very possibility of such an act of representation. It is thus a cultural style that conjoins Catholic Europe, with Habsburg Austria, (formerly) Habsburg Spain, France, and Italy as principal coordinates.

Because it originated as an attitude both pan-European and parochial (distinguishing Catholic from reformed Europe), the baroque could be reconstituted in the nineteenth century in terms of the modified dialectic of cosmopolitanism and parochialism (now nationalism). The baroque claimed to represent an entire cosmos from the vantage point of a Catholic center that controlled the principles and the process of representation. In this respect the cultural history of the baroque and the intellectual history of the term *baroque* converged in the late nineteenth and early twentieth centuries.

In a 1943 essay called "The Spanish Baroque," the Austrian-born literary historian Leo Spitzer looked at the history of the word *baroque* to suggest that only in his own generation, that is, between 1915 and 1940, did the term enter scholarly usage, and furthermore that a cultural as well as an intellectual agenda specific to this period in fact generated the analytical category. The actual historical origin of the word, Spitzer wrote, is unknown, but "baroque" in seven-

---

4. Eric Hobsbawm, "Introduction: Inventing Tradition," in *The Invention of Tradition*, ed. Eric Hobsbawm and Terence Ranger (Cambridge, 1983), pp. 1–2.

teenth-century French meant "bizarre" or "fantastic." It was Heinrich Wölfflin's *Principles of Art History* (1915) that first removed the pejorative hue that had colored the term ever since and instead used it to speak of a legitimate form of artistic intention (*Kunstwollen*) to be distinguished from the classical. From Wölfflin, Spitzer argued, "the German soul"—in other words the practitioners of cultural history—created "the myth of the baroque man."[5] Literary historians such as Karl Vossler, Ernst Robert Curtius, Josef Nadler, and Hugo von Hofmannsthal himself adopted it as a marker of "the deep Catholic faith that lay at the heart" of the "violent dynamism" of Spanish literature and painting. "And thus it can be explained," Spitzer continued, "that for an Austrian like myself, brought up beside the baroque architecture of the Karlskirche in Vienna, educated in Grillparzer's studies of Spanish theater and in Hofmannsthal's imitations of them, it never seemed problematic that Mediterranean Catholicism (Spanish or Italian) should have found in sensuality itself the expression of the transcendent."[6] For Spitzer, the culture of the baroque bespoke for its modern historians and admirers two polarities: the sensual and the eternal, life and dream. It became thus a wish fulfillment, he suggested, for twentieth-century conservative intellectuals, such as T. S. Eliot, who felt "the tragic tension of a lost Christian past and an intolerable present."[7]

The original baroque culture that becomes the referent for the neobaroque must be dated slightly differently in various national contexts. José Antonio Maravall locates the Spanish baroque between 1600 and 1675.[8] These dates may hold in the French case as well, as they span roughly the reign of Louis XIII and the first and more successful half of the reign of Louis XIV, the period associated with the Colbert ministry and the building of Versailles, in other words, with a politics of representation. In Austria the periodization

---

5. Leo Spitzer, "The Spanish Baroque," in *Leo Spitzer: Representative Essays*, ed. Alban Forcione, Herbert Lindenberger, and Madeline Sutherland (Stanford, 1988), pp. 125–26, 128.

6. Ibid., pp. 129–30.

7. Ibid., pp. 131, 134, 138.

8. José Antonio Maravall, *The Culture of the Baroque*, trans. Terry Cochran (Minneapolis, 1986), pp. 3–15. Maravall uses the baroque as a "concept of epoch," i.e., a *Zeitgeist*.

may be later, perhaps from the final defeat of the Ottoman invaders in 1683 to the second defeat of Austria by Prussia in 1763, the end of the first and more successful half of the reign of Maria Theresa.

This dating of the Austrian baroque seems to be confirmed architecturally, because the liberation of Vienna from the Turks was commemorated by the construction of the Karlskirche, Vienna's most celebrated baroque structure. Fischer von Erlach's building, which in the history of architecture represents the apogee of the Austrian baroque, also embodies the baroque in the sense of a historically and politically specific ideological cosmology. The church celebrates the Habsburg emperor whose name it carries as the center of a political and religious totality. Architecturally, the baroque style expresses this totality by compressing the forms inherited from the Renaissance so that the cupola absorbs the entire building: Charles, the house of Habsburg, and hence Austria are thus represented as a circle that fills the cosmos and renders the outside irrelevant. The "above," however, is still relevant: structurally and ornamentally the cupola leads anyone who would experience this building into a concentration on the divine mystery that is the symbolic referent of earthly Habsburg rule.

The urban context of the building has a different set of symbolic coordinates: the structure announced the newly assured security of Vienna by its very position outside the city walls. In its embodiment of the Habsburg cosmology, therefore, the church also guards the circular and still walled city of Vienna, with the imperial residence (Hofburg) competing with St. Stephen's cathedral (Stefansdom) for the center of that circle. By standing outside and, so to speak, gazing at the old city, the Karlskirche absorbs and hence claims to resolve the symbolic tension between the Hofburg and the Stefansdom. In its structural language, therefore, the Karlskirche baroque expresses a political totality legitimated by symbolic reference to divine mystery; in its contextual language, to the political totality created, or enabled, by the strength of that reference to the divine.

The history of art and architecture has its own modes of defining periods and styles, but the classification of a building or painting made according to those criteria notwithstanding, the focus and hence the classification of what is baroque at stake here have to do with the contextual discourses of the original periods as well as with

The Karlskirche, Vienna. Engraving by S. Kleiner, from *Vera et accurata delinatio*, 1724–1737. Courtesy of the British Library.

the conceptions later eras had of those periods and the ideological agendas for which they were evoked. As a discursive style, the baroque seems to me to embody the two principles of theatricality and totality, and it is these properties, associated with a particular idea of a cohesive, Catholic, imperial past, that the neobaroque discourses of the late nineteenth century seek to reappropriate, stylistically and hence culturally and politically. By totality I mean a dialectic of power, identity, and coherence that united nation, monarch, and God. Theatricality is the second and equally important principle and the one that renders historically specific the political principles just stated, which on their own do not speak to any particular period. Theatricality refers to the claim not merely that this political cosmology could and should be represented through action and images (festivals, ceremonies, rituals, performances, art, architecture, and so on), but that it comes to exist through representation. Representation is thus constitutive rather than reflective of cultural and political identity and power; the baroque refers just as much to a process of representation as to an object—physical or temporal—of representation. Similarly, the reappropriative agenda of the neobaroque refers to a goal of cultural reformation through representation and reconstitution, again with totality and theatricality as guiding principles. Between the period of the baroque and that of the neobaroque, the religious dimension of Catholic theatricality and totality dissipates, so that the modes of representation become, in the Weberian sense, rationalized.

Another Viennese example: It seems to me thoroughly plausible to read the entire process of the late-nineteenth century development of the Ringstrasse, a process that indeed quite appropriately provided the era with its name, as stemming from a neobaroque ideological agenda, in other words as a refashioning of the spatial language set by the Karlskirche, rather than as the result of a liberal program. Although there is no necessary contradiction between historicism and modernism, Ringstrasse historicism expresses bourgeois appropriation of aristocratic hegemony as much as it does the celebration of a triumphant liberalism.[9]

9. The argument for the Ringstrasse as embodiment of triumphant liberalism is Carl Schorske's; see his chapter "The Ringstrasse, Its Critics, and the Birth of Urban Modernism," in *Fin-de-siècle Vienna: Politics and Culture* (New York, 1980), pp. 24–

To argue that the appropriation of a past style, as a way of mapping the desires of the present onto the claims of the past, is essentially ideological is not to absolve the original period's style or claims of ideology. For Hermann Broch, all historicism is morally suspect because it reveals an era's inability to produce its own discursive language. This notwithstanding, it seems necessary to penetrate into the dialogue that occurs between model style, model era on the one hand, and the agendas of the imitating period and style on the other. In the phrase of Pierre Bourdieu, an era reveals itself through its nostalgias. As both a period and a style, the baroque claimed totality, and did so through theatricality.

II

In Paris, in Vienna, and, contiguously, in Bayreuth, projects of national redefinition, reconstitution, and reinvigoration unfolded in the 1860s and 1870s with three common elements: national identity was represented theatrically through baroque traditions and the claim to recapture those traditions; explicit theatrical practice, opera in particular, took its place at the center of this cultural assignment; the opera house thus became a crucial vessel of national rededication through the appropriation of the baroque. Not only were the historical origins of opera as a genre in the baroque era; the operatic claim to unite all art forms into a single expressive totality also spoke directly to the aestheticizing claim to formulate and represent a national culture precisely as a coherent and powerful totality. In this sense, nineteenth-century operatic culture served conservative ideology. But there were also places in that culture for contestation, in other words for an ambivalent relationship to dominant cultural practices and norms, and even for cultural resistance—a relationship of opposition to those practices and norms. These phenomena must be analyzed with reference to operatic texts (words and music) as well as institutional contexts. The cultural history of French and Italian opera

115. Broch sees the Ringstrasse as historicist and hence antimodernist, an association that is, for him, essential and hence, in my view, essentialist. See Broch, pp. 1ff.

from the 1840s through the 1870s reveals many realms of contestation. The place where operatic resistance is traditionally identified is
Wagner, but within his music dramas, musical modernism is often
offset by cultural conservatism. Furthermore, a look at the institutional Wagner and the interplay of Bayreuth with the music-dramas
performed there reveals the Wagnerian agenda to have been perhaps
even more bourgeois-reactionary and indeed neobaroque than it was
revolutionary. Nietzsche as well as Adorno and Broch can help us to
see these dynamics.[10]

The history of opera in Paris and Vienna is framed by the baroque
at the beginning and the neobaroque at the end. In both cities opera
was imported in the first half of the seventeenth century as an exotic
and expensive Italian entertainment, ideal for the court. Yet the
ideological use of opera took variant forms in the two places as it
began to serve French self-representation as nation and Austrian
self-representation as empire. That is, opera as genre and institution
quickly became a national, French institution in Paris, but tended
to retain much Italianate quality in Vienna, up to the Palladian
design of the 1869 opera house. This Viennese proclivity must be
understood, however, in terms of an imperial attitude in which
Italy was an internal rather than an external cultural contributor,
and not as a sign of inherent internationalism.[11] At every moment
opera as a genre and a public institution served to represent the
nation or empire from the points of view of ideology, contestation,
and resistance. (Indeed, with a new opera house scheduled to open
on the site of the Bastille in conjunction with the bicentennial of the
1789 revolution, another chapter in the history of French opera as
national representation will have to be written.[12] The new opera

10. Nietzsche's position on these issues must be traced of course through his
own transformation from Wagnerian (as manifest in *The Birth of Tragedy*) to a position
of ambivalence ("Richard Wagner in Bayreuth") to the anti-Wagnerian positions of
Beyond Good and Evil and *The Case of Wagner*. See also Theodor Adorno, *Versuch über
Wagner* (Frankfurt, 1952) and Broch, chaps. 1 and 4, passim.

11. Rossini's success in Paris may argue for an Italian presence there that is as
strong as that in Vienna. But it can also be said that Rossini was successful because,
royalist that he was, he wrote French-style opera, complete with the ballet that every
Italian composer had to insert into an opera for it to be accepted in Paris.

12. It will be interesting to see in the next few years whether an attempt is made
to revive a sense of a national operatic genre, perhaps through a focus on Berlioz
and Meyerbeer, in conjunction with the new Bastille Opera. The initial signals are

house, indeed like the contemporary architectural transformation of Paris into which it fits, would be unthinkable in Vienna, where high culture wears its historicist architectural costumes in strict adherence to their nineteenth-century ideological origins.)

In both Paris and Vienna, seventeenth-century opera followed and only rarely rivaled the leading baroque carriers of theatrical self-representation, the Comédie Française and the Hofburg-theater. Until the neobaroque 1860s, opera in Paris and Vienna moved from hall to hall, whereas the court theaters were ensconced in the royal residences, the Palais Royal and the Hofburg. When Colbert instructed impresario Pierre Perrin to found an opera company in 1669, the shadow of the Comédie Française was apparent. He charged Perrin with "l'établissement des académies de l'Opéra ou représentation en musique, en vers français, à Paris et dans les autres villes du royaume pendant l'espace de douze années": "the establishment of academies of opera or of representation in music, in French verse, in Paris and in the other cities of the realm for a period of twelve years."[13] Note the phrase "representation in music": the object of representation is not stated but tacitly evoked as the nation. Consistent with this evocation is the stipulation that the texts must be in French verse, and that, as with the Comédie Française, the capital city will serve as the source of a national culture. Perrin's main opposition was an anti-operatic sensibility that finds adherents in the twentieth century, as the seventeenth-century verse that attacked Perrin and his new institution bears witness: "Ce beau mais malheureux Orphée/Ou pour mieux parler ce Morphée, /Puisque tout le monde y dormit": "This handsome but unhappy Orpheus/ Or to be more accurate this Morpheus/ Since the entire audience slept."[14] Lully took over the administration of opera in Paris after Perrin was imprisoned for debts, and in

---

mixed: the choice of architect was made in the same way as that for the Palais Garnier in 1860: by open contest. But the winner was a Uruguayan, Carlos Ott. The Socialist government's January 1989 dismissal of Daniel Barenboim as director of the Bastille Opera suggests that some kind of national program is desired; Barenboim's plans would have emphasized Mozart and Wagner.

13. Cited in Jean Gourret, *Histoire de l'opéra de Paris, 1669–1971* (Paris, 1977), p. 16.

14. Ibid.

1673 he was able temporarily to move the opera company into the Palais Royal, which had become vacant following the death of Molière.

Because my subject is the dialogue between the nineteenth-century neobaroque and the seventeenth-century baroque, it would be senseless to attempt a quick survey of opera in Paris between the two periods. A few points, however, will reinforce the sense of persisting ideology and contestation in the operatic representation of the nation. The dominant polarity in the mid-eighteenth century was that of Rameau and Rousseau, with the dominant controversy that between the persistence of baroque principles and forms of representation and theatricality versus the well-known Rousseauean attack on theater and theatricality.[15] During the period of the revolution, the name of the institution changed five times, from the obviously unacceptable Académie Royale de Musique to the Académie de Musique to the Opéra to the Opéra National to the Théâtre des Arts to the Théâtre de la République et des Arts, the last a name that carries on the claims of national representation first expressed in Colbert's phrase "représentation en musique." The "royalist" operas of Lully, Rameau, and Gluck were suppressed, and a new genre of revolutionary opera developed, with Grétry as its most celebrated practitioner.

On 13 February 1820 the duc de Berry was assassinated at the opera and received the sacrament in the theater; the archbishop of Paris closed the house because, once sacralized, it could not be profaned. Among other things, this episode shows how far apart in their ideas of national representation, at least it terms of clerical perception, the modes of opera and national religion really were in restoration France. (It's a long way to Wagner's placement of communion on an operatic stage.) Between 1821 and 1875 Parisian opera was

15. The text in question is the *Letter to d'Alembert Concerning Spectacles* of 1758, a reply to an article in the *Encyclopédie* that had argued for the establishment of a theater in Geneva. Profiting from the dual meaning of the French word *représentation* as "representation" and "performance," Rousseau engaged the Platonic dichotomy between real knowledge (achieved through philosophy) and false knowledge (the "representation" of knowledge)—the alleged transgression of the theater. The specific relevance of the problem to Rousseau's home city of Geneva revealed the survival of Calvinistic moralism in the Catholic convert, as did the campaign against Calvinism's classical enemy—the baroque theater and its representational claims.

thus housed in the temporary theater on the Rue Le Peletier; this period has recently received a very helpful historical analysis in Jane Fulcher's book *The Nation's Image: French Grand Opera as Politics and Politicized Art*. Fulcher argues that the genre of spectacular French grand opera rose and declined between 1821 and 1870 according to the dynamics of mediation between the state production and control of forms of national representation on the one hand and on the other a "dangerous realm, one of contestation over the voice of the 'people.' "[16] She then surveys the period through an analysis of the performance history and reception of several major works: Auber's *Muette de Portici* (premiered in 1828) in the context of the Bourbon restoration's most conservative and proclerical years, and Meyerbeer's *Robert le Diable* (1831), *Les Huguenots* (1836), and *Le Prophète* (1849) in the context of the monarchy of Louis Philippe, the 1848 revolts, and the Second Republic. She leaves little doubt that the libretti of all these works offered an unquestionable but imprecise and therefore contestable symbolic portrayal of a society in upheaval. Yet the portrayal of medieval religious fanaticism in *Robert*, of Protestant-Catholic conflict in *Les Huguenots*, and of a radicalized and revolutionary John of Leyden in *Le Prophète* do not add up to revolutionary allegory, and the conservative embedding of these plots within the music of Meyerbeer and the performance traditions of grand opera diffuse radical tendencies.

Perhaps because Fulcher's analysis ends with the opening of the new opera house in 1875 as a convenient marker for the end of the period that is her focus, she does not stress to what extent the enormous project of the Palais Garnier was an attempt by Napoleon III and his prefect, the baron Haussmann, to recapture state, imperial control over opera as national discourse, and hence by means of neobaroque architecture and cultural policy to extend the Second Empire's process of imitative self-representation back not only to the obvious model of the First Empire but to the baroque model of the realm of Louis XIV.

The "Palais Garnier," the popular name for the new opera house, is a felicitous compromise formation between the name of its bour-

16. Jane Fulcher, *The Nation's Image: French Grand Opera as Politics and Politicized Art* (Cambridge, 1987), pp. 2, 8.

geois architect and its imperial, baroque agenda (its official name is the Académie Impériale de Musique). The building became the centerpiece of the so-called second network of Haussmannization. Along with the Gare St. Lazare and the "grands magasins," it anchors the system of the "grands boulevards" completed with the Avenue de l'Opéra, which connected the Palais Garnier with the Palais Royal at unparalleled cost to the preexisting neighborhood. The symbolism of this urban network is crucial. By connecting the new opera house with the Palais Royal, the Avenue de l'Opéra (originally named the Avenue Napoléon) connected not only two national theaters, but two historical periods and styles defined by a national discourse of baroque theatricality and totality. The fact that the Palais Royal meant both theater and royal palace recalled the seventeenth-century unity of theater and monarchy (theatricality and totality) and declared its relevance for the Second Empire.

All the same, grand designs have short-term pretexts. If the assassin of the duc de Berry chose the old opera house for symbolic as well as logistical reasons, the would-be assassin of Napoleon III, Orsini, had much to imitate when he tried his luck on 14 January 1858. True to the tested formula of Second Empire farce imitating First Empire—or more precisely in this case First Restoration—tragedy, Orsini failed, but he did, like his more talented predecessor, cause the closing of an opera house, this time for reasons of security. An architectural competition was announced with the stipulation that the winning design incorporate a separate carriage entrance for the emperor. Charles Garnier won on the second round with an elaborate baroque design that symbolically as well as topographically claimed a new center for Paris. The Guide Michelin may still measure distance from the western door of Notre Dame, but as far as the Second Empire was concerned, the Opéra was the omphalos. Or, to propose a more symbolically relevant sacred counterstructure, the Opéra was the Second Empire's Karlskirche. The architectural historian Monika Steinhauser has suggested that that neobaroque style of the Palais Garnier "is not only a stylistic posture, but a mode of representation of a restorative regime.[17]

---

17. Monika Steinhauser, *Die Architektur der Pariser Oper* (Munich, 1969), p. 174. The translation is my own.

The farcical, and indeed pathetic, aspect of the Palais Garnier plays itself out in the fact that its opening came only in January 1875, over four years after the collapse of the empire it was to represent. The exterior structure was unveiled and admired in 1867, and the last facades and statuaries were uncovered in 1869, but in 1870 an English tourist revealed that the building was an empty shell. The calamities of 1870–1871 delayed completion, and the interior was finished in 1874. Before its first use, therefore, the building had acquired a double historicism: it referred back to the seventeenth-century French baroque, and now also to the neobaroque of the vanished Second Empire. Significantly, the house opened with an evening of operatic fragments.

The suggestion that the Palais Garnier inherits the theatrical posture of the Karlskirche is abstract; that the project for a new opera house for Vienna's Ringstrasse consciously followed the Paris project is indisputable. An architectural competition was announced in Vienna by imperial decree within weeks of the Paris announcement in 1860. (Thirty-five entries were received, against seven hundred in Paris). Despite the sizable Austrian political and military upheavals of the 1860s, the new Hofopern-theater was completed by 1869. Its neo-Palladian style was reviled by the public and critics, and the house achieved legendary proportions when its two architects, Eduard van der Nüll and August Siccard von Siccardsburg, suddenly died, the first a suicide, the second—according to journalistic legend—of grief a few weeks later.[18] The Italian baroque style was to blame for the public hostility; clearly modeled on the Basilica Palladiana in Vicenza, the building was decried as foreign. Perhaps the Austrian loss of the Italian territories, including Vicenza, a decade before, had placed Venetian forms into the category of foreign and enemy. Italianate representations were not despised as long as they bespoke Austrian control: thus the opera house opened on 25 May 1869 with a performance of Mozart's *Don Giovanni*.[19]

18. See Wilhelm Beetz, *Das Wiener Opernhaus, 1869 bis 1945* (Zurich, 1949).

19. The politics of *Don Giovanni* and its status as mediator between German and Italian aspects of Austrian culture is a crucial and long-lived issue that will retain prominence in the history of the Salzburg Festival. The work was often performed in German translation, in which case it was billed as *Don Juan*. The posters for the

Like the Palais Garnier and like the neighboring Karlskirche, the new Hofopernhaus redistributed architectural and symbolic emphasis in its urban surroundings. Carl Schorske has analyzed its setting within the Ringstrasse development. It bears repeating, however, that the literal street in question divided the old city from the new, the Hofburg from the new buildings—university, town hall, parliament, and others—that symbolized the new era. The only structures that were built on the Hofburg side of the street, and indeed on either side of the Hofburg, were the new Hofburg-theater and the Hofopernhaus.[20] Hermann Broch has suggested that a principle of theatricality, inherited from the baroque, deter-mined imperial representation and pageantry and was thus the principle that held the empire together. A mere glimpse of the emperor on his route between the Hofburg and the suburban Schönbrunn castle granted the Viennese burgher a sense of high moral participation in imperial glory.[21] Of the two, now literalized, imperial ballasts of Burgtheater and opera house, the former claimed priority and sacredness in its service to imperial theater. To begin with, its old home had been nestled within the Hofburg, on the Michaelerplatz side. Second, the theater it presented was German, and thus suggested a national tradition as opposed to the imperial tradition of the Italianate opera house. The sacredness of the institution is revealed in the comportment of the audience: Broch is right to suggest that the young Hugo von Hofmannsthal received not only his aesthetic but his ethical education from the ritual outings to the Burgtheater initiated by his father, and this ritual aspect its confirmed by the tradition of prohibiting applause and curtain calls at Burgtheater performances (a tradition that did not survive the move to the house on the Ringstrasse).[22]

25 May 1869 performance read *Don Juan;* it can therefore be assumed that the performance was in German.

20. It may be noted that the new stock exchange, which neither architecturally nor ideologically inhabits the baroque world, was also built "on the baroque side" of the Ringstrasse. Its location, however, was far on the western side of the horseshoe-shaped street, removed from the unified area of the Hofburg, Burgtheater, and opera house.

21. Broch, p. 74.

22. See Broch, pp. 101–2. For Burgtheater performance tradition, see Fred Hen-nings, *Heimat Burgtheater: Wie ich ans Burgtheater kam, 1906-1923* (Vienna, 1972), p.

If sacredness in the Viennese theater is measured by service to
and participation in imperial theatricality and representation, in
other words by its appropriation of baroque style and purpose,
then the new opera house, which carried a gold inscription to Franz
Josef on its crown, came to mediate between the courtly, baroque
sacredness of the Burgtheater and the solidly middle-class style of
the third major performing-arts structure to go up in Ringstrasse
Vienna: the concert hall of the Musikverein, just off the Ring and
opposite the Karlskirche. The Vienna Philharmonic, then as now,
inhabited the new concert hall and also served as the opera house
orchestra. But the Musikverein, and the various instrumental and
choral organizations associated with it, exemplified, as Leon
Botstein has argued, the growing middle-class focus of aesthetic
enjoyment in Vienna.[23] Instrumental and choral music, for their lack
of conventional theatricality, were a- or anti-baroque and therefore
powerful symbolic vehicles for the self-representation of a still aesthetically oriented Viennese *Bildungsbürgertum*. Compromise for-
mations persisted, however: just as the bourgeois Vienna Philharmonic formed the pit orchestra for the opera house, the sternly
neoclassical exterior of the Musikverein was countered on the inside
by plump golden caryatids, which hold up the balconies.

As a final note, it is important to see how the style of the entire
Viennese spectrum of bourgeois self-representation, from the Burgtheater to the Musikverein, differed from the Parisian case. In Paris
the continuum of aesthetic enjoyment and the acquisition of commodities (and hence the admission that culture had become a commodity) operated with little camouflage. Thus the baroque Palais

---

24 and passim; also Friedrich Schreyvogel, *Das Burgtheater* (Vienna, 1965). Stefan
Zweig's memoir *The World of Yesterday* (New York, 1943) contains the following
apposite account: "When the 'old' Burgtheater, in which Mozart's *Marriage of Figaro*
was first given, was torn down, all of Vienna's society was formally and sorrowfully
assembled there; the curtain had hardly fallen when everybody leapt upon the stage,
to bring home at least a splinter as a relic of the boards which the beloved artists
had trod; and for decades after, in dozens of bourgeois homes, these insignificant
splinters could be seen preserved in costly caskets, as fragments of the Holy Cross
are kept in churches" (p. 16).

23. See Leon Botstein, "Music and Its Public: Habits of Listening and the Crisis
of Musical Modernism in Vienna, 1870–1914," work-in-progress, forthcoming, University of Chicago Press.

Garnier emerged unbothered in the context of the grands magasins and the Gare St. Lazare, which had been placed next to them to deliver the suburban bougeoisie into their clutches. The grands magasins were themselves baroque palaces; as Philip Nord has suggested, "Expensive materials, statuary, wrought iron grillwork, golding and multichrome mosaics dazzled the stroller, the potential shopper, with an opulence and grandeur which the new Opera House itself could scarcely match." Not that this practice went uncriticized: in his 1883 novel *Au bonheur des dames* (about a department store of that name), Emile Zola disapprovingly compared the grand magasin to the cathedral where, in Nord's words, "under vaulting metallic naves, celebrants practiced the rites of commodity worship."[24] In Vienna all connection between culture and commodities was suppressed. Department store culture existed, but tucked away on the Mariahilferstrasse and further marginalized from official culture by the significant involvement of Jews, as in the renowned Herzmansky store. The relatively explicit Parisian juxtaposition of culture and commodities may explain the playfulness in cultural representation in that city, as opposed to the deadly seriousness and "museality," as Broch referred to the cultural claims of fin-de-siècle Vienna.[25]

III

The period of the second network in the redesign of Second Empire Paris (1860–1870) and the periods of Ringstrasse and fin-de-siècle Vienna (1860–1914) can be compared not only in terms of the dominant ideology of the baroque but also in those of the battle for control of modern life between the baroque on one side and an emergent critical modernism on the other. Although in France the terms of this battle altered with the collapse of empire in 1870, they survived in Austria until the Habsburg collapse of 1918, and, as this book argues, reemerged in reconstructive ideology between 1918

24. Philip G. Nord, *Paris Shopkeepers and the Politics of Resentment* (Princeton, 1986), pp. 71, 74.
25. Broch, p. 61.

and 1938. Second Empire modernism involved the reclaiming of the street and of public life (as the paintings of Manet and the essays and poems of Baudelaire reveal); Viennese modernism rejected the city and its architecture for its false historicism and its mendacious representation of shallow liberalism—as a process of "poverty masked by wealth," in Hermann Broch's formulation.[26]

The dominance of the baroque coexisted with the life of empire. The Second Empire's dialectical relationship between high culture and commodities, as indeed between bohemians and bourgeois, coupled with the obvious presence of revolutionary tradition and political fragmentation and then with the severity of the crises of 1870–1871, precluded the continuing hegemony of baroque forms of cultural and political self-representation beyond the life of the empire.[27] By the time of its opening in 1875, the Palais Garnier was more a circus than a temple. It represented the arena of fragmented and commodified cultural consumption governed by a dynamic of distance in which culture becomes a possession rather than a unmediated representation of personal and collective identity. In Austria, however, where the centrifugal realities of spatial and temporal fragmentation were belied by the theatrical continuity of the reign of Franz Josef—in other words, where political representation controlled political reality—baroque culture remained dominant to the Habsburg collapse of 1918 and persisted as a competing mode of national representation through to the *Anschluss* of 1938. After 1890, baroque culture was countered by a small but incisive critical avant garde, intellectuals who are all too often conflated with the majority culture they despised. After 1918, baroque culture survived as the ideology of a conservative minority, but a persistent and energetic one. One of its legacies is the Salzburg Festival. The

---

26. Broch, p. 1.

27. For an analysis of the interdependence of bourgeois and bohemian, see Jerrold Seigel, *Bohemian Paris: Culture, Politics, and the Boundaries of Bourgeois Life, 1830–1930* (New York, 1986). As Seigel introduces his argument, "Bohemian and bourgeois were—and are—parts of a single field: they imply, require, and attract each other" (p. 5). The most profound texts on this theme, to my knowledge, are Walter Benjamin's *Charles Baudelaire: A Lyric Poet in the Era of High Capitalism*, trans. Harry Zohn (London, 1976), especially the essay "The Paris of the Second Empire in Baudelaire," and the untranslated *Passagen-Werk*.

enormity of the final and retarded collapse of 1918 is nevertheless by no means to be underestimated, and the trauma of its effect on intellectuals can be measured in the intensity of the ideology of cultural reconstruction.

The neobaroque cultural discourse that ultimately produced the idea of the Salzburg Festival thus represented a conservative departure from the thought of the pre–World War I Viennese intelligentsia, and the biographical trajectory of the ideological founder of the festival, Hugo von Hofmannsthal, can be mapped onto an increasing marginalization of avant-garde intellectual culture in Austria. The fin-de-siècle Viennese thought that cultural historians and, as of the 1980s, a large portion of the museum-going public in Europe and the United States, have all come to associate with the origins of much twentieth-century modernism spanned fields from the language philosophies of Mauthner, Kraus, and Wittgenstein, to Freud, to the critique of style and form of Loos, the Secession and Wiener Werkstätte movements, the literary-social critiques of Hofmannsthal himself, Schnitzler, and later Broch and Musil, and Kafka (who can be included in the broad Austrian context but clearly not in the Viennese one), and the music of the Second Vienna School. All these intellectual trends, innovations, and radicalisms tended to eschew any conception of participation in a coherent intellectual or critical avant garde that would itself mirror the totalizing (and theatrical) *Weltanschauung* of the baroque culture they were in the process of undermining.

In a late essay called "The Question of *Weltanschauung*," for example, Freud explicitly rejected the labeling of psychoanalysis as a *Weltanschauung*, which he defined as "an intellectual construction which solves all the problems of our existence uniformly on the basis of one overriding hypothesis, which, accordingly, leaves no question unanswered and in which everything that interests us finds its fixed place." For Freud, the opposite of *Weltanschauung* was science, in particular a specialized science, "marked by negative characteristics, by its limitation to what is at the moment knowable and by its sharp rejection of certain elements that are alien to it."[28]

---

28. Sigmund Freud, "The Question of *Weltanschauung*," *New Introductory Lectures on Psychoanalysis*, trans. James Strachey (New York, 1965), p. 139.

The underside of this mode of critical, negative thinking is the predicament of Adolf Loos, of the Hofmannsthal of the "Letter of Lord Chandos," and to an extent of the early Wittgenstein: the rejection of all existing conventions of form, style, and coherence as false, with the proclamation of nothingness as the result, failing a totally new system of representation. (Music is the only field that can claim the establishment of a new representative system, and even that one can be accurately described, as Schönberg was prone to do, as a return to classicism.) Hermann Broch, a supporter of Loos and the scandal-provoking minimalist 1908 Michaelerplatz apartment building that Loos placed opposite the neobaroque wing of the Hofburg, nevertheless criticized Loos for his rejection of all ornament. Whereas Loos's rejection of imposed, theatrical ornamentation was, for Broch, an epistemologically and ethically necessary step, the rejection of ornament per se was self-defeating, because artistic expression and aesthetic knowledge, Broch argued, depends on a system of organic—not imposed—ornamentation. Indeed, Broch's favorite example of an elaborate system of organic ornamentation was the music of Bach.[29]

Freud, who in this respect shares an agenda of Max Weber's, participates with Loos in the critique of an ideology that they describe alternatively as a claim to intellectual totality (Freud) and to a representational, stylistic totality (Loos). Freud was a systematic scientist whose work was at least formally independent of political events; Loos, like Karl Kraus and Hofmannsthal, was somewhat of an apocalyptic. Kraus continued in his apocalyptic style after the Habsburg collapse of 1918, a style that never abjured his own tormented dependence on baroque theatricality.[30] Hofmannsthal felt the necessity of turning to a task of cultural reconstruction, a kind of neo-neobaroque, blind to the possibility that this process and style of reconstruction would itself turn into an ideological construction of the kind he and many of his generation had striven to reject.

29. I refer to Broch's early essays of cultural criticism. See my introduction to Broch, *Hugo von Hofmannsthal and His Time*, p. 7.

30. For an elaboration of this argument, see Kari Grimstad, *Masks of the Prophet* (Toronto, 1983).

IV

The Salzburg Festival was inaugurated in the summer of 1920, less than two years into the fifteen-year life of the "republic that no one wanted." Defeat on the battlefield and at the conference table had made Austria into a dysfunctional fragment, severed both from Germany and from the former national components of the Habsburg Empire. Vienna had become an imperial capital with almost no territory to administer. The Habsburg industrial base lay beyond the new Austrian boundaries; the vast railroad network that connected Vienna with that base was useless. In this condition, Austria had little chance of economic survival. Two alternatives seemed possible: some kind of de facto unification or economic federation with the former national components of the empire, or a true annexation or union (*Anschluss*) with Germany (the Weimar Republic).

The *Anschluss* question is a complicated political phenomenon. The Austrian Social Democrats were at the core of the pro-*Anschluss* majority after 1918; Weimar Germany presented itself as a Social Democratic republic, and the idea of German national unification followed the Wilsonian rhetoric of national self-determination that the Habsburg nationalities were invoking. Otto Bauer and Karl Renner, the Social Democratic leaders, were thus prominent among the pro-*Anschluss* faction. (Renner remained in favor of the *Anschluss* until its realization in 1938 and was ultimately installed, nevertheless, by the Soviets as Austrian chancellor in 1945. Bauer opposed *Anschluss* after 1933.) Those who opposed *Anschluss* immediately after 1918 did so in the name of a complicated belief in Austrian national identity. They believed that German Austria (*Deutschösterreich*) embodied not only an authentic German cultural heritage, but the most authentic one. The majority of the nationalist Austro-Germans were conservative Catholics, proclerical, and Christian Social. Yet some considered themselves liberals and saw Austria's political and economic revival in terms of a federation with the former component nationalities of the empire.

The Salzburg Festival and the cultural program it embodied were thus Austro-German, anti-*Anschluss*, Catholic, and conservative, but with a distinct federalist surface to their rhetoric. Yet although the definition and embodiment of an Austro-German national identity that would be compatible with a pluralistic, republican society formed the manifest goal of the Salzburg Festival, there was never any doubt that national culture would and should outweigh pluralist politics. Though the new Austrian republic was to live in putative egalitarian harmony with its Hungarian and Slavic neighbors, there was never any consideration of including Czech, Hungarian, or Yugoslavian works in the Salzburg Festival repertory. Austrian national identity and its representative aesthetic discourses would remain German, Catholic (and hence distinct from the Protestant German state), and baroque.

The Salzburg repertory, and hence the desired new Austrian culture, were to be grounded in a classical literary and aesthetic pantheon that ranged from Mozart and Goethe to Franz Grillparzer and the festival's principal founder himself, Hofmannsthal. Hofmannsthal sought to restore an alleged ideal of a nonmilitaristic, literary and aesthetic Germany, but one refashioned along the baroque lines suggested above. The festival repertory was to consist, as Hofmannsthal wrote in "Die Salzburger Festspiele," of a "German national program" of Goethe, Mozart, Grillparzer, and Gluck, "German and national in the sense in which the great Germans of the end of the eighteenth and the beginning of the nineteenth centuries, the true teachers of the nation, thought of a national style."[31] ("Die Salzburger Festspiele" was a publicity pamphlet written in the form of a catechism, a significant stylistic choice in view of the Catholicizing intentions of the projected festival. The quotations that follow form the answers to questions that Hofmannsthal poses rhetorically.) *Faust* and *Don Giovanni* were to be interpreted as Catholic morality plays, and to form a trinity Hofmannsthal provided his own version of the Everyman drama, a version which dated from 1911 but gained new purpose and a new fame through the festival. *Jedermann* opened the inaugural festival in an outdoor performance on the steps of the cathedral of Salzburg, a telling combination of Hofmannsthal's baroque aesthetic and Max Reinhardt's theatrical savvy, and the initiation of a tradition that con-

31. Hugo von Hofmannsthal, "Die Salzburger Festspiele," *Gesammelte Werke,* 15 vols., ed. Herbert Steiner (Frankfurt am Main, 1945–55): *Prosa IV* (vol. 6), pp. 88–94. Hofmannsthal's essays appear in two volumes (5 and 6) of this series. These volumes will henceforth be referred to as *Prosa III* and *Prosa IV.*

tinues to the present day. The city of Salzburg itself, which Hermann
Bahr had once praised as the spot where stone turns into spirit, became the baroque stage/altar on which Austrian identity could be
resanctified.

The festival program revealed on every level a convergence of
explicitly cosmopolitan and pan-European ideals with a Bavarian-
Austrian—that is, a baroque—nationalism. As the alleged geo-
graphic center of Europe as well as of the Catholic-German "nation," Salzburg promoted the "belief in a Europeanism, as it was
fulfilled and illuminated in the period from 1750 to 1850." The
paradoxical convergence of nationalism and cosmopolitanism is a
crucial component of the Salzburg ideology: Hofmannsthal never
relinquished the notion that cosmopolitanism is essentially a German virtue. The Salzburg repertory was indeed to include non-
German works, but works that the *Aufklärer* and the romantics had
long classified as German classics—Shakespeare above all.

As to whether the audience was to be limited to German speakers,
Hofmannsthal wrote, "We hope to the utmost degree, that the
members of other nations will come to us in order to find what they
would not be able to find anywhere else in the world." Salzburg
was to reestablish the cultural roots of which the branches were
Berlin, Vienna, Bayreuth, and Oberammergau. Unlike Bayreuth,
which served the art of one man, Salzburg wished "to serve the
entire classical possession of the nation"; unlike Oberammergau,
the site of the renowned decennial passion play, Salzburg was to
serve a broad, formally secular but inwardly baroque and Catholic
theatrical tradition. Salzburg was to emerge "from the same spirit"
as Oberammergau but would be built "on different fundaments,"
those being the "theatrical ability" of the "Bavarian-Austrian tribe
[*Stamm*]." Unlike larger cities, Salzburg as festival city signified a
collectivity that would embrace both performers and audience into
a communitarian solidarity. Every major city was, Hofmannsthal
suggested, a "place of dissipation"; to go to Salzburg was to under-
take a pilgrimage, to be cleansed of urban, secular modernity. The
"eternal ethos [*Ortsgeist*]" of Salzburg was to symbolize the rejection
of profane society in favor of a sacred, rediscovered community.
The clichés are in place: community over society, *Geist* over politics.

As to how embracing that community would be—in other words,

Jedermann, staged before the Salzburg cathedral, 1920. Courtesy of the Max
Reinhardt Archive, State University of New York, Binghamton, New York.

as to the hypothetical question of whether the appropriate audience
for this national program would be an elite one or a popular one—
Hofmannsthal provided a *völkisch* answer: "He who has the concept of the *Volk* in his soul rejects such a dichotomy." Just as the
works of Mozart transcend their rococo style and become eternal
("the great is always new for the heart of the *Volk*"), Goethe's *Faust*
is not "a difficult work, food for the cultured," but rather the "play
of all plays, formed from the theatrical elements of many centuries,
and rich enough in spectacle, color, and movement so as to capti-
vate the most naive public just as much as the highly cultured one."
Hofmannsthal resorted to the ideal of the *Volk* to avoid the issue
of elite versus popular, or indeed any kind of cultural fragmentation.[32] Yet although he continued to speak of art for the nation, he
cultivated the patronage of the old European aristocracy, and ticket
prices were immediately so high so as to forbid access to anyone
who did not belong either to the old rich or to the German industrial
elite.

V

If the ideology of the baroque surfaced in the manifest representations of the Salzburg Festival, then the ideology of Bayreuth
can be said to have informed its latent identity. The Bayreuth
Festival, inaugurated in 1876, had from the start declared itself,
through Wagner and his legions of epigones, a ritual and site of
pilgrimage for a national elite—or, in Nietzsche's eyes, for a
middle class that was defining itself as an elite. Although the
rediscovered national identity consecrated and celebrated at
Bayreuth was *völkisch*, the festival, like Salzburg, was not for the
Volk.

Bayreuth has been studied, texts and contexts; Salzburg has not
been. The Salzburg "texts" are not so clearly connected to ideologi-

---

32. I use the terms *Volk* and *völkisch* to describe the ideological projection of a
preindustrial, preurban, harmonious, and homogenous Christian population. For
elucidations of this ideology, see the now classic books of Fritz Stern (*The Politics of
Cultural Despair* [Berkeley, 1961]) and George Mosse (*The Crisis of German Ideology*
[New York, 1964]).

cal contexts, to be sure; indeed the choosing of texts formed the most deliberate and careful aspect of the festival conception. Despite Hofmannsthal's crucial role as planner and author, Salzburg was not conceived as the celebration of the alleged union of national art and one national genius. But insofar as Hofmannsthal genuinely felt himself to be the most genuine representative of an Austrian identity (a notion that the critical Hermann Broch only confirmed), his personality did determine the personality of the festival, even though megalomaniacal self-assertion was never his style. Hofmannsthal is to Salzburg as Wagner is to Bayreuth, but the texts of Hofmannsthal—one, *Das Salzburger grosse Welttheater* (the *Salzburg Great World Theater*), was written for the festival, as *Parsifal* was for Bayreuth—were complemented by those of others. As for the festival context, questions of its identity and significance have never been asked as they have been endlessly in the case of Bayreuth. The Bayreuth ideology was explicit from the start and was ultimately appropriated with ease and great power by the National Socialist regime. Wagner's own writings on Bayreuth have been analyzed critically as Hofmannsthal's have never been. In fact, the very proposal that Salzburg may fit into an ideological context at all, let alone into one similar to Bayreuth's, is one that raises defensive eyebrows—in Austria of course but also among its worldwide enthusiasts.

Hofmannsthal's own contextualization of Salzburg within a national ideology is no less significant than Wagner's of Bayreuth. It is only more complicated, and certainly less explicit. The Salzburg Festival itself is therefore more difficult to interpret as an ideological formation. The Bayreuth ideology is monolithic; the Salzburg ideology is elusive and overdetermined. Wagner appealed to a nationalistic mythology that was easily interpreted by his public. His anti-Semitism, in an archetypical manner the negative determinant of his German nationalism, was expressed implicitly but recognizably in his dramas (Loge the crafty adviser, Mime the swindler, and gold, for example, as opposed to Wotan the god, Siegfried the hero, and love), explicitly in his essays ("Das Judentum in der Musik," and others). Hofmannsthal was a Viennese Catholic of Jewish extraction (his great-grandfather was the Bohemian textile merchant Isaak Hofmann), married to a Jewish woman. His chief collab-

burg" proposed the construction of a 1,500-seat festival theater
on the Mönchsberg, the cliff overlooking the town. Mozart, still
present, was clearly being joined by Wagner. Just in case the example of the "green hill" that holds the Bayreuth Festspielhaus was
not clear, the proposed Salzburg structure was referred to as a
Kunsttempel, a temple of art. The realization of the festival in 1920
resulted to a large extent from Hofmannsthal's convincing combination of the traditions of Salzburg with the example of the sacred
celebration of national mythology à la Bayreuth. Nevertheless, the
ideological example of Bayreuth was in fact less evident to Hofmannsthal than it was to the Salzburgers of 1890, for whom Bayreuth remained, fourteen years after its inception, a cause célèbre.

Without the music of Richard Strauss that combined with Hofmannsthal's libretti, there is not much stylistic similarity between
Wagner, the megalomaniacal Saxon Protestant, and Hofmannsthal, the delicate Viennese Catholic. Yet the *völkisch* ideology which
they both came to embrace and around which they created festivals
received corroboration in their own creative work. Both tried to
recapture a national mythology. Wagner's method was to reclaim
Germanic and Norse myths for modernity through the revitalizing
process of music. Hofmannsthal passed from the appropriation
of Greek mythology (the Elektra myth, the first of his texts to be set
by Strauss) to Catholic mythology, rooted in the tradition of the
morality play and thus formally autonomous. As far as the religious
content of the national mythology was concerned, for Hofmannsthal Austro-German culture was defined by Catholicism. For
Wagner, a Saxon caught between Catholic Bavaria and Protestant
Prussia, between the existing patronage of the declining King Ludwig II and the potential patronage of the rising Emperor Wilhelm
I and Bismarck, the geographical compromise of Bayreuth, technically in Bavaria but removed from Munich, was an ingenious so-
lution.

The *völkisch* qualities of the Bayreuth ideology do not render the
ideology of the baroque irrelevant. It is more than circumstantial to
Wagner's project that Bayreuth first attracted him for its baroque
opera house, built for its margraves by Giuseppe da Bibiena. If the
explicit architectural forms of the austere festival hall that Wagner
ultimately had built speak to *völkisch* and neo-Attic themes rather

than baroque ones (Cosima Wagner wrote to Nietzsche that Wotan
and Siegfried could not "appear amidst amoretti, shells, and the
whole apparatus of the eighteenth century"[35]), the hall's physical
engagement of baroque ceremonial theatricality was clear. Like the
Karlskirche and the Palais Garnier, it declared a displacement of its
town's ceremonial center.

Wagner himself was Protestant; are his creations, among which
Bayreuth itself must be included, at all Catholic, or indeed—beyond
Bayreuth itself—baroque? Thomas Mann, in his 1933 essay "Suffering and Greatness of Richard Wagner," recognized the Catholicity
in the final music-drama, *Parsifal*, the only work written explicitly
for Bayreuth and allowed by Wagner's will to be performed no-
where else: "Wagner's last work is also his most theatrical . . . the
art of the theater is already baroque, it is Catholicism, it is the
church; and an artist like Wagner, used to dealing with symbols and
elevating monstrances, must have ended by feeling like a brother of
priests, like a priest himself."[36] The dramatic and ideological claims
of *Parsifal* rest in the claim to reexperience theatrically and hence
be reconsecrated by the passion of Christ. The story is Christian in
a general sense, but the theatrical modality of the work as well as
its festival context is baroque. Wagner labeled *Parsifal* a "stage
consecration festival play" (*Bühnenweihfestspiel*); the candidates for
consecration were the work itself (and by extension the art of
Wagner in general), the house of Bayreuth, and the restored German culture and mythology that the first two instantiated. Bayreuth
had already been declared sacred: it was the new Wartburg where
Wagner—once the rebellious Tannhäuser, now the conservative
Hans Sachs—could celebrate "die holde Kunst." *Parsifal* was now
written for the house and was to be performed only in that house.
Wagner's widow enforced that term of his will with uncompromis-
ing ferocity (until the Metropolitan Opera successfully challenged
her in 1903, in an assault on the Grail that Cosima attributed to the
origins of its general manager, Heinrich Conried, né Cohn).[37]

It will be recalled that the plot of *Parsifal* concerns the reconsecra-

35. Quoted in Robert Gutman, *Richard Wagner: The Man, His Mind, and His Music*
(New York, 1968), p. 322.
36. Thomas Mann, *Essays* (New York, 1957), p. 200.
37. Gutman, p. 409n.

tion of the monastery of Monsalvat in which the Holy Grail is kept; the place has fallen into disarray because the high priest Amfortas (a Wagnerization of the mythical fisher-king) has an unhealing wound in his side that of course symbolizes spiritual and cultural decadence. He is the incapacitated Prometheus who can only sit in a bath (Marat?). He was wounded by the same spear that had pierced Christ's side (this originated with Wagner). The only curing agent is the "pure fool" who will touch and heal the wound and take over the monastery. As in previous operas, the principal characters assume dimensions of Wagner's own psyche.[38] Just as Wagner was himself both Wotan and Siegfried, here Wagner is both Amfortas, the priest of a decaying culture, and Parsifal, the restorer. He is also Gurnemanz, the monk who narrates the story to us and to Parsifal, and who guides Parsifal to Monsalvat in the suspicion that this may be the pure fool of mythical expectation. The old Gurnemanz is sage, storyteller, and cultural planner. Parsifal is escorted into the hall of the monastery, where he is instructed to witness an actual communion ritual which Wagner placed on the Bayreuth stage. To emphasize the sacred nature of this theatrical procedure, Wagner requested that his audience not applaud at the first act curtain. Cultural restoration is achieved at the opera's conclusion, after Parsifal has undergone his own personal ritual of purification. (He is able to resist the sexual advances of the seductress Kundry, the Jewess who witnessed the Crucifixion and laughed, and who is the Hetaera Esmeralda responsible for Amfortas's condition.) The baroque quality of *Parsifal* consists, it can be argued, in its claim to merge sacred theater (communion and Monsalvat) and secular theater (the performance of the Parsifal myth and Bayreuth) into a representation of a mythically determined cultural renewal. It is not coincidental that the Salzburg Festival planners were more fascinated by *Parsifal* than by any other of Wagner's works.

Wagner's music dramas and his creation of Bayreuth as an institution to celebrate them and further their message have parallels in the case of Salzburg. Each festival was established at a point in the

---

38. See Michael P. Steinberg, "Portrait of the Artist: Wotan and Amfortas Reflect Wagner," *Opera News*, 9 April 1983.

life of its founder when he was expressing the desire to move from a socially withdrawn life to a politically involved one. This shift meant not the rejection of art for politics but the integration of art into politics. For Wagner, unmediated political action had not been in question since his marginal participation in the Dresden uprising of February 1849; his 1851 essay "Art and Revolution" had established the program for the sublimation of political into aesthetic revolution. For Hofmannsthal, however, a festival was part of a drive toward political participation, a chief component in his developing notion of "conservative revolution." For both men, a festival as an institutionalization of their own art was a conservative phenomenon, a convergence of artist and society. This self-institutionalization is paralleled, in the works of both, by theatrical creations that explore the reintegration of social outcasts into society— male characters in Wagner's works, female characters in Hofmannsthal's. The redeemer-heroes of Wagner's early operas, the Flying Dutchman, Lohengrin, and Tannhäuser, had been antisocial and inherently unable to join the societies with which their interaction forms the relevant drama. It is a long way from the romantic, revolutionary, and tortured artist Tannhäuser to the (ultimately) integrated, comprehended, and appreciated mastersinger Walther von Stolzing, hero of *Die Meistersinger von Nürnberg*. The very plot of *Die Meistersinger* is the reconciliation of artistic inspiration and innovation with the rules and traditions of the masters; this is the lesson the young knight Walther learns from the folk-hero Hans Sachs, whom Wagner selected because he already enjoyed that status in popular German folklore.

It may be accurate to describe Wagner's Dresden politics as political theater in which he was unable to play a star role. While in Dresden he had written "Draft for the Organization of a German National Theater for the Kingdom of Saxony." Robert Gutman has suggested that Wagner's radicalism in fact increased after the debacle of 1849; Wagner spoke of a "fire cure" and flood, which he predicted for 1852. "From the ruins," he wrote, "I shall then find those whom I need. Then shall I erect a theater on the banks of the Rhine and issue invitations to a great dramatic festival.[39] The

39. Gutman, pp. 238, 126.

Götterdämmerung symbolism is clear. Yet when he returned from his Swiss exile to Munich to accept the patronage of Ludwig in 1864, he returned as an institution in search of an institutional base. He set out immediately to form a conservatory that would complement the performances of his works, as well as founding a weekly polemical journal to be written by the conservatory faculty and a second newspaper "elucidating," in Robert Gutman's words, "the concept of civic rejuvenation through the Wagnerian drama."[40]

By 1867 Wagner had come to the belief that his institutionalized *Gesamtkunstwerk* could not thrive in "Catholic-Jewish Munich."[41] Although *Die Meistersinger* was premiered in Munich (27 June 1867), Wagner had by that time turned to Nuremberg itself as the potential site of his academy. He took seriously his own Hans Sachs's recognition of Nuremberg as "the center of Germany."[42] Nuremberg was technically Bavarian, but Protestant and a dominion of the Hohenzollern (earlier, that of the Hohenstaufen). As well as the premiere of *Die Meistersinger*, the year 1867 saw a substantial shift of political weight to Prussia and Berlin. By July, as Gutman writes, Wagner, his mistress Cosima (née Liszt) von Bülow, and her husband Hans (Wagner's conductor and a Berliner) "were toasting Bismarck at Triebschen and crying out in unison 'Delenda Austria!' "[43] In addition, Cosima's divorce from von Bülow later that year entailed her abnegation of Catholicism. There were thus many factors in the growing momentum to move the *Gesamtkunstwerk* into a Protestant cosmos. (For a Hungarian Catholic educated in Paris, Cosima Liszt von Bülow Wagner's crusade for Protestant German nationalism centering in Bayreuth, a crusade she pursued until her death in 1930, was quite a tour de force. Perhaps it even upstages the crusade of Max Reinhardt, a Viennese Jew reared in Pressburg and living in Berlin, for an Austro-German Catholic theater in Salzburg.)

In September 1867 Wagner wrote fifteen anonymous articles for the newspaper *Süddeutsche* titled "German Art and German Poli-

40. Ibid., p. 237.
41. Quoted in ibid., p. 264.
42. Wagner's Sachs refers to Nuremberg as "friedsam treuer Sitten . . . in Deutschlands Mitten" in the third act "*Wahn* monologue." See Chap. 3, note 7.
43. Gutman, p. 269.

tics," using rhetoric that duplicated Hans Sachs's final address to the gathered Nuremberg *Volk* at the conclusion of *Die Meistersinger*. The mission of Germany, he wrote, was to civilize the world through a revitalized German theater. (In these articles he also praised the *Burschenschaften*, student associations, of Father Jahn as allies in the same cultural mission.)[44] The Battle of Sedan, which he interpreted as a cultural as well as a military victory over the barbarians he had had Hans Sachs decry, increased Wagner's loyalty to Berlin.

Robert Gutman has compared Wagner's new institutional posture with his contemporaneous musical style: "He began the closing act of *Siegfried* on the first of March [1869, after a fourteen-year hiatus], and was working on its full score by the end of summer. Its love music, dazzling and somewhat overweening, has none of the neurotic ecstasy of *Tristan* and the Venusberg scene in *Tannhäuser*, but rather moves with the self-satisfied strut of Nuremberg's burghers. Having started as revolutionaries in the political ferment of Dresden following Louis Philippe's fall, Siegfried and Brynhild are united two decades later in bourgeois German Switzerland during the heyday of Bismarck."[45]

Bayreuth, then, represented a turn to bourgeois Protestantism both for the festival location and in the form of the first complete performance of the *Ring of the Nibelung* that inaugurated the festival in 1876. Yet *Parsifal* in 1882 represented an ambiguous but distinctive turn to neo-Catholicism. Robert Gutman dismisses the Protestant-Catholic duality by asserting the primacy of Wagner's hatred of all Christianity "as Judaic error perpetuated, a situation he was determined to correct."[46] The ceremonial seriousness of *Parsifal* alone would seem to belie this judgment. Presenting an alternate view, Winfried Schüler has argued that Bayreuth represented the restoration of "German Christendom" and hence a victory of (indigenous) Protestantism over (external, international) Catholicism.[47] It seems

44. Ibid., p. 278.
45. Ibid., pp. 287–88.
46. Ibid., p. 335.
47. Winfried Schüler, *Der Bayreuther Kreis von seiner Entstehung bis zum Ausgang der Wilhelminischen Ära: Wagnerkult und Kulturreform im Geiste völkischer Weltanschauung* (Münster, 1971), pp. 268–78.

more probable that, even beyond his unquestionable political opportunism, Wagner tried to rally some kind of eclectic Christianity into
his German mythology. The unity of Germany and German mythology is the ultimate ideological principle for him, and cultural, political, and religious heterogeneity had to be resolved in order for the
cultural *Gesamtkunstwerk* to emerge. This purpose was well served
by a convergence of Protestant myth and Catholic theatricality and
ritual. In the principle of a *deutsches Christentum* the emphasis is on
the national priority, and that is the key to the continuity between the
religiously eclectic Bayreuth and the religiously monolithic Salzburg.
Yet it is clear that for Wagner the sanctification (and conservability)
of Bayreuth depended on the Catholicized *Parsifal*.[48]

If *Parsifal* reveals an infusion into Bayreuth of the ideology of the
baroque (along with the more typically cited *völkisch* ideology) and
hence tightens the relationship between Bayreuth and Salzburg,
it can be said in addition that as a "dedicated text," *Parsifal* is
complemented in the Salzburg context by Hofmannsthal's *Jedermann* and by its calculated sequel of 1922, the hyperbaroque *Salzburger grosses Welttheater*. It will be argued in Chapters 5 and 7
that the aesthetic inferiority of these works informs their historical
significance. Nevertheless, a note on *Jedermann* is in order here, as
it is the text that encapsulates the formation of the Salzburg baroque

---

48. The fact that Bayreuth's ideological content is as manifest as Salzburg's is
latent (the religious eclecticism of Bayreuth notwithstanding) is confirmed by the
post–World War II continuation of the two performance traditions. Without address-
ing at this early point the difficult question of the ideological relationship of either
Bayreuth or Salzburg with National Socialism or with Germany and Austria between
1933 and 1945, I suggest only that the postwar rebuilders of the new Bayreuth, led
by Wagner's grandsons Wieland and Wolfgang Wagner, deliberately endeavored to
root out all *völkisch* images and associations from the productions of the music
dramas. They asserted tacitly that the invented tradition of Wagnerism had to be
reinvented if Wagner and Bayreuth were to survive as legitimate aesthetic entities.
Hence, although the same works of course continued to be staged, an entirely
new, minimalist and ahistorical style was developed with the purpose of detaching
Wagner from the Germanic mythology that had had such relevance to Nazi ideology.
With the exception of *Die Meistersinger*, the operas were stripped of the mythical-
historical trappings that had become emblematic of prewar Wagnerism, from the
neoclassical set designs to the naturalistic representation of nature. (*Die Meistersinger*,
explicitly *völkisch* and naturalistic, could not be dehistoricized.) This was not the case
in Salzburg, where the latency of ideological content enabled absolute stylistic
continuity in subservience to the myth of Austrian historical continuity.

Alexander Moissi as Jedermann and Luis Rainer as Death in the 1926
festival production of *Jedermann*. Courtesy of the Max Reinhardt Archive,
State University of New York, Binghamton, New York.

ideology. As a text written not for the festival but autonomously between 1903 and 1911, it became a model for rather than a model of the festival ideology.

Theatricality and totality dominate with the opening scene. An announcer (literally the "announcer of the play": *Spielansager*), who is not listed in the dramatis personae, steps forward to frame the impending drama in terms of a moral lesson and hence to incorporate the audience into the play's sacred cosmology and ritual process. The first character listed in the dramatis personae to speak is the Lord God (Gott der Herr), who, according to Hofmannsthal's stage directions, "becomes visible on his throne and speaks." He declares the advent of the day of judgment and names Jedermann (Everyman) as the human paradigm who is to be judged. He then dispatches Death to find him. Jedermann appears, a rich man who will not share his money, despite the entreaties of his mother. A banquet follows, and Jedermann is the first in the crowd to hear the distant tolling of bells. Voices call "Jedermann!" Death appears. On his final path to a Christian death and salvation, Jedermann is distracted by Lust, Mammon, and the Devil, and reclaimed by the sisters Good Works and Faith. The Austrian baroque cosmology of a matriarchal Catholicism is reaffirmed. (In the same year that he completed *Jedermann*, Hofmannsthal placed on the operatic stage a secular personification of a fantasied baroque heroine and matriarch—the Marschallin in *Der Rosenkavalier*—and named her Maria Theresa.)

CHAPTER 2

Festival Planning and
Cultural Planning

I

THE Salzburg Festival had a long period of germination, but when
it was finally born in 1920 it attempted to rise to a challenge of
national self-definition. This chapter will begin by charting the
evolution of the festival from the first stirrings in the 1840s to its
inauguration and final endowment (spiritual as well as financial) in
1925 and 1926. It will propose an answer to the question that many
observers of the festival have asked: why did it take so long to get
started? The proposed answer: it took the collapse of Habsburg
Austria and the inception of the culturally undefined first republic
to transform the sleepy traditions of Salzburg—Mozart and the
church—into the unified *mythos* of Salzburg, to energize and conse-
crate the traditions of the past into defining principles of the present
and the future. Salzburg became a celebration not of tradition but
of a reforged link with the past, a past that was adapted, if not
invented, to serve the spiritual as well as the political desires of
future-minded conservatives.

The momentum that ultimately produced the 1920 festival ac-
crued through the efforts of different kinds of people: performing
artists, entrepreneurs, armies of music-journalists, and cultural critics with elaborate ideological models for the symbolic reconstruction of Austria. If Hugo von Hofmannsthal spoke for this last category, he did so while assimilating the cultural roles and styles of

37

the others as well. This chapter charts the formation of an institution and an ideology; the two processes and the people involved cannot be separated. In Hofmannsthal the formation of an institution found a champion; in a long sequence of cultural entrepreneurs, journalists, and critics, the intellectual and ideological campaign for the festival found its infantry.

By 1918, national redefinition had become the most urgent project to everyone committed to the idea of a Salzburg festival. The festival had become a symbol, but also a component of what was being symbolized: an Austrian, in other words a Catholic German culture that claimed the title of keeper of German high cultural tradition. The theater pieces that were to be performed at the festival were to create their audience out of Austro-German Catholic congregants. The actual spectators were to serve as a paradigm for the nation as a whole. They were to see themselves—their "passion"—mirrored onstage. Audiences from 1920 on understood this charge, and often showed it by wearing the regional folk-costume of Loden suits and dirndls, a style that itself represents a Catholic world incorporating Austria, Bavaria, and the Tyrol.[1] Thus, in speaking of the theatrical structure one can describe the onstage action as the symbol, the spectators as the symbolized, one the mirror of the other. The symbol, though, has the instrumental value of creating the symbolized.

In its function the symbol was instrumental; in its character, however, the symbol was static. Both symbol and symbolized, theater-piece and audience, were representations of a fixed ideal of national character, and therefore the theater as represented at Salzburg assumed the status of a monument. In this respect one can posit a difference between theater and theatricality on one hand and drama on the other. The first can be said to suggest a closed system of ideas and representations; the second, an open one. The first presents a coherent tableau in which problems of theme and plot are solved according to a predetermined set of ethical principles

---

1. Hermann Broch suggested that the wearing of "medieval costume" was intended to reinforce the morality-play ambience, especially at performances of *Jedermann* and *Das Salzburger grosse Welttheater* (Broch, p. 177). His son, Hermann Friedrich Broch de Rothermann, who attended, confirmed to me that Broch was referring to Austrian folk clothing.

(the morality play is a prime example); the second presents conflict and tension that are irresolvable, even if the plot of the drama resolves itself. This dichotomy between theater and drama was applied by Theodor Adorno to Wagner, in an example that holds equally well for Salzburg: "Wagner's talent was primarily theatrical rather than dramatic . . . all tension is removed from the operas by the element of 'consecration.' "[2]

Nineteenth-century tourists knew Salzburg for the splendor of its baroque architecture and its evocations of Mozart. Those attributes complemented each other while adding a symbolic "southernness" to the city, which was geographically a main gateway between Germany and Italy. The south, Italy in particular, had garnered in the age of Winckelmann and Goethe the aura of purity and rejuvenation. Nietzsche had renewed that symbolism in musical terms in the 1880s, identifying Mozart (along with Bizet) as the symbol of the youth and health of the south, and Wagner as the voice of the stifling and diseased north.[3] The spirit of the south was in addition, for Nietzsche, an international spirit, combining German and Italian attributes. In a similar reflection on southern Germany in general and why it had resisted the Reformation in particular, Hegel had alluded to the "mingling of elements which is the general characteristic of its nationality.[4]

Spurred by its nebulous national identity, the history, or perhaps the mythos, of Salzburg is one of autonomy. From the fifteenth century until the advent of Napoleon, Salzburg remained under the rule of an autonomous archbishop or church-prince (Kirchenfürst). Many of these rulers gained reputations as lavish spenders for secular as well as religious projects. In 1618, during the rule of Markus Sittikus (1612–1619), the first opera in a German-speaking country was performed at the Schloss Hellbrunn. Under Johann Ernst Graf von Thun (1687–1709), Fischer von Erlach, architect of the Karlskirche in Vienna, was commissioned to build the Kolle-gienkirche in Salzburg. Opinions differ as to the origin of the style of the more mundane architecture of Salzburg. Hermann Bahr

2. Theodor Adorno, *In Search of Wagner*, trans. Rodney Livingstone (London, 1981), pp. 59, 125.
3. See Nietzsche, *Beyond Good and Evil*, aphorisms 240, 245.
4. Hegel, *Philosophy of History*, trans. J. Sibree (New York, 1956), p. 419.

wrote of its Roman origin; others have considered it the product of the taste of the local princes. It was Bahr who coined the celebrated paean to Salzburg as the city where "nature is turned to stone and stone turned to spirit," a statement that contains the Salzburg Festival's ideological cornerstone: the continuity from nature to culture to divinity.

Salzburg's self-fashioning as the center of German Catholicism was not a cosmopolitan process. In 1498 the church-prince Leonhard von Keutschach banished the city's Jews, and in the 1740s the Protestants were similarly expelled. (Savannah, Georgia, and its surroundings were settled largely by exiled Salzburg Protestants.) Salzburg's last church-prince, Hyeronimus Colloredo, was exiled by Napoleon, who placed Salzburg under the authority of the Elector of Bavaria. Ten years later it fell under the authority of the Habsburgs. Technically, then, the city that after 1918 was to embody Austria and "the Austrian idea" had been a part of Austria for only a hundred years. And as for the alleged unity of Catholic spirit in Salzburg and Mozart, it can be recalled that Mozart hated Salzburg and was driven out of it by Colloredo himself.

In 1549 the German mastersinger Hans Sachs visited Salzburg and wrote a paean to it, "Ein Lobspruch der Stadt Salzburg." The verse was reprinted in the *Österreichische Rundschau* during the Salzburg Festival in 1921, a gesture that certainly reinforced the symbolic continuity between early modern and contemporary Salzburg as well as that between Salzburg, Wagner, and Bayreuth.[5]

In 1841 the city of Salzburg celebrated the founding of the Dom-Musikverein und Mozarteum, and academy for the study of church music and Mozart. The Mozarteum, separated in 1880 from the Dom-Musikverein, became the institutional base for musical life in Salzburg and the springboard for the ambition to start some kind of music festival there, with an emphasis on Mozart. In 1870, in collaboration with the Breitkopf publishing house, a group of Viennese financiers led by Carl Freiherr von Sterneck and Karl Spängler founded the Internationale Stiftung Mozarteum (International Mozarteum Foundation), with the intention of publishing a complete new Mozart edition. It seems to have been Carl von Sterneck who

5. *Österreichische Rundschau*, 17 July 1921, pp. 781ff.

in the same year also came up with the idea of building a Mozart festival hall in Salzburg.[6] The first decisive support for the idea came from the celebrated conductor Hans Richter, active with both the Vienna Philharmonic and the Bayreuth Festival, who conducted on a fairly regular basis in Salzburg from 1879 on. In that year he conducted the Vienna Philharmonic in their second appearance there (the first had been in 1877), and in August 1887 he conducted a series of centennial performances of *Don Giovanni* in Salzburg. It was apparently at a roundtable of artists participating in that 1887 production that Richter proposed a permanent Mozart festival in Salzburg and offered his help in gathering together the necessary artists.[7] He himself was instrumental in founding a committee to investigate the possibility of both a festival hall and a regular festival.

In 1890, under the leadership of a Professor Karl Demel, the committee that Richter had helped form was named the "'Actions-Comité' für ein Mozart-Festspielhaus in Salzburg." The committee expressed its goal in a short, collectively signed article titled "The Mozart Festival Hall in Salzburg." "Similar to the Wagner theater in Bayreuth," it read, "[the Salzburg theater] should be a nurturing ground for good music in a broader sense, but should in no way be considered a competitive undertaking to Bayreuth." In the spirit of the action committee's ideas, Ferdinand Fellner, one of central Europe's most renowned theater architects, suggested an opera house for Salzburg reminiscent of the Bayreuth Festival Hall. In the tradition of Bayreuth, as noted above, the theater was to be built on the Mönchsberg, the imposing cliff overlooking the town. In supporting the plan, the action committee argued that the Mönchsberg possessed the dignity befitting a festival as well as the tranquility that could not be found in town, with "the noisy activity of everyday life, the screeching of wheels and the shrill whistle of locomotives." The Mönchsberg theater was to seat 1,500; 300 seats were to be inexpensively priced. The projected price for the whole

---

6. Although this particular enterprise contains no explicit political references, the year 1870 obviously rings with the context of an emergent *kleindeutsch* German empire against which a recently humiliated Austria might wish to assert itself.

7. "Das Mozart-Festspielhaus in Salzburg," Salzburg: Selbstverlag des Actions-Comités, 1890, p. 1.

endeavor was quoted at 600,000 florins: 350,000 for the construction of the theater, 80,000 for its appointments, 100,000 for the first two operative productions, 20,000 initial deposit, and 50,000 for a reserve fund.[8] The proposed theater building itself was described as a baroque structure, whose interior would be in the style of a concert hall rather than an opera house, with nearly the entire audience placed in front of the proscenium rather than on balconies—an unacknowledged debt to Bayreuth. The exterior, of which a sketch was provided, nearly duplicated the Bayreuth theater. The entire conception, however, met with opposition from Salzburg conservationists who protested the potential use of the Mönchsberg for a theater site. (Fellner went on in 1893 to build the Landestheater in downtown Salzburg theater, which housed the indoor performances of the Salzburg Festival until the first festival hall was built in 1926).

Interrupted by long gaps due to deficits, music festivals of some sort were held in Salzburg in 1877, 1879, 1887, 1891, 1901, 1904, 1906, and 1910. In 1901 Lilli Lehmann sang the role of Donna Anna there; in 1906 Richard Strauss conducted the Vienna Philharmonic; in 1910 Gustav Mahler conducted *The Marriage of Figaro*, a staged production with scenery by Alfred Roller. Except for Mahler (who died in 1911), all these people later played at least marginal roles in the formation of the Salzburg Festival.

II

The process that created the Salzburg Festival of 1920 and beyond really began in 1903 with a dialogue between two well-known Austrian figures, the cultural critic and essayist Hermann Bahr and the director-impresario Max Reinhardt. Born in Linz in 1863, Bahr had been active as a theater critic in Vienna in the 1890s. Reinhardt had begun his acting career in Salzburg, and in 1894 at the age of twenty-one had been engaged by the director Otto Brahm for the Deutsches

---

8. Ibid., pp. 4, 8, 11. In 1880 the Austro-Hungarian florin was worth slightly under half the value of the U.S. dollar. See Charles P. Kindleberger, *A Financial History of Western Europe* (London, 1984), p. 475.

Theater, Berlin, an institution that he was himself able to purchase in 1906. The ideas these two men shared for a possible dramatic festival in Salzburg coincided to a great extent with the program Hofmannsthal would formulate fifteen years later, though Bahr and Reinhardt referred neither to a "German national program" nor to Mozart. At first, Reinhardt spoke of a combination of Shakespeare and "romantic theater." Bahr had written an essay in 1900 called "The Capital of Europe: A Fantasy in Salzburg," which consisted of a conversation between a narrator and an imaginary, unnamed interlocutor about a festival in Salzburg. On a stroll through Salzburg, the narrator (Bahr) exclaims, "To play theater here! Imagine . . . leaves would rustle and the water would spring up. Wouldn't that be beautiful?"[9]

In 1903 Bahr enlisted Hofmannsthal, Richard Strauss, and the *art nouveau* architect Henry van der Velde for a projected 1904 festival that would highlight Eleonora Duse and Isadora Duncan. In 1906, on the recommendation of Reinhardt, Bahr went to Berlin as the "traveling director" of a "theater of five cities" that would tour Berlin, Hamburg, Munich, Salzburg, and Vienna. Among the participants were the architect Otto Wagner and the designer Alfred Roller. The venture failed for lack of funds, was resurrected in 1908, and failed again. In a letter of 1908 to Reinhardt, Bahr returned to the idea of a stationary festival in Salzburg and proposed a program of Shakespeare, Lessing, and Gorki.[10] (He was probably referring to Gorki's *A Night's Lodging*—*Nachtasyl* in German, a play often alternately translated as *The Lower Depths* in English—with which Reinhardt had had a large success in Berlin.[11]) Bahr moved to Salzburg in 1912, into the baroque Schloss Arenberg across the river from the old city and its fortifications, and adopted the role of intellectual promoter of Salzburg precisely as the "capital of Europe." He became well respected by city and church officials, and became henceforth a key middleman in the negotiations between

9. Hermann Bahr, "Die Hauptstadt von Europa: Eine Phantasie in Salzburg," in *Essays* (Leipzig, 1911, pp. 235–41), p. 235.
10. Oskar Holl, "Dokumente zur Entstehung der Salzburger Festspiele: Unveröffentlichtes aus der Korrespondenz der Gründer," *Maske und Kothurn* 13 (1967): 151, 159.
11. See J. L. Styan, *Max Reinhardt* (Cambridge, 1982), p. 10.

Hofmannsthal, Reinhardt, and the festival promoters on one hand and the church officials on the other, once the festival got going in 1920. (In 1922 he moved to Munich, where he died in 1934.)

Despite Bahr's presence in Salzburg, however, and his continued, if sporadic, efforts to promote the idea of a festival there, talk of a festival and the potential building of a festival hall was supplanted by the rebuilding of the Mozarteum, for which the cornerstone was laid in 1910. The first major step toward a refocusing of attention on the festival idea came in October 1913 with the initiation of a correspondence between the Salzburg merchant Friedrich Gehmacher (1866-1942) and the Viennese music critic Heinrich Damisch (1872-1961).[12] Gehmacher had been instrumental in the rebuilding of the Mozarteum, which he considered only the first stage in the creation of an institution whose culmination would be a festival in its own festival hall. Only when the festival hall is built, he wrote, "will validity be given to the saying that was often quoted to me as encouragement during the construction of the Mozart-house: 'We are creating an Austrian Bayreuth in Salzburg.'"[13] Damisch agreed with this principle, and wrote in 1918 that Salzburg should be to Mozart as Bayreuth is to Wagner. Thus, unlike the early ideas of the 1890 action committee, those of Bahr and Reinhardt, and the later ones of Hofmannsthal, those of Gehmacher and Damisch focused more exclusively on Mozart. In their minds, then, the relevance of Bayreuth and its cultism had more to do with the celebration of one man than with the celebration of some kind of national mythology.

Based in Vienna, Damisch looked into potential Viennese support for the Salzburg enterprise. In August 1916 he wrote to Gehmacher with a list of names, including those of the conductor (*Hofopernkapellmeister*) Franz Schalk and the industrialist Emil Ronsperger, both of whom would become important figures in the festival. (Also on Damisch's list were the engineers Erwin Mayer and Wilhelm Gorlitzer, the conductor Alfons Blümel, and the Prussian opera singer Josef Groenen. He also suggested that in addition a women's committee be formed by Maria Mayer and Nikita Gor-

---

12. The correspondence was published in Holl, pp. 148–79.
13. Quoted in ibid., p. 152.

litzer.)[14] Damisch also wrote to Rudolf von Lewicki, a Viennese musicologist associated with Lilli Lehmann. He received negative responses from both Lewicki and Lehmann, who made disparaging remarks about Gehmacher's qualifications as festival promoter. Damisch informed Gehmacher of this development and suggested to him that neither of them might be important enough for Lehmann and Lewicki: "You are not called 'your excellence' and I am not of the *Neue Freie Presse*."[15] (The *Neue Freie Presse* was often disparaged in Austria; as both the leading Viennese paper and a Jewish paper, it was alleged to be the kingpin in Jewish control of the press. This remark does suggest anti-Semitic undertones, although there is no corroborating evidence for that whatsoever as far as Damisch and Gehmacher are concerned.)

Gehmacher and Damisch, like the participants in Hermann Bahr's imaginary dialogue, had first discussed the idea of a festival in Salzburg while walking in the mountains overlooking the town. Like their predecessors, they assumed that any festival hall would be built outside the town and with a panoramic view at its doorstep. The spot they had in mind was not the Mönchsberg but the Maria-Plainer Gelände, across the river and north of town. The land would have to be bought, however, and there Gehmacher foresaw difficulty, since, as he wrote to Damisch in September 1916, "it is peasants we are dealing with, who become untrustworthy in precisely such matters."[16] Whether the festival might have some meaning for the Salzburg peasants was clearly not an open question for Gehmacher; his formulations and projections, as this small episode shows, carried no pretensions for involvement of the *Volk*. By 1917 the price of the site on the Maria-Plainer Gelände and the projected construction costs had risen, and they were expected to soar once the war was over. The plan was abandoned.

On 1 August 1917, largely because of the efforts of Gehmacher and Damisch, the Society for a Festival Hall in Salzburg (Salzburger Festspielhausgemeinde) was formed in Vienna. The society had headquarters in Vienna and Salzburg and intended to divide its

14. See ibid., p. 156.
15. Quoted in ibid., p. 164.
16. Quoted in ibid., p. 161.

meetings between the two cities, but it set itself up in Vienna first in order to attract the Viennese financial support that was clearly necessary for the project. (Because of the uncertainties of war, activity began slowly, and the inaugural meeting was not held until the following summer.) Gehmacher's motives for the formation of the society, as he expressed them to Damisch in a letter of 6 February 1918, were the following: "Among other things the purpose of our society was to prevent Reinhardt from building the festival hall. The open-air performances he can have. Eventually we might have to strike some kind of contact with him, just as long as we gain a definite influence on the festival hall and Reinhardt doesn't rule alone."[17]

The reasons for Gehmacher's antipathy to Reinhardt are difficult to determine. It might have resulted from a perceived difference in purpose; Gehmacher wanted a Mozart festival and may have expected Reinhardt to work for a more eclectic theater festival—as Reinhardt had himself envisioned some fifteen years earlier. It might have stemmed from the general unease of a conservative in relation to a perceived theatrical innovator, and it might have been a case of tacit anti-Semitism. In any case, when the society held a general meeting on 15 August 1918, Reinhardt was appointed to the artistic advisory board, along with Richard Strauss and Franz Schalk.

Ferdinand Künzelmann, a critic, writer, and member of the Festspielhausgemeinde, had proposed himself as the society's contact man with Reinhardt. He arrived at the 15 August 1918 meeting armed with a supposedly confidential letter from Reinhardt, written in Bad Gastein on 21 July 1918, which revealed that his interest had altered from a pure theater festival to a Mozart festival. This letter may indeed have changed Gehmacher's mind about Reinhardt, as Holl argues. Beyond that, however, Reinhardt's letter is a rich document that reveals much about his ideas for Salzburg.[18]

17. Quoted in ibid., p. 173.
18. Ibid., pp. 174–78. The letter is all the more valuable a document because Reinhardt rarely wrote letters and has therefore not left much documentation of his ideas. (According to the Hofmannsthal scholar Rudolf Hirsch, Reinhardt felt awkward with words and was therefore particularly reticent in writing to the poet Hofmannsthal. Almost no correspondence between the two exists—Rudolf Hirsch, personal communication.)

So strong was his apparent desire to convince Künzelmann of his earnestness and enthusiasm for a festival in Salzburg that he described the project as his "life's task." He suggested further that his entire career in Berlin amounted to a "great and comprehensive preparation for what is in question here." Rhetorical passion increases as the letter proceeds, and, whatever the measure of sincerity, Reinhardt shows very clearly his understanding of the ideological incentives for the Salzburg Festival: sacred theater as a representation of sacred culture and Austro-German nationalism as joint foundations for post-war reconstruction.

"The merry and pious genius of Salzburg" itself, Reinhardt writes, suggests the two sides of the festival character: the secular and the lighthearted, and the popular on one side; the sacred ("mystery plays and Christmas pageants") on the other. These elements would be united "under the sign of Mozart."

Salzburg would also return the roots of European theater to their original soil. The theater is essentially Austrian for Reinhardt. Even in Berlin, the leading theatrical talents, he writes, come from Austro-Hungary; he mentions the names, among other, of Max Pallenberg, Hermann and Helene Thimig, Ernst Deutsch, and Alexander Moissi. He is writing only months before the dissolution of the monarchy, but it is clear that Austrian identity is for him still firmly connected to the monarchy, to its "fortunate population mix." Austrian theater must, he writes, "reach once again these proud heights, reconquer the banner of leadership and plant it in Salzburg—this is a task as enticing as it is achievable. With beauty, spirit, and cheerfulness, above all with the deep belief in this mission, with godly sparks of joy, the world can be conquered and fraternized." (This last phrase, *mit dem Götterfunken Freude ist die Welt zu erobern und zu verbrüdern*, appears to be a somewhat muddled evocation of Schiller's "Ode to Joy" and hence to the choral verses of Beethoven's Ninth Symphony.)

The Austrian mission of purification through theater has been made more urgent by the war, and Salzburg, "with its wonderfully central location, its natural and architectural splendor, its historical curiosities, its memories, and not least its unspoiled virginity, has therefore a calling to become a place of pilgrimage for the countless people who long to be redeemed through art from the bloody horror of our time." "This very war," Reinhardt continues, "has shown that the theater is not a dispensable luxury for an elite of ten thousand, but rather an indispensable nourishment for everyone."

Certain measures will have to be taken, Reinhardt warns, if the Salzburg Festival is not to lose its sense of mission and become instead a "theater-hotel, in which art would never feel at home." To be avoided at all costs is a festival composed of imported, guest performances with no indigenous identity. Reinhardt warns first of practical consequences, then of spiritual ones. Productions transplanted from urban theaters will lose their freshness, terseness, and sparkle. Productions designed for one theater will not work in another. The festival will sink "to the level of a summer theater that will surely be visited with pleasure during rainy weather by the hotel guests who happen to be around." But he goes on: "The solemnity, celebration, and uniqueness that all art has, and the theater of ancient times and of the time of the infancy of the Catholic church—this must be returned to the theater. In this virtue lies the very strongest justification, indeed the burning necessity, for the festival hall away from the big city, whose atmosphere in turn produces substantial and fruitful work to be sure, but no more, and at most in the rarest cases the miracle that alone raises the theater to the level of art."

In a short discussion of possible repertory, Reinhardt reveals that his imperial sense of Austria (his use of the term "Austro-Hungary" included) does not displace his dedication to an essentially Germanophone theater and culture. "I can even imagine that the Hungarian, Czech, and other national theaters might make guest appearances here" (as well as Russian theater, opera, and ballet and English, French, Italian, and Scandinavian troupes), "but the core of the festival must unconditionally be a local, homegrown art. That art must be the master of the house who chooses to extend the hand of friendship to guests." The nationalistic and imperial resonances of the "house" metaphor are intensified by the accompanying image of non-German speaker as "guests."

Reinhardt concludes with a plea that charitable causes be considered and that "a mite be collected from every festival visitor for this purpose." Again, he considers the practical as well as the spiritual. "None of us today has the right to think about art without having fulfilled his duty toward the poor victims of these difficult times," he suggests. But a concern for charity would also "assure the required official promotion of the project." It is hard to tell whether he has in mind civic or church support, but his model for the collection of charity money clearly shows a view of a theater audience in terms of a church congregation.

III

Despite his references to the war, Reinhardt's miniaturist focus on performance ideas suggests a separation from and even a trivialization of politics rather than a concerned synthesis of politics and theater. This was not the case with Hugo von Hofmannsthal, for whom political developments became the defining motivation of cultural representation.

In 1919 the artistic advisory committee that had been formed the year before and included Reinhardt, Strauss, and Schalk was joined by Alfred Roller and Hofmannsthal, a sequence which led Oskar Holl to suggest that Hofmannsthal arrived late to the festival project and hence proved less important to it than his predecessors.[19] Because the earliest of Hofmannsthal's propagandistic essays on Salzburg dated from 1919,[20] there is no question that his participation in the festival ideal postdated that of Reinhardt and Bahr. Once initiated, however, his presence became crucial in two aspects beyond (or beneath) the level of ideological contextualization: the provision of the central works of the festival repertory, *Jedermann* and *Das Salzburger grosse Welttheater*, and international fundraising beyond the reaches of the Salzburger Festspielhausgemeinde. That process underscored the "cosmopolitan" character of the festival and thus became for Hofmannsthal a consistent as well as necessary extension of the festival idea.

During 1917 and 1918, Hofmannsthal had garnered firsthand experience in the practical area of the Austrian theater through his participation in what he and others referred to as "the crisis of the

19. Ibid., p. 178.
20. The essay is "Die Salzburger Festspiele," discussed in Chapter 1.

Vienna Burgtheater." His manipulation of that crisis in favor of his old friend Leopold von Andrian-Werburg reveals much about the convergence of ideology and administration in the Austrian theater.

The overseer of all the imperial theaters in Vienna, including the Burgtheater and the Hofoper (now Staatsoper), was appointed by the emperor, and it was his responsibility to appoint the directors of the individual theaters. In 1918 the position was held by Count Colloredo, with whom Hofmannsthal was on very good terms. Hofmannsthal exerted his influence on Colloredo to have Andrian appointed *Intendant*, or general manager, of the Burgtheater. Aside from the fact that he was the maternal grandson of the composer Giacomo Meyerbeer, Andrian had no professional theatrical experience whatsoever.[21]

It is clear that Hofmannsthal saw Andrian's appointment as a way of gaining virtually direct influence over the Burgtheater and hence over Austrian theater in general. His goal, as he expressed it in a letter to Andrian in August 1918, was with the help of Max Reinhardt to return the Burgtheater to its true tradition, away from the modernism and naturalism of Gerhart Hauptmann and Otto Ernst.[22] Hofmannsthal and Reinhardt had worked well together for years in both drama and opera; *Ariadne auf Naxos* had been dedicated to Reinhardt. Judging from Hofmannsthal's letter to Andrian and Reinhardt's letter, quoted above, to Künzelmann, one sees clearly that both men saw themselves as preservers of an Austrian, baroque theatrical tradition. This similarity exists despite the difference in their views of the political context of Austrian theater. For Reinhardt, baroque theater signified a performance tradition; for Hofmannsthal it formed a symbolic discourse of Austrian identity. Both nevertheless viewed a regrounded theater in Austria as a bulwark against the modernism that was becoming more and more associated with and characteristic of Berlin. Whereas the Berlin theater, as it was developing from Hauptmann through Erwin Pis-

21. He had been educated by the Jesuits and trained as a lawyer, and had spent his entire career as a diplomat, stationed in Rio de Janeiro, Buenos Aires, St. Petersburg, Bucharest, Athens, and finally in Warsaw, where he spent the First World War.

22. See Hofmannsthal and Andrian, *Briefwechsel*, ed. Walter Perl (Frankfurt am Main, 1968).

cator to Bertholt Brecht, tended to represent mundane brutality from a Marxist, class-oriented perspective, Reinhardt had become famous in Berlin for exactly the opposite: a production of Shakespeare's *Midsummer Night's Dream* that emphasized the dream quality and unreality of life.[23] Whereas the new Berlin theater strove to bring the audience down to harsh reality, Reinhardt strove to use the theater to redefine and sublate reality through the representation of an all-encompassing dreamworld. (One suspects that the exhaustion Reinhardt speaks of in his letter to Künzelmann had something to do with a growing feeling of superfluousness in postimperial Berlin.[24])

Theater as the locus of a dreamworld was the principle of the Vienna Burgtheater and the crux of its importance to those personal ambitions and aesthetic sensibilities that Reinhardt and Hofmannsthal unquestionably shared. Hermann Broch has argued that Hofmannsthal's frequent visits to the Burgtheater as a child in the 1880s formed the basis of his aesthetic and ethical education. The Burgtheater became a dreamworld that Hofmannsthal strove to redefine as reality. As Broch suggested: "from the very first moment, the Burgtheater gave to [Hofmannsthal's] work a decisive ethical significance. For everything the Burgtheater added up to, the elevation of the naturalistic and the psychological into the realm of ethical motive, the unveiling of a higher reality which, through the reality of the stage, does not deny its Platonic heritage, this orderly transformation of the dreamlike into the cold dream of art and, through art, into a new warmth—in short, this attitude of 'self-transcendence'—became for Hofmannsthal the basic principle of all ethicality and the basic attitude of his life."[25]

23. See Styan, p. 55. In an article called "The Magician of Leopoldskron," Reinhardt's supporter and colleague Rudolf Kommer wrote of the 1905 premiere of the production: "it seemed a new play entirely. . . . it had a message that did away in one evening with all the voluptuous pessimism and sordidness of the preceding fifteen or twenty years of naturalism." See Oliver Sayler, ed., *Max Reinhardt and His Theatre* (New York, 1924), pp. 1–15.

24. Erwin Piscator himself, in *Das politische Theater* (Reinbek bei Hamburg, 1979 [1929], p. 32), referred to the pre-1918 Berlin theater world—the period before his own arrival there—as Max Reinhardt's heyday. Piscator's point was that, contrary to much assumption, he was neither influenced by nor interested in Reinhardt's theater.

25. Broch, p. 102.

The "life is a dream" thematic reached Hofmannsthal via Calderón and Grillparzer and became a crucial component of his middle and late drama, as it had been of his early lyric poetry. It is probably the connecting link between the aestheticizing poetry of his youth and the socially conscious drama, indeed the social criticism itself, of the latter part of his career. Thus his turn to social criticism during the First World War represented more a refocusing than a complete change of concern and attention. Theater politics in general and the ideology of the Burgtheater in particular served as the linchpin between artistic production and social action.

The "crisis of the Burgtheater" received almost daily coverage in the *Neue Freie Presse* during the summer of 1918. This level of attention paid to the Burgtheater, often on the front page, during a time when fighting was escalating fiercely in the last summer of the war, reinforced its centrality as a symbol of Austrian national consciousness. The editors of the *Neue Freie Presse* consistently positioned articles about the reorganization of the Burgtheater next to articles about the projected postwar reorganization of Austria and Europe in general, as if to suggest that these were components of a single process. On 3 July 1918 the paper reported the resignation of the previous director of the Burgtheater, Hofrat Max von Millenkovich. Two days later, an editorial declared that the new director "must possess a conception that is high, orderly, and Austrian every bit as much as European . . . a natural patriotism and a natural cosmopolitanism." On 7 July a long front-page *feuilleton* suggested that Millenkovich's failure resulted from his ambition to transform the Burgtheater into a representative of "Christian-German" (*christlich-germanisch*) culture: "it is to be hoped that this was the first and the last attempt to attach to the Burgtheater a political direction entirely foreign to it. This stage belongs to no political party, but can rather subscribe only to a single and sole politics: it has always been a brilliant emblem of German Austria, and must always remain so. It is lamentable indeed that an institution so important, so indispensable to German art and German culture, for the entire position of the Germans in Austria, has in recent times been reeling from one crisis to the next." The editorial concluded with the plea for a change in the course of events in the form of a new director: "the long awaited Messiah, the healer, who will redeem this house from the heavy curse of the last decades."[26]

On 17 July the *Neue Freie Presse* carried a small article saying that Max Reinhardt had assumed temporary direction of the Burgtheater; on 20 July it announced the appointment of Andrian. The next day the same columnist who had written the rhetorical plea two weeks before scathingly attached Andrian as "a cavalier who understands nothing of the theater, has never had his finger, to say nothing of his soul, in the theater business, and knows about opera and drama only from the perspective of a box, from the boudoir of a ballerina, or from hearsay." By 25 August the paper suggested in a front-page editorial that Hermann Bahr, whom Andrian had appointed to the board of directors of the Burgtheater (along with Alfred Roller—and in both cases certainly under the eye of Hofmannsthal), should follow the example of Napoleon, on whom he had written, and appoint himself director.

Among Andrian's few supporters was the conservative writer Rudolf Holzer, editor of the *Wiener Zeitung*, a charter member of the Salzburger Festspielhausgemeinde and later its press attaché. Holzer accused Andrian's detractors of attempting to jettison the traditions of the Burgtheater by placing it in the hands of a group of directors. This he labeled a "symptom of the time," which— clearly in the shadow of standard antiliberal rhetoric—he in turn called "parliamentarization." The theater, he argued, must be directed by one man, and it is precisely the tradition of the Burgtheater that its director be removed from the everyday operations of the theater, so that the purity of his cultural vision can remain intact. In a somewhat tongue-in-cheek fashion, Holzer compared the relationship between Hermann Bahr and Andrian to that of Hans Sachs and Walther von Stolzing. Andrian the impresario might well be a puppet of Bahr's, Holzer suggested, but ultimately that would serve Austrian theater and national culture well, as it would assure a solid connection between Salzburg and Vienna.[27]

Andrian lasted in the job only until November. Because his ap-

---

26. The piece is signed "W."

27. Rudolf Holzer, "Der neue Kurs," *Mitteilungen der Salzburger Festspielhausgemeinde*, I, no. 2 (October 1918), 20–23. Archive of the Musikverein, Vienna (see note 35 below).

pointment was an imperial one, it did not survive the empire. It is quite possible that this debacle had something to do with Hofmannsthal's intense refocusing, from late 1918 on, toward Salzburg. Although the Burgtheater never wavered from its essential conservatism, it seems that Hofmannsthal felt his power to be waning in Vienna, as Reinhardt felt his to be waning in Berlin.

IV

On 30 July 1918 the *Neue Freie Presse* announced the formation of the Salzburger Festspielhausgemeinde, with its headquarters at Karlsplatz 6, the Musikverein building, in Vienna. Headquarters were set up in Vienna as well as in Salzburg on grounds of accessibility to the centers of Austrian finance. Prince Alexander von Thurn und Taxis, president of the Musikverein, was named president of the society. Mauriz Krumpholz was named secretary; Heinrich Damisch and the financier Emil Ronsperger were placed in key directorial positions. On the board of directors were the writers Theodor Antropp and the *Wiener Zeitung's* Rudolf Holzer, the music critic and *Neue Freie Presse* editor Josef Reitler; Karl August Urtaria, president of the Wiener Konzerthaus Gesellschaft; Albrecht Claus, insurance executive; the banker Gustav Frid; the engineers Wilhelm Gorlitzer and Wilhelm Techen; the merchants Emil Löwenbach, Adolf Graf, and Leo Taussig; the baritone Richard Mayr; the foreign ministry official Ernst Hermann Sommert; and Dr. Rudolf Hans Steiner.[28] On 20 August 1918 the *Neue Freie Presse* reported the inaugural meeting of the society in the Schloss Mirabell in Salzburg; the meeting was run by Vice-president Urtaria because Thurn and Taxis had suffered an accident.

The festival committee immediately embarked on a membership drive, attempting to draw support from Germany as well as Austria. Membership fees started at an annual rate of 100 kronen, and climbed to the status of founding member at a cost of 100,000 kronen. The flyer that contained the membership information was headed by a call to arms: "Join the Salzburg Festival Society! *Help*

28. *Neue Freie Presse*, 3 August 1918, p. 1.

the construction of the Salzburg Festival Halls in the Hellbrunn Castle Park! *Help* build a mountain of the Grail for the most genuine and great art! *Enable* at the same time *the reconstruction of Austria*, of which the Salzburg Festival will always be a most important factor! *Prepare* the way for the lasting harmonization of spirits from the bedrock of all-encompassing art!"[29] Perhaps the most interesting image in this highly rhetorical plea is that of the mountain of the Grail. This is a sure reference to Wagner's *Parsifal*, the music drama that, in its combination of a Catholic mythology with a festival setting, provided a repeated example for the spiritual builders of Salzburg.

The language of the flyer is in general very revealing of the vantage point of the Salzburg inner sanctum. The international character of the festival and its proposed repertory, especially in these early planning stages, always came second to the festival's prime purpose of national cultural reconstruction. A great difference in tone separated this flyer from a short piece by Ernst Ehrens which appeared in the liberal Berlin theater journal *Schaubühne* on 7 March 1918. The latter was also a piece of propaganda and urged the public to contribute to the festival cause. But instead of stressing Austrian cultural reconstruction as the goal of the enterprise, Ehrens stressed its international character. He expressed the hope that the festival could cultivate international guest appearances, and that specifically the Opéra Comique would be invited from Paris to perform *Carmen* in Salzburg. The choice of example seems a touch on the deliberate side; Ehrens seems to be responding to the Salzburg idea in the style of "Nietzsche contra Wagner".[30]

In a clever fundraising move, the Salzburger Festspielhausgemeinde published a pamphlet of testimonials from the more enthusiastic celebrity respondents to the membership drive.[31]

29. Unpublished pamphlet, Festspielhausarchiv, Salzburg. The italics are in the original. This is an uncatalogued archive. At one time two festival halls, a small one and a large one, were envisaged. Both were to be built in the park where in 1618 the first opera was performed in a German-speaking county, a crucial event in the Salzburg history-mythology.

30. Ernst Ehrens, "Das Salzburger Festspielhaus," *Schaubühne*, 7 March 1918. Festspielhausarchiv, Salzburg.

31. "Kundgebungen zur Errichtung des deutschösterreichischen Festspielhauses in Salzburg." Festspielhausarchiv, Salzburg.

Among those who sent encouragement—and some money, one would assume—between February and May of 1918: Alfred Roller, Prussian *Geheimrat* Ludwig Barnan, Karl Hauptmann (Gerhart's brother), Siegfried Jakobson, editor of *Schaubühne*, Friedrich Funder, editor of the conservative Catholic Viennese paper *Die Reichspost*, conductors Max von Schillings of Stuttgart and Bruno Walter of the Munich Opera, opera singers Leo Slezak, Heinrich Hensel, Hermine Bosetti, and Lola Artot de Padilla, writers Gerhart Hauptmann, Anton Wildgans, and Josef August Lux. Forming the largest group were German theater directors and managers (*Intendanten*): Eugen Kilian of Munich, Baron zu Putlitz of Württemberg, Von Reichel of Bremen, Alexander von Fielitz of the Stern Conservatory in Berlin, von Holfen of the Königliche Schauspiele, Berlin, Dr. Zeitz of the Städliche Bühne, Frankfurt, Cortolezis of the Karlsruhe opera, Paul Eger of the Grossherzogliches Hoftheater, Darmstadt, Karl Hagemann of the Hof und Nationaltheater, Mannheim, and Otto Lohse of the Dresden opera.

Most of the letters contained general words of support and encouragement; three contained substantive suggestions. Karl Hauptmann warned that the Salzburg Festival Hall must differentiate itself from existing theater structures by presenting "something of the future"; it must be grandiose. "A chamber theater cannot be a festival hall. [A festival hall] must be the new, great instrument of the true popular theater (*Volkstheater*)." The conservative Catholic, Austrian poet Anton Wildgans suggested that the festival repertory revitalize a purely Austrian literary canon, Grillparzer above all, and that the performances of these works be conceived in a unique festival style. Bruno Walter, later to become a major figure in Salzburg, offered a suggestion that went in the opposite direction: he proposed an alliance with the Vienna opera, so that operatic performances of high quality, with all the trimmings, would be assured.[32]

Early in 1919 the Vienna and Salzburg branches of the Festspielhausgemeinde each circulated a pamphlet restating the general

---

32. The first series of Mozart operas presented in Salzburg, in 1921, were productions imported from Vienna. But this was the result of temporary circumstance rather than plan.

purpose of the Salzburg Festival within the general context of Austrian cultural reconstruction. The Viennese pamphlet was signed by the entire board of directors of the society, which now included the artistic advisory board of Hofmannsthal, Reinhardt, Roller, Schalk, and Strauss. The piece opened with the proverbial homage to the "magic" of Salzburg and the reminder that the idea for a Salzburg Festival had existed for a long time. The current context, the article suggested, redefined and gave a new urgency to that festival idea. The article called on "state and nation" to take up the festival cause and lend it the necessary "legitimation." At stake was the construction of an—printed in bold type—Austro-German (*deutschösterreichisches*) festival hall, which would house "spiritual and earthly festivals of the musical and dramatic art of all nations under the leadership of German, in particular Austro-German art." The resulting spiritual rejuvenation would be supplemented by economic benefits in the form of new tourism in the city and province of Salzburg. These new revenues could in turn, the pamphlet suggested, be used for an expansion of the Mozarteum into "a new center of intellectual life for central Europe (*Mitteleuropa*)." The festival idea, the pamphlet concluded, was testimony to the cultural consciousness that the Austrians had retained through the war, and would serve as a cornerstone of the "reconstruction of destroyed intellectual life and shattered cultural contacts."[33]

The Salzburg pamphlet made the same points with more inflamed rhetoric. It opened with the suggestion that the current Austrian condition was one of peace without hope, that the cruel peace that had been inflicted was all the more cruel for the fact that Austria had never been understood by her allies, to say nothing of her enemies. The Salzburg Festival was to be a "visible symbol" of the Austrian "summoning of spiritual strength": "We are not concerned with the foundation of a theater, with the project of dreamlike fantasies or the local affairs of a provincial town. We are concerned with European culture, and one of eminently political, economic, and social significance." Like the Vienna article, this one combined a pan-European perspective with one of Austro-German

---

33. "Festspielhaus in Salzburg," unpublished pamphlet of the Verein der Salzburger Festspielhausgemeinde, Festspielhausarchiv, Salzburg.

superiority. The festival, it proposed, would "show our specifically Austrian essence in the works of our masters." The strength of the festival vision, it proposed, lay in the "selfless devotion to the dream of artists and of the people (*Künstler- und Völkertraum*)" shown by the greatest living Austrian and southern German artists. (Presumably this reference is to the testimonials cited above, though the vast majority of German respondents were Berliners, not southern Germans.) The Salzburg Festival, the article concluded, would reestablish Salzburg as the "spiritual bridge" between East and West, the traditional Austrian prerogative, and make of it a bridge between North and South as well, and hence the true cultural pivot of *Mitteleuropa*.[34]

In the summer of 1918 the Festspielhausgemeinde had inaugurated a regular forum for the expression and discussion of the Salzburg Festival idea: the "Newsletter of the Salzburg Festival Society" (*Mitteilungen der Salzburger Festspielhausgemeinde*). It was edited in Vienna by the entire board of directors of the society; a Herr Neumayr was the managing editor. Friedrich Gehmacher directed the Salzburg office. The newsletter was published through 1921 in a consistent format: five or six articles followed by a review of recent press coverage of festival plans and a section of festival society news and events.[35]

The newsletter was originally intended to be a quarterly publication, but in January 1919 it began appearing on a monthly basis as a manner of response to the Austrian cultural crisis. The December 1918 issue, published a month after the final Habsburg collapse, opened with a short column, "To Our Readers": "The content of the drama on the world-stage has not been able to cripple or hinder the quiet, determined work of the festival idea." The baroque image of the world-theater was clearly at work. The column continued: "The last weeks have brought epochal tremors and changes to the development of German theater culture as well. The individual charge of the art of the stage, the noble, old culture of the dynasties and courts has for the time being come to an end. New vistas and

34. Untitled, unpublished pamphlet of the Verein der Salzburger Festspielhausgemeinde, Festspielhausarchiv, Salzburg.
35. Copies of the newsletter, *Mitteilungen der Salzburger Festspielhausgemeinde*, are held in the archive of the Musikverein, Vienna.

possibilities present themselves. The theater is entirely in the hands of the nation and the people."[36] There is no doubt that it was in the interest of the directors of the Festspielhausgemeinde to campaign for the ongoing importance of their project during a time of crisis when other things were clearly judged more vital by everyone else. But their earnest belief that their project was crucial to the reformation of Austrian identity should not be undervalued, and the fact that the festival did begin to take form during this period suggests further that the importance its promoters attached to it was accepted by a much larger number of people.

This tone was reinforced in an article of 24 January 1919 in the *Wiener Allgemeine Zeitung*, entitled "Das Erste" ("The First Thing"), and signed "B.Z." It opened: "An empire is destroyed. A throne tumbles. A people rises up. A new state order is forged. New world orders dawn. Of the old traditions nothing remains. And what is the first thing to rise from this chaos? A Mozart Festival Hall in Salzburg! A temple dedicated to the divine, to be erected in the park of Hellbrunn as a living symbol (*Sinnbild*) of an indestructable Austria, as a sign of the indestructability of the essential character of German Austria's religious confession of faith. The first thing! Even before misery, insecurity, worry, and suffering are eliminated . . . we erect a structure dedicated to art in the place where Mozart was born. . . . Reconstructed from the Austro-German spirit, true to its *völkisch* mission, it has been chosen as mediator between South and East, between North and West. May it be an auspicious sign for us. . . . Behold, one day it will be said: This was German Austria's first deed."[37]

The inaugural issue of the *Mitteilungen der Salzburger Festspielhausgemeinde* opened with an article titled "The Mozart Festival Hall in Salzburg," by Konrad Lindenthaler. Its argument was that it would be "unmozartly" (*unmozartlich*) to perform *only* Mozart in the new hall, and that works of other composers should be presented as well (with the exception of Wagner, for technical reasons). This first issue also reprinted the celebrity testimonials of the spring of 1918,

36. *Mitteilungen*, I, 4.
37. "Das Erste," reprinted in the *Mitteilungen der Salzburger Festspielhausgemeinde*, II, 2 (February 1919), 8–9. Archive of the Musikverein, Vienna.

discussed above. In its review of press coverage of the festival plans it recorded the support of "the Salzburg press of all parties," as well as that of the conservative Catholic Vienna *Reichspost*, which carried a column expressing the hope that the festival would effect a "reawakening of the old mystery plays."[38]

The October 1918 issue contained an article by Josef August Lux called "Ideas for the Festival Hall." It set an example for future articles by continuing the tradition of discussing the proposed Salzburg Festival as a foil to Bayreuth. Lux argued that whereas Bayreuth was an artificial construction that promoted tourism, Salzburg was a natural and holistic place of pilgrimage. In Bayreuth the festival atmosphere is limited to the interior of the festival hall; in Salzburg the entire city and surrounding landscape share in the creation of the sacred, festival atmosphere. In other words, the Salzburg Festival is a totality. For the first time since the creation of the Olympics, Lux writes, the Salzburg Festival presents "a total aesthetic realization (*Durchbildung*) of the festival character, which here in Salzburg is to embrace art, architecture, landscape *and social structure*."[39] That all of Salzburg serves this total festival identity is symbolized by the panoramic vista of the town, beneath the fortification that Lux calls the "mountain of the Grail." (The Parsifal imagery returns.)

Lux's spirit was matched by the *deutschnational* Theodor Antropp in a January 1919 article called "The Festival Idea."[40] Antropp offered a new perspective on the Bayreuth-Salzburg connection by placing both festivals as late examples in a historical process that began with Attic tragedy. Not surprisingly, he relied heavily on Richard Wagner's theoretical writings. Antropp provides the theoretical underpinning for the aestheticism he shares with Lux: Greece, he proposes, was rediscovered as an aesthetic whole by the Renaissance, only to be challenged by the "nature evangelist" Rousseau. Rousseau was then countered by the "art evangelist" Schiller, who in his *On the Aesthetic Education of Man* revitalized the Renaissance world-view by uniting it with idealism. The post-

38. *Mitteilungen* I, 1.
39. *Gesellschaftsbild* (emphasis mine), with its suggestion of a totalistic picture or image (*Bild*) of society.
40. See the *Deutsches Biographisches Archiv*, ed. Bernhard Fabian (Munich, 1982).

Schillerian artist, of which Wagner is the greatest example, must view his universe aesthetically, as a totality. His duty, according to Antropp, is "to purify his century," a fearsome task that parallels the purifying mission of "Agamemnon's son." Through the works of Mozart and the playwright Ferdinand Raimund, the Salzburg Festival has the potential "to fulfill the ethical demand of Richard Wagner 'to bring about an elevation of the ethic of the nation through an ennobling of taste, and to encourage, through the cultivation of an ever growing public the liberation of a richly talented spirit of the people (*Volksgeist*).' " Salzburg could thus take up the unfinished task of Bayreuth: "The Bayreuth example has indeed proved effective, and the resumption of folkloric passion plays, the Lutheran plays, the festive folkplays of Rothenburg and Kochel, the achievements of the Worms Volkstheater as well as the Harz Mountain Theater enjoy an ideal communion with the Wagnerian festival idea. Yet all these undertakings are only attempts, and however deserving of praise and gratitude they may be, they have nevertheless not succeeded in offering us what goes hand in hand with Bayreuth's service to the tragic muse: a worthy counterpart, which through artistically perfect presentations is capable of holding up next to raw reality the alternate, ideal mirror image of spirited art."[41]

Bayreuth retained its presence in a three-part article by Paul Marsop titled "On the Way to the Salzburg Festival Hall." For Theodor Antropp, Bayreuth and Salzburg both had been late links in a long chain; for Marsop, "Bayreuth is no goal, but a starting point" for the Salzburg endeavor. The crucial element of the Salzburg Festival is the sacredness of Austro-German folk culture (*Volkskultur*). In order for that character to be retained, the festival planners must guard against the victory of tourism—Bayreuth's scourge—which turns the opera house into a "hairdo museum" (*Zopf-Museum*) full of "hare-brained philistines." The most powerful instrument for retaining sacred atmosphere is the architectural style of the festival hall, which must avoid the "mechanical opportunism" of Fellner and Helmer and the predilection of all German theater designers (except for Karl Friedrich Schinkel and Gottfried

41. *Mitteilungen* II, 1 (January 1919), 1–5.

Semper) to concentrate on the facade as opposed to the stage and technical areas, and on profane decoration as opposed to sacred festival atmosphere. The design of the Salzburg Festival Hall, Marsop proposed, must be dictated by two stylistic principles: Salzburg's topographical uniqueness and its baroque traditions. The interior must be acoustically perfect and fireproof, with enough inexpensive seats to pay homage to German "democratic consciousness." "The choice," Marsop suggested, "is between the anti-German, antidemocratic, money-swallowing tiered theater which leads to catastrophe in a fire or a panic, and the German theater, or rather, festival hall." The theater must be used for the festival only: "Festival means worship. A house of worship is not rented out." Marsop's sensitivity to the issues of fire and panic was perhaps inspired by the infamous fire in Vienna's Ringtheater in 1881, which killed four hundred people. His synthesis of issues of ideology and public safety suggest a Wagnerian conflation of fire and punishment for decadence. (When Wagner himself heard of the 1881 fire, he is reputed to have exclaimed that the disaster should have occurred during a performance of Lessing's *Nathan der Weise*, when most of the casualties—so he thought—would have been Jews.)

The second choice to be made, Marsop wrote, is that between the society parades of the Berlin Lessing Theater and the Munich Volkstheater and "a temple of Austro-German artistic genius." Austro-German, not German: although German participation, encouragement, and funds are to be solicited, the festival must remain an Austrian phenomenon, in support of the principle that "German culture is the product of the decentralization of the German character."[42]

The newsletter also solicited columns from more celebrated advocates of the cause. Hofmannsthal's well-known essay "A German Festival in Salzburg," cited in the first chapter, was originally published there in April 1919.[43] Proposals for the physical layout of the festival theater were contributed by Alfred Roller and the architect Hans Poelzig.[44]

---

42. Paul Marsop, "Auf dem Wege zum Salzburger Festspielhause," *Mitteilungen,* II, 2 (February 1919), 1–8 (part I); II, 9 (September 1919), 1–8 (part II); II, 11 (November 1919) (part III, unavailable).

43. *Mitteilungen,* II, 3–4.

44. Alfred Roller, "Festspielhaus in Salzburg," *Mitteilungen,* II, 6 (June 1919), 1–4; Hans Poelzig, "Festrede anlässlich der III. ordentlichen General-Versammlung der

Roller's main point was the familiar one that a festival hall must be physically different from a repertory theater. He proposed a 2,000-seat theater, "without ornament and colored with very dark tones." Poelzig, who had just completed the celebrated 3,000-seat Grosses Schauspielhaus in Berlin for Max Reinhardt, agreed with the emphasis on the festival character of the proposed Salzburg theater, but disagreed with Roller's proposal for a stark, dark structure. The Salzburg Festival Hall, he argued, should instead be a symbol of revitalized German art, which is essentially baroque: "All German art is more or less baroque, intricate, irregular, unacademic, from the Romanesque through German Gothic period up to Rococo." Poelzig characterized the German baroque tradition as a convergence of German Gothic and Italian baroque, and Salzburg was of course the prime example, geographically and architecturally, of that convergence. A resumption of that style would provide a "confrontation with the magic of the past." The mission of Salzburg as the recapturing of a glorious past inspired Poelzig's architectural proposals in the same way it did the choice of repertory made by Hofmannsthal and Reinhardt.

The new Salzburg architecture, Poelzig proposed, would counter the impoverished architectural trends of the nineteenth century, which he characterized as the loss of plasticity, dimensionality, and sense of space. His proposal was described by the Salzburg architect Karl Ceroni as "a fantastic structure, reminiscent of east-Asian temple buildings, with the main structure rising like a cone, surrounded by terraces and staircases."[45] Surviving photographs of the Gaudi-like Grosses Schauspielhaus in Berlin give an idea of what Poelzig's Salzburg Festival Hall would have looked like, had it been built.

The newsletter rounded out its coverage of the festival idea with articles about tangential issues, including a two-part history of the morality play tradition and a series, written by Hofopernsänger Anton Schittenhelm, analyzing the Bayreuth staging of *Parsifal*.[46]

Salzburger Festspielhausgemeinde in Salzburg," *Mitteilungen*, III, 9–10 (September-October 1920), pp. 1–10.

45. Karl Ceroni, "Der Entwurf Poelzigs für das Mozart-Festspielhaus," *Mitteilungen*, III, 9–10 (September-October 1920), pp. 10–11.

46. Joseph Ridler, "Geistliche Schauspiele," *Mitteilungen*, II, 3 (April 1919) and 7 (July 1919); Anton Schittenhelm, *"Parsifal," Mitteilungen* II, 6 (June 1919) and 7 (July

Almost every article perpetuated the Salzburg rhetoric of the reawakening of Austro-German culture. In October 1919 the newsletter reprinted the initial publicity pamphlet of the Festspielhausgemeinde about the goals of the festival. It replaced the original
ending with a call to the national governments for supporting
funds, and therefore adopted a more practical tone, stressing the
potential benefits for tourism and local employment. Yet the rhetoric remained: the festival would revive Austria's "wounded national
pride" and recapture "the Europe of the late eighteenth and early
nineteenth centuries with its supranational spirit . . . whose highest
expression was German music, [and which] lies behind us like a lost
paradise.[47] This superb example of the Salzburg idea as "nationalist
cosmopolitanism" concluded with the leitmotif of the Salzburg Festival as the "Grail-mountain of art of all peoples, under the aegis
and leadership of German, and in particular Austro-German art."

The almost parenthetical stress on the Austro-German face of the
endeavor reveals its ultimate place in conservative German ideology
per se. It was not difficult to sublimate the Austrian cultural ambitions of Salzburg into German ones, despite the essentially anti-
German rhetoric of Austrians such as Hofmannsthal and Bahr.
They spoke only of Austria when they spoke of Salzburg, but the
Salzburger Festspielhausgemeinde often spoke of the festival as "a
question of the German people, of German culture."[48] Perhaps the
most sweeping appropriation of the Salzburg program into a pan-
German cultural ideology came from the Berlin representative to
the Festspielhausgemeinde, a Herr Merkel, in a 1921 speech. Salzburg, he claimed, should become not so much an Austro-German
as a German festival, striving against the present world cultural
situation, in which "culture is losing more and more ground to
civilization."[49]

1919). Schittenhelm discussed the original, 1882 Bayreuth staging of the work, which
remained in use until 1934, when the new designer was Alfred Roller.

47. "Aufruf" and "Die kulturelle, volkswirtschaftliche und politische Bedeutung
des Festspielhauses in Salzburg," Mitteilungen, II, 10 (October 1919), pp. 1–7.

48. Salzburger Wacht, 23 August 1920, p. 4, report on the 21 August meeting of
the Festspielhausgemeinde. Also, Salzburger Volksblatt, 23 August 1920, pp. 2–3.

49. Neue Freie Presse, 18 August 1921, p. 3. The culture/civilization dichotomy
activates a principle of nineteenth-century German nationalist ideology that will be
discussed in Chapter 3.

V

On 19 August 1922, on the eve of the opening of the third Salzburg Festival—the first full festival season, including the premiere
of Hofmannsthal's *Welttheater* and four Mozart operas performed
by the Vienna State Opera—a group of leading festival committee
members and Salzburg luminaries gathered in the Hellbrunn Castle
park to lay a cornerstone for the Salzburg Festival Hall. They recorded the ceremony with their signatures on a piece of "ancient
Salzburg parchment."[50] The leading signature was that of Salzburg
archbishop Ignaz Rieder, followed by, among others, those of Gehmacher and Damisch, Ronsperger, Ridler and Holzer, Poelzig,
Strauss, and Schalk. Hofmannsthal does not seem to have attended.

The parchment proved to be more the death warrant for the
Hellbrunn theater than its birth certificate. The inflation of 1923
seemed to preclude any festival at all; Max Reinhardt ultimately
staged Molière's *Malade imaginaire* at his own Schloss Leopoldskron,
and thus provided, at least pro forma, a festival for 1923. In 1924
there was no festival at all. These general problems were further
exacerbated by a growing feud between the Salzburg and Vienna
branches of the festival society; the Salzburgers felt that all the
decisions came from Vienna while they bore all the responsibility.
As a result of these differences, President Thurn und Taxis
resigned. Salzburger vice-mayor Richard Hildmann and Richard
Strauss each occupied the presidency for a short time, before it was
passed to Baron Heinrich Puthon.[51]

Josef Kaut writes that during this period Hofmannsthal began
earnestly to fear that the whole enterprise would dissolve. Financial
worries were exacerbated by a lack of confidence, on the part of
Hofmannsthal and others, in Reinhardt's reliability. There is no
question that, with the resumption of the festival in 1925, Hofmannsthal's involvement with mundane planning and fundraising
had become decisive. He wrote regularly to festival administrator
Erwin Kerber about repertory and casting, as well as funding and

---

50. A copy of this parchment is held in the Theatersammlung, Nationalbibliothek,
Vienna.
51. Kaut, *Die Salzburger Festspiele*, pp. 40–41.

the diplomacy of the handling of celebrities (especially the competing conductors Franz Schalk and Bruno Walter). He seems to have
followed the budget carefully, and it seems to have been he who
initiated the decision to cancel the 1926 new production of *The Magic
Flute*, a decision that angered Schalk, who was to have conducted.
(Schalk conducted only *Don Giovanni* that year, while the much
younger Walter conducted *The Abduction from the Seraglio* and *Die
Fledermaus;* Schalk got his new *Magic Flute* in 1928.)[52]

Hofmannsthal worried about Reinhardt's commitment. In an October 1927 letter to Kerber he complained about Reinhardt's unrelia-
bility, his "demonic playing around with a hundred projects."[53]
Hofmannsthal also corresponded during this time with the British
actress Diana Cooper, who performed the role of the Madonna in
the 1925 festival staging of Karl Vollmöller's *The Miracle*, a modern
passion play in the form of a pantomime which Reinhardt had taken
to America, with Cooper, in 1923. In an undated letter from the
spring of 1925, Cooper wrote to Hofmannsthal (in English) that "we
should be familiar by now with Reinhardt's method of arriving a
week before the festival and having neither time nor calm to perfect
anything."[54]

The 1925 festival opened with the *Welttheater*, performed no
longer in the Kollegienkirche—a relief for the Salzburg church hierarchy and a victory for a large part of the conservative Salzburg
citizenry—but in the new, temporary festival hall next to the old
and revered Felsenreitschule. (This old riding school, carved into
the rock of the Mönchsberg, had itself been used in 1921 for several
performances of *Jedermann* when rain prevented the use of the
cathedral square. It has been used repeatedly ever since, most
notedly for Reinhardt's 1933 production of *Faust*.) In 1926 the festival hall was remodeled and made into a permanent theater struc-

52. Hofmannsthal-Kerber correspondence, 20 undated letters between January
1926 and June 1928: Frankfurt, Hofmannsthal archive, Freies Deutsches Hochstift,
catalogue number 106—Kerber—1–20; letter 2.

53. Hofmannsthal-Kerber correspondence, Frankfurt, letter 15. That this was
Hofmannsthal's general opinion of Reinhardt was confirmed by Rudolf Hirsch in a
personal communication.

54. Frankfurt, Freies Deutsches Hochstift, third of three letters from Cooper to
Hofmannsthal.

ture, designed by architect Clemens Holzmeister (who ultimately designed the new "large festival hall" in 1960).

This project needed money. Much of it came from the new, Christian Social, pro-festival governor of the province of Salzburg, Franz Rehrl, who will be discussed at greater length in the following section. Much of it, however, came from the fundraising efforts of Hofmannsthal, who generated a correspondence with Europe's old nobility and thus created the lasting international, aristocratic profile for his national, popular festival.

Hofmannsthal's goal was to create a group known as the Friends of the Salzburg Festival with a total membership of about one hundred of the most prominent figures in the major European countries and the United States. Prominence was defined by money, aristocratic position, a place in high culture, or a combination of those attributes. Hofmannsthal himself handled most of the recruiting of Austrian members of this elite committee. In Germany, England, and France he worked in close consultation with representatives: his personal friends Baron Georg von Franckenstein, Austrian ambassador in London, and Paul Zifferer, the Austrian press-attaché in Paris, as well as Baron Edgar Uexküll in Berlin. American recruitment was left to a great extent to Strauss, who had conducted in the United States in 1920 and had done some footwork for the festival.

Hofmannsthal drafted list after list of potential committee members. Although one cannot simply assume that every figure to appear on one of his lists actually joined, there is no evidence that anyone refused an invitation to do so since invitations were always worded in flattering terms and did not formally obligate recipients to contribute financially to the cause. (The available evidence suggests that only one respondent, Lord Haldane, joined on the explicit condition that he not be obliged to contribute money.) Hofmannsthal's list for the Austrian contingent included Andrian, Thurn und Taxis, Colloredo, Franckenstein, Madame Nelly Grünberger, Dr. Pauker, Baron K. Rothschild, Josef Redlich, and Paul Hellmann (Redlich's brother-in-law).[55] The German list: Graf Wolfgang Cas-

---

55. This list and all the following are found in the Hofmannsthal archive, Freies Deutsches Hochstift, Frankfurt. Since the time of my research much of the material

tell-Castell, Dr. h.c. Otto Deutsch, Karl Henkel, Count Gerhard von Kanitz, Richard von Kahlmann, Thomas Mann, Mrs. Paul von Mendelssohn-Bartholdy, Helene von Nostitz-Wallwitz, Prince Heinrich XXXIX, Prince Adolf Schaumburg-Lippe, Countess Schaessburg-Rhedern, and Baron Uexküll. The English list: the Marchioness of Anglesey, the Earl of Balfour, Lady Beatty, Arnold Bennett, Lord Berners, the Viscountess Chilston, Lady Colefax, Lady Cunard, Sir Edwin [sic] Elgar, Lord Haldane, Sir Henry Hadow, Lady Lavery, Miss Olga Lynd, Professor Gilbert Murray, H. G. the Duchess-Dowager [sic] of Rutland, and the Earl of Oxford and Asquith. The French list: Madame Maurice de Beaumarchais, Madame Dagny Björnson-Sautereau, Prince de Beauveau-Craon, Madame Renée Dubost, Professor Marcel Dunan, Paul Géraldy, Madame Octave Homberg, Charles Luquet, the Duchess de Liancourt, the Countess Emmanuel de Larochefoucault [sic?], the Countess Mathieu de Noailles, Paul Painlevé, and Maurice Ravel.

Franckenstein, Zifferer, and Uexküll shared with Hofmannsthal the task of writing soliciting letters to potential committee members and reported to Hofmannsthal the results of their inquiries. Franckenstein also provided Hofmannsthal with biographical information—occasionally in the form of extracts from "Who's Who"— on figures such as the Earl of Balfour, Edward Elgar, Sir Henry Hadow, Viscount Haldane, and Gilbert Murray. (The last of these at least, as a groundbreaking Oxford classicist, was already well known to Hofmannsthal for a glowing article about *Elektra* of some years before.) Franckenstein was particularly keen on Sir Henry Hadow, vice chancellor of Sheffield University and a musicologist specializing in Austrian music. He also urged the establishment of a women's committee, led by Mrs. Courtauld, "who with her husband provided the financial guarantee for the recent local opera season." Letters of acceptance, addressed to Franckenstein (except in the case of Gilbert Murray, who wrote directly to Hofmannsthal) invariably expressed sympathy, in Lord Balfour's words, "with the artistic and international objects on which you dwell in your letter."

Zifferer, in Paris, was in general more pessimistic than Franck-

---

has been published in Hugo von Hofmannsthal–Paul Zifferer, *Briefwechsel*, ed. Hilde Burger (Vienna, 1984[?]).

enstein. He provided most of the names that ultimately made up the French list, but he complained that it was difficult to inspire interest, and that two or three letters and often a personal visit were necessary to receive any answer at all—positive or negative. Soliciting money was even more difficult, he wrote, since an incentive such as a private box in Salzburg would not tickle the "snobbism" of "rich people" the way it would if it were in Paris. Zifferer therefore suggested that Hofmannsthal himself appeal directly to the French government with a letter to Alfred Grünberger, Ignaz Seipel's foreign minister from 1922 to 1924 and ambassador to France since early 1925. Grünberger was in close contact with French cabinet minister and former minister of war Paul Painlevé, and could impress him with the potential rise of French popularity in Austria that would be gained by French support of the Salzburg Festival.

All of Hofmannsthal's emissaries were aware of the character and significance of their cause. Franckenstein summed it up, in a 1937 speech at the unveiling of a bust of Hofmannsthal in Salzburg: "The idea of the Salzburg festivals sprang from [Hofmannsthal's] profound belief that it was our country's mission to preserve and consolidate its inheritance of intellectual and cultural supremacy— despite poverty, the hard struggle for survival, and our restricted national frontiers."[56] The tact and success of the pan-European Salzburg propaganda came from the fact that this nationalist program could be expressed as a cosmopolitan ideal that would in turn seem like pure internationalism to the English and the French.[57]

VI

Both Hofmannsthal and Reinhardt agreed with Bahr's celebrated characterization of Salzburg as the city where nature is turned to stone and ultimately to spirit, and despite the new festival hall, they went on using Salzburg's nature, stone, and spirit for settings

56. Franckenstein, *Facts and Features of My Life*, p. 321.
57. See Chapter 3 for a discussion of the differences between (German) cosmopolitanism and (non-German) internationalism.

and scenery. The carved rock of the Felsenreitschule continued to be used for opera, the cathedral facade for *Jedermann*, and in 1922 the actual altar of the Kollegienkirche became the stage for *Das Salzburger grosse Welttheater*. No chance was missed to reinforce the idea that the festival emanated from indigenous Salzburg soil and spirit. The indigenous Salzburgers, however, did not necessarily accept this idea, and in planning their theatrical coups Hofmannsthal and Reinhardt were profoundly fortunate in finding the unequivocal support, from 1922 on, of the Salzburg governor, Franz Rehrl and, from the beginning of their enterprise, the somewhat more equivocal support of Salzburg archbishop Ignaz Rieder.

Rehrl, born in Salzburg, a life-long Christian Social, pro-*Anschluss* in 1918 all the same, but staunchly anti-Nazi after 1933 despite a definite strain of anti-Semitism, was governor (*Landeshauptmann*) of the province of Salzburg from 1922 to 1938 (when he was imprisoned). From that vantage point he paid close attention to the perilous development of the Salzburg Festival, especially when the concern was the physical construction project in 1925 and 1926 and the renovation in 1937 of the old stables, adjacent to the Felsenreitschule, into the festival hall. (It was Rehrl who engaged the architect, Clemens Holzmeister.) He expressed the motive for that attention with the formula "Festspiele=Wirtschaft": festivals=economy or economic growth. Federal aid for the festival amounted to a subsidy of 400,000 Kronen, awarded in 1920.[58]

Yet purely economic considerations do not adequately explain Rehrl's interest, as the festival, especially during the mid-1920s, could not be counted on as a secure money-making enterprise. Beyond economic rationality lay what Ernst Hanisch has called Rehrl's "emotional aversion to Vienna."[59] Rehrl felt that Salzburg had, since 1816, been "colonialized" by Vienna, and in a Christmas eve, 1924, article in the *Salzburger Chronik*, he repeated the claim that "Salzburg had been a powerful cultural center way before Vienna had earned its place of significance."[60] According to Rehrl, Salzburg had a closer affinity with Bavaria than with Vienna, an

58. *Salzburger Volksblatt*, 17 August 1920, p. 1.
59. Ernst Hanisch, "Franz Rehrl—Sein Leben," *Franz Rehrl, Landeshauptmann von Salzburg, 1922–1938*, ed. Wolfgang Huber (Salzburg, 1975), pp. 5–42; quote on p. 5.
60. Quoted in ibid., p. 5.

affinity that could be reinforced by the festival. For Rehrl, Bavarian tourism was a crucial prospect, and a practical consideration which therefore reinforced his festival ideology. This is an attitude markedly different from that of the Viennese Hofmannsthal, for whom Salzburg presented a national image compatible with and even complemented by that of Vienna.

In local politics, Rehrl's provincialism was manifest in the disputes between his own Christian Socials, traditionally strong in Salzburg, and the Social Democrats, traditionally strong in Vienna. Festival politics played an important role in those disputes, in particular the funding of the festival hall construction in 1925. Inflation and budgetary irresponsibility had within a few months raised the projected cost of the project from 50,000 schillings (500 million kronen) to two million schillings. The situation was all the more embarrassing since the current president of the Festspielhausgemeinde was Richard Hildmann, the Christian Social vice-mayor of Salzburg. The Viennese press commented maliciously on the predicament and that tone reached an international audience with an article in the New York-printed, London-circulated *Musical Courier* called "Financial Tricks in Salzburg Festival Society," which compounded accusations of incompetence with allegations of embezzlement.[61] The article stirred a personal protest on Rehrl's part, which he put into a letter to the Austrian ambassador in London, Georg von Franckenstein, demanding that he unmask the anonymous author.[62] The situation in general fueled Social Democratic antipathy to the festival, and Rehrl and Hildmann waged a long battle against Salzburg Social Democratic chairman Karl Emminger. Rehrl won the battle and rescued the festival by removing its direction from the private Festspielhausgemeinde to the government. Under governmental control the festival's deficit was reduced, with the substantial help of the Bavarian Bank (Bayernbank).

Rehrl's Bavarian politics and finances, which extended beyond the festival into more mundane projects such as railroad renovation,

---

61. *Musical Courier*, New York, 15 April 1926, p. 46.
62. See Albin Rohrmoser, "Der Kulturpolitiker Franz Rehrl," *Franz Rehrl*, pp. 169–213.

represented the limit to which he could pursue his essentially pro-
Anschluss politics (another profound political variation from the
Viennese festival planners). The Salzburg Festival retained a Bavarian tint—especially in the constitution of its audience—until 1933,
when Hitler exacted a 1,000 mark fee from any German crossing
the Bavarian-Austrian border.

Archbishop Ignaz Rieder also cooperated productively with the
festival and with Max Reinhardt in particular. By allowing the
cathedral facade and the Kollegienkirche altar to be used as stage
sets, Rieder had much to do with the theatrical success of the
Hofmannsthal-Reinhardt-Roller miracle plays. Yet his relationship
with the Salzburg impresarios was always one of compromise, for
Rieder had continually to balance his sincere belief in the religious-
ness of the Salzburg plays with the skepticism and the anti-Semitism of his constituents.

The initial contact between Reinhardt and Rieder was secured by
playwright Alois Ausserer, who first suggested to Reinhardt that
the archbishop might be receptive to the festival idea. On 16 July
1920 Reinhardt wrote to Rieder and sketched the planned staging
of *Jedermann* in front of the cathedral. He stressed the fact that this
setting would allow a large enough audience to include the "less
well-off" and would therefore assure widespread popularity for the
festival among the local Salzburgers. Rieder promptly answered,
on 21 July, that he "would rejoice from the bottom of his heart, if
this penetrating play came to fruition; it will make a powerful and
purifying impression."

Reinhardt concluded that first letter by explaining that one
technical problem had still to be solved. At the moment of
Jedermann's death the text called for the ringing of church bells.
In an outdoor performance, these bells would have to ring from
the surrounding churches, and Reinhardt was concerned with
the problem of sound balance between the bells and the onstage
voices. Those bells did come to cause a major problem, but not the
technical one that Reinhardt feared. A contingent of Salzburgers
protested the use of church bells for what they considered
purely theatrical and profane purposes. These protests, as Hans
Spatzenegger has suggested, ranged from "anonymous anti-
Semitic insults to difficulties within the church hierarchy." The

result was that in 1921 Rieder withdrew the permission for the ringing of the bells.[63]

With the planning of the *Welttheater* performances for the summer of 1922, Hofmannsthal took over the correspondence and negotiations with Rieder, often with the mediation of Hermann Bahr. In a letter to Hofmannsthal of 16 January 1922, Rieder expressed his doubts about staging the new play in the Kollegienkirche. He suggested that the acoustics were not good, and that several other locations would serve better: the cathedral square (as it had for *Jedermann*), the Felsenreitschule, or the armory of the baroque palace across the river. However "noble and beyond reproach" the new play may be, "a house of God cannot be turned into a theater." Rieder then suggested that if the church were to be closed for two weeks for restoration, the play could be performed during that time—when the building would not really be serving as a church—and the proceeds from the performances could contribute to, indeed enable, the restoration. One cannot know whether the suggestion represents the first time the idea of the play supporting the restoration was brought up, but this letter does suggest that an ideological as well as a financial deal was in the making.[64]

Hofmannsthal answered on 6 February, and argued for the importance of the Kollegienkirche. To perform a sacred play like the *Welttheater* in an ordinary theater, he wrote, would be "to abandon spirit for money." To perform it in the cathedral square would be all right with him, but not with Reinhardt, whose already tense rehearsal process would be made unbearable by the logistical worries of an open-air performance—the worry of the usual rainy weather most of all. The riding school and the castle armory, he added, did not have enough doors. Finally, he argued, the *Welttheater* needs "beautiful, old, worthy music, choruses, trumpets, and most of all the organ; the music must amount almost to an oratorio," and this could be achieved only in the church or on the

---

63. Hans Spatzenegger, "Erzbischof Rieder und Max Reinhardt," unpublished account, Konsistorialarchiv, Salzburg.

64. Rieder's letter of 16 January 1922, Hofmannsthal archive, Freies Deutsches Hochstift, Frankfurt.

square, which might ultimately be used for a few performances anyway, weather permitting.[65]

On 12 March Friedrich Gehmacher of the Salzburger Festspielhausgemeinde wrote to Rieder with a formal appeal for permission to use the Kollegienkirche. Rieder agreed, and agreed that the play deserved a background appropriate to the "sacred character" that "explicitly raises it beyond the profane theatrical." He went on to list in detail the renovations that would be covered by the proceeds of the play, and suggested that the rector of the cathedral, Jakob Obweger, be contacted about the details of the restoration. This Hofmannsthal did himself on 20 May. On 12 June the Festspielhausgemeinde announced that an agreement had been reached: the play would be performed in the church, and proceeds would go toward its restoration. The Festspielhausgemeinde would immediately contribute four million kronen from its own funds, and there would be a special category of inexpensive tickets for the local population.[66]

Beneath all these negotiations lay the knowledge that the Austrian state was too poor to contribute to the restoration. Hofmannsthal wrote to his friend and London representative Georg von Franckenstein, and asked whether he might be able to raise some additional funds in England. His ultimate fear, he wrote, was that the whole project would collapse and thus bring about "dissent and antipathy toward the whole thing from a segment of the Christian population."[67] The most revealing aspect of this letter is Hofmannsthal's apparent realization—at this early point—of the flimsy ground on which his national Catholic folk festival stood among the people of Salzburg.

VII

In Chapter 1's discussion of the ideology of the baroque, I suggested that the history of baroque cultural representation between

65. Hofmannsthal, letter of 6 February 1922, Konsistorialarchiv, Salzburg; published in the Salzburger Nachrichten, 25 July 1970, p. 3.
66. Ibid.
67. Hofmannsthal to Franckenstein, 10 March 1922, "Was ist das Leben für eine Mysterium," Unveröffentlichte Briefe von Hugo von Hofmannsthal, mitgeteilt und kommentiert von Rudolf Hirsch, Neue Zürcher Zeitung, 5 August 1983, Fernausgabe No. 179, pp. 21–22. I am grateful to Fritz Fellner for this reference.

The set at the altar of the Kollegienkirche for the 1922 production of *Das Salzburger grosse Welttheater*. Courtesy of the Max Reinhardt Archive, State University of New York, Binghamton, New York.

1860 and 1938 finds a parallel in the history of scholarly interest in baroque culture. A similar situation holds for the history of the Salzburg ideology. The ideologically informed institutional history that I have been recounting so far in this chapter emerges in dialogue with trends in the contemporary intellectual history of Austrian and German conservatism. Hofmannsthal himself bridges these discourses most clearly. The rhetoric of the Salzburg Festival, from Hofmannsthal's elegant pronouncements to the more prosaic campaign literature of the festival committee, drew its power from its emblematic position in the general process of cultural planning for the first Austrian republic. The efforts of the members of the Festspielhausgemeinde and the musical journalists (Antropp, Marsop, Lux, and others) helped piece together a Salzburg ideology as well as the festival through instinctual expressions of received cultural and aesthetic loyalties to Austria, Salzburg, Mozart, sacred high culture, Bayreuth. Hofmannsthal was a grand synthesizer. The fact that the Salzburg Festival planners—including Hofmannsthal—did not concern themselves with programmatic planning beyond the bounds of their one project does not displace the universal claims of their ambitions into the realm of rhetoric without concrete intentions. Neither does it sever "theater politics" from national politics. Salzburg involved the invention of a national culture, the invention of a state of mind. Once in place, that state of mind could be transferred and applied to more detailed and programmatic contexts, such as secondary education.[68]

In my own view, the mechanics of the application of the Salzburg state of mind is secondary to the fact that it was conceived as a totality, as a *Weltanschauung*, in Freud's use of the term.[69] The fact that the Salzburg ideology was conceived as a poetic whole, as the "mirror of the nation"—to use a phrase of Hofmannsthal's—

---

68. A recent Austrian dissertation has charted the increased use in Austrian secondary schools of Hofmannsthal's own works. This study leaves two questions unanswered in relation to the current context: the possible connection between the increased attention to Hofmannsthal and the dissemination and acceptance of the "Salzburg ideology" as a fitting program for secondary education, and the possibility of parallel increased attention to other Salzburg authors and works—Grillparzer, for example. (Gerlinde Huber, "Hugo von Hofmannsthal der Österreicher in den Lesebüchern der Ersten und Zweiten Republik," Diplomenarbeit, Klagenfurt, 1970.)
69. See Chapter 1, section III.

dictated that it was a program to be accepted in full, on faith, as the definition of national- and self-identity. It was absolutely a cultural program, but one that worked through a principle of totality, and hence total adherence, rather than a principle of rationality, and hence rational application.

The juxtaposition of totality and rationality as cognitive categories parallels the elusive heuristic distinction between ideology and science. In a more specific and more specifically German and Austrian intellectual context, it parallels the no less crucial distinction between practices of cultural criticism and of social theory. Cultural criticism, at least in the German context, has tended toward a utopian posture that defines culture as an essential totality which must be either preserved or regained. The major trajectory of this kind of German cultural criticism is that of *völkisch* ideology and post-Nietzschean criticism from Paul de Lagarde to Julius Langbehn, Moeller van den Bruck, Ernst Bertram, and Rudolf Pannwitz (*post*-Nietzschean; Nietzsche does not fit in here and was fundamentally misread by his epigones).[70] Such a posture is not surprising when taken by explicitly conservative thinkers, but non- or even anticonservative thinkers (Hermann Broch and Karl Kraus are two examples) engage it as well. Social theory is, in the German context, to a great extent a reaction against the totalizing and ideological tenets of cultural criticism. The major trajectory of German social theory is the antitotalistic reaction begun by Max Weber, the intellectual and political fight to understand and represent society as a nonorganic system that is no more than the sum of its parts. Cultural criticism uses normatively the category of community, *Gemeinschaft* to define, represent, and judge society; social theory the category of society, *Gesellschaft*. Weber and German Weberian social theory project a reaction against Nietzscheanism, if not against Nietzsche.

Hofmannsthal was, at least by 1918, a conservative cultural critic; Salzburg, a product of cultural criticism. As an exercise in cultural planning, Salzburg is thus fundamentally different from the cultural planning of a Weberian social theorist such as Karl Mannheim,

70. The first three are treated in Fritz Stern's *Politics of Cultural Despair* (Berkeley, 1961). Ernst Bertram and Rudolf Pannwitz will be introduced below.

who actually made the expression current. For Mannheim cultural planning was a necessary rational policy tool in a mass society, and mass society is precisely the social category not acceptable to conservative cultural theorists, Hofmannsthal among them, who replaced it with the notion of the *Volk*. For Mannheim, planning was the "rational mastery of the irrational," against the grave danger which, he thought, could not be prevented by unplanned, uncontrolled democracy, the "eruption of crowd behavior." Mannheim's concept of cultural planning is foreign to a sense of liberalism in the Anglo-American, pluralistic sense, which might decry any notion of cultural planning, but it is rationalistic and antitotalitarian.[71]

In Hofmannsthal's intellectual milieu, the Salzburg ideology grew in the ferment of a vital new spurt of Nietzscheanism in post–World War I Germany and Austria. As an exercise in cultural planning, Salzburg is a romantic redefinition of society as a community, an aesthetic totality. It stands between, on the one side, the rationalistic planning of Mannheim, and, on the other, the deromanticized, de-aestheticized politics of totality of Carl Schmitt, for whom totality was purely a situation created and enforced by power. There is, however, an intellectual continuity between the aestheticizing totality of the Salzburg ideology and the de-aestheticized totality of Schmitt and Nazism in general. Hence the intellectual—and in many cases political—continuity between the Salzburg ideology and Austrian Nazism, a problem that will be addressed in the last chapter.[72]

---

71. See Karl Mannheim, *Man and Society in an Age of Reconstruction*, trans. Edward Shils (London, 1940), especially pp. 265, 344. It is interesting to note that the drive to understand mass society and the character of mass hysteria led three Austrian novelists to turn to the writing of social theory: Broch in *Massenwahntheorie*, Canetti in *Massen und Macht* (translated as *Crowds and Power*), and Musil in several short essays.

72. This hypothesis is likely to offend many contemporary Austrian observers who retain the long-standing idea of the separation of (sacred) culture from (profane) politics, and especially the separation of Austrian culture from German, and Nazi, politics. Yet their association was frequently maintained (of course with a different agenda) between 1933 and 1945. It can be observed that the longtime director of the Institut für Theaterwissenschaft of the University of Vienna, Heinz Kindermann, in 1933 wrote an essay called "The Mission of the Contemporary German Poet," in which he extolled the continuity from Moeller van den Bruck through Stefan George

The testimonial that caused Hofmannsthal to be embraced by conservatives (including, some years later, some Austrian Nazis) and rejected by some moderates (including Thomas Mann) was his famous 1927 address "Writing as the Spiritual Space of the Nation," in which he coined the phrase and proclaimed the goal of a "conservative revolution."[73] The piece itself, and especially the notion of conservative revolution, constitute a companion position to the Salzburg ideology. Of immediate interest and importance is Hofmannsthal's metaphor of the nation's spiritual *space* (*geistiger Raum*). This image is imbued with his sense of baroque form as a static representation of cultural totality. It is the same sense of space that informs the cosmology of the Karlskirche and the image of the stage as "world-theater."

The essay is an affirmation of the unity of the German intellectual and spiritual tradition, a unity that provides a sense of community (*Gemeinschaft*) fundamental and unique to the German national spirit. The fact that the address was delivered in Munich no doubt contributed to its pan-German tone, yet there is no contradiction between this and Hofmannsthal's earlier, explicitly Austrian definitions of the German spirit of the pre-Salzburg years. The legacy of the German spiritual *Gemeinschaft* Hofmannsthal discusses here was still, for him, the spiritual possession of the Austrians. The essay calls for an extension of the Salzburg process, the redefinition of a unified German spirit from the legacy of German letters. He concludes: "The process of which I speak is nothing other than a conservative revolution of an import unknown by European history. Its goal is form, a new German reality, in which the entire nation can participate."

---

and Hofmannsthal to National Socialism: *Des deutschen Dichters Sendung in der Gegenwart* (Leipzig, 1933). Moeller's idea of the "third Reich," George's idea of the "new Reich," Hofmannsthal's "conservative revolution," and Hitler's "German renewal," Kindermann suggested, all combined ideals of religion, art, and economy into an image of the "spiritual organic totality (*Gesamtorganismus*) of our nation." Kindermann (whose career stretched into the late 1980s) is himself an embodiment of the continuity between Austrian Catholic conservatism and Austrian National Socialism, but this continuity must in no sense be taken to imply either a universal relationship or an implied determinism or causality that may have led one form of cultural allegiance to the other.

73. Hofmannsthal, "Das Schriftum als geistiger Raum der Nation," an address given at the University of Munich, 10 January 1927, *Prosa IV*, pp. 390–413.

Throughout the essay, Hofmannsthal posits the image of the cultivated German against that of the cultural philistine (*Bildungsphilister*), an image he accurately, if somewhat prosaically, credits to Nietzsche. Hofmannsthal does a profound injustice to Nietzsche, however, in positing a (German) national type as the necessary counterpart to the cultural philistine. Hofmannsthal's misreading of Nietzsche as a nationalist is in the tradition of the contemporary Nietzscheanism by which he was affected. Between 1917 and 1920, works of Ernst Bertram and in particular Rudolf Pannwitz bore heavily on Hofmannsthal and hence on the cultural ideology he was then producing.

The book of Bertram's in question was his August 1918 bestseller *Nietzsche: In Search of a Mythology*. It began with an explicit rejection of the Rankean concept of scientific history and proposed instead a revitalized mythology as a national imperative. Germany must rediscover a national mythology, Bertram argued, and Nietzsche had defined all the major principles of that new national mythology.[74] Hofmannsthal and Bertram had known of each other at least since 1907, when Bertram wrote a pamphlet titled "On Hugo von Hofmannsthal," in which he relied heavily on Nietzsche's *Will to Power* to argue for the continuity between baroque style and musical structure as the hallmark of Viennese culture.[75]

There is no evidence of a personal relationship between Bertram and Hofmannsthal, however. It is otherwise with Rudolf Pannwitz, who between 1917 and 1920 played the monster to Hofmannsthal's Dr. Frankenstein and held him as well as Bahr and Redlich under a personal and intellectual spell. Pannwitz was twenty-six years old in 1917 and had apparently been an admirer of Hofmannsthal's for some years. In that year he published his first and most famous book, *The Crisis of European Culture*, and sent Hofmannsthal a copy. Hofmannsthal's reaction was intensely enthusiastic, and he wrote to Leopold von Andrian that "a new figure has entered my life."[76] In October Hofmannsthal wrote to his fellow morality-playwright Max Mell about his discovery of Pannwitz in tones that suggest the

74. See Ernst Bertram, *Nietzsche: Versuch einer Mythologie* (Bonn, 1918).
75. Ernst Bertram, *Über Hugo von Hofmannsthal* (Dortmund, 1907), p. 343.
76. Hofmannsthal and Andrian, *Briefwechsel*, letter of 27 September 1917, p. 252.

coming of a prophet: "What I expect from him seems incalculable, not for me, but for the spiritual life of the epoch. I would dare to risk invoking the name of Herder as a comparison."[77] A prolific unpublished correspondence between Hofmannsthal and Pannwitz exists and constitutes a rich source of Hofmannsthal's intellectual biography.[78]

Hofmannsthal's first letter to Pannwitz is dated 31 July 1917; it expresses his "extreme passion and agreement" with Pannwitz's book and ends with the plea, "Again, forgive me for writing as if to an acquaintance; perhaps you will accept this as an expression of the effect of your writing."[79] Indeed, Pannwitz entered Hofmannsthal's life at the appropriate moment to be influential on two fronts: the formation of a conservative cultural theory and the formation of a cultural and political attitude toward the Czechs (the latter to be discussed in Chapter 4).

On 9 November 1917 Pannwitz informed Hofmannsthal of a manuscript he was planning called "Österreichische Kulturpolitik," with the projected subheadings "The State of the Future," "Austria's Eternity," "Spirit," "Politics," and "Church." There is no evidence that the work was ever written. Pannwitz also informed Hofmannsthal that although he was German-born, he wanted to live the rest of his life in Austria, the only potential soil for a viable German culture.[80] He found "much more vitality in the people than in Germany," and found it possible that "Germany has suddenly come to an end, while Austria has taken over its old role and removed it to another plane . . . everything depends on finding the right direction *now*. The Austrian is more elastic than the German."[81] The Prussian domination of central Europe was for Pann-

77. Letter of 3 October 1917, in Hugo von Hofmannsthal and Max Mell, *Briefwechsel*, ed. Margret Dietrich and Heinz Kindermann (Heidelberg, 1982), p. 139.

78. The correspondence is housed in the Deutsches Literaturarchiv, Marbach. I am grateful to Werner Volke of the archive for the permission to quote from it.

79. Hofmannsthal-Pannwitz correspondence, Deutsches Literaturarchiv, Marbach: Hofmannsthal's letters to Pannwitz are filed under the heading "H:Pannwitz," file numbers 70.630 to 70.634. This is a sealed file. Pannwitz's letters to Hofmannsthal are filed under heading "P:Hofmannsthal," file numbers 60:742a-d. This file is open. All subsequent quotations from this correspondence are drawn from these files and consequently no further references will be given.

80. Pannwitz, letter of 1 August 1917.

81. Pannwitz, letter of 11 August 1917.

witz an "intermezzo"; Prussian power would give way to Austrian
power as Babylon gave way to Egypt and the Western to the Eastern
Roman Empire.[82]

Pannwitz's cultural criticism rested on several fundamental principles: organic culture, antidemocratic (anti-Wilsonian) politics, a
recognition of an organic Austria out of the union of the German
Austrians and the Czechs, an antipathy to anything Prussian and
hence to the German state (where he held organic culture to be
impossible), and—ultimately a factor in his break with Hofmannsthal—an antipathy to cultural spectacles and performers, categories
that came to include Salzburg, Strauss, and Reinhardt.

Pannwitz considered Salzburg a rationalization and falsification
of "organic" Austro-German culture and stated that it had been
the German equivalent of the Salzburg *Gründerjahre* (a pun on the
German *Gründerzeit* or "take-off" period of Bismarck days) which
caused him to leave his native Germany. He warned Hofmannsthal
that Strauss "doesn't belong in Vienna, let alone Salzburg," but
should rather "go to Budapest unless he prefers the pseudo-mozar-
tification of the Yankees."[83] As far as Reinhardt was concerned,
Pannwitz wondered whether his enthusiasm for Salzburg was the
result of honest and new ideas or of a lack of financial remuneration
in Berlin.[84] Pannwitz thus provided Hofmannsthal with many of
the Salzburg metaphors, but turned away from Salzburg itself because its theatricality rendered it an impure manifestation of its
cultural-political principles. In October 1920, Pannwitz reproached
Hofmannsthal for having allowed *Jedermann*, "which I love and
revere as a religious work," to be profaned by having it performed
in Salzburg.[85] For Hofmannsthal, however, the Salzburg Festival
embodied that conception of conservative revolution and cultural
reconstruction, and he was not about to entertain Pannwitz's criti-
cisms of it. The elevation in 1922 of *Das Salzburger grosse Welttheater*
to the central position in the festival repertory reinforced the metaphor of the festival as the mirror of an idealized social totality. The

82. Pannwitz, letter of 24 October 1917.
83. Pannwitz, letter of 4 November 1919.
84. Pannwitz, letter of 28 February 1920.
85. Pannwitz, letter of October 1920.

Catholic world-theater represented onstage mirrored the *Gottes-staat*, the godly state, which was held out as the image of Austria's future.[86]

86. For a contextualization of the *Welttheater* theme with Austrian conservative political and literary theory of the time, see Walter Weiss, "Salzburger Mythos? Hofmannsthals und Reinhardts Welttheater," *Zeitgeschichte* 2 (February 1975): 109–19. This theme and Weiss's article will be discussed in Chapter 4.

CHAPTER 3

Nationalist Cosmopolitanism

I

Fʀᴏᴍ the perspective of the Salzburg Festival and Austro-German intellectual attitudes at the inception of the First Republic, this chapter attempts a retrospective interpretation of a crucial and elusive discourse in German intellectual history: that of cosmopolitanism. The intellectual promoters of Salzburg and its world-view called themselves cosmopolitans and the Salzburg Festival a celebration of cosmopolitanism. The cosmopolitan tradition they evoked and claimed to follow was that of the German enlightenment and early romantic thinkers between 1780 and 1800. The very term "German enlightenment"—or *Aufklärung*—has a sacred aura to it. More than the French, Scottish, or Italian enlightenments, it is almost always invoked as a golden age of culture, and has therefore had very few critics in later periods. Whether the term is used to refer to a coherent totality of an age enlightened in both intellectual life and politics, or more modestly to mean an intellectual tradition that is held to be apolitical or prepolitical, it almost always invokes a model and an ideal that is to be repossessed.

The texts that have transmitted the German enlightenment have been read in various ways from the moment the period began to be considered a past age. If we tentatively date it from the beginning of the reign of Frederick the Great to Napoleon's sweep into Germany, we can see how the enlightenment has almost always been discussed in terms of the intellectual traditions of cosmopolitanism, or rather in terms of the achievement of a cosmopolitan national

84

culture. The period is seen to end with the emergence of an explicitly national consciousness—romanticism in literature, nationalism and statism in politics. Yet although the age of enlightenment cosmopolitanism predates and differs from the so-called century of nationalism, the relationship between these two national styles has been seen in different ways. The enlightenment is a golden age for all. For nationalists, the achievements of Lessing, Kant, and Goethe (the most politically neutral giants, as opposed, say, to Herder) prefigure and make possible the transitional discourses of Humboldt, Fichte, and Hegel, figures who can be seen as standing on the threshold of nineteenth-century nationalist consciousness. This is the celebrated view of Friedrich Meinecke in his most nationalistic phase, as developed in his study of cosmopolitanism and the national state of 1907.[1]

The experiences of the two world wars, especially the second, dampened—or at least censored—the proclivity to see the German enlightenment as the progenitor of a legitimate nationalist discourse, and thereby generated the view of the period that prevails today: that of the noble cosmopolitan tradition contradicted and betrayed by the narrowing and ultimately destructive attitudes of nationalism. (But if nationalism was fired by Napoleon, then "c'est la faute à la France.") According to this view, the *Aufklärung* is a paradise lost. It had its isolated defenders in the nineteenth century; seen in this light, the lonely voice of Heinrich Heine has acquired heroic proportions in post–World War II historiography and literary criticism. And, immediately after that war, the shaken and now postnationalistic Friedrich Meinecke wrote a meditation called "The German Catastrophe," in which with almost deliberate naiveté he recommended that Germany rediscover its cosmopolitan roots through the rediscovery of Goethe and the formation of local Goethe Communities.[2]

1. Friedrich Meinecke, *Weltbürgertum und Nationalstaat* (Berlin, 1907); translated by Robert B. Kimber as *Cosmopolitanism and the National State* (Princeton, 1970).
2. Friedrich Meinecke, *Die deutsche Katastrophe* (Wiesbaden, 1946); translated by Sidney B. Fay as *The German Catastrophe* (Cambridge, Mass., 1950), p. 120. The following passage reveals Meinecke's surviving nationalist cosmopolitanism: "it has always been a fact that a specifically and genuinely German spiritual production has succeeded in having a universal Occidental effect. What is more German than Goethe's *Faust* and how powerfully has it cast its radiance upon the Occident!

Yet although these historiographical styles differ in their valua-
tions of enlightenment and nationalism and in their concepts of
historical continuity and discontinuity, they share a certain underlying nationalism—manifest in the first instance, latent in the second.
Even if the German enlightenment is seen as the heroic antagonist
to German nationalism—and here the case of Heine is paramount—
the very concept of a German enlightenment is in itself a nationalistic identification of a nationally defined tradition or style. The two
approaches can converge, and have, on the principle that enlightenment and even more specifically cosmopolitanism are German
virtues.

The reception of the enlightenment in general and this convergence of interpretive and ideological strategies in particular are
themes crucial to German intellectual life between 1914 and 1933.
In both crumbling empires and both nascent, precarious republics,
intellectual as well as political models of past golden ages became
crucial components in strategies of survival, self-representation,
and reconstruction. During the war but even more after the war,
the turn to the enlightenment signified the turn away from an ideal
of a nationalist, militaristic Germany to the rededication to the
rediscovered ideals of the *Goethezeit.* The cosmopolitan "Weimar
Republic" symbolized this about-face to the world. The Austrian
Republic revealed similar tendencies. Yet the desire to return to
the cosmopolitan ideals of the German enlightenment was often a
nationalistic program. In this respect more will be said later in this
chapter about Hugo von Hofmannsthal and Thomas Mann—an
Austrian Catholic and a north-German Protestant, but, during the
war and Weimar years, both nationalist cosmopolitans.

For both Mann and Hofmannsthal in those years, cosmopolitanism and nationalism were not contradictory at all. Because national
identity is a much simpler notion for a German than it is for an
Austrian, Mann found the passage from one style to the other more
straightforward (à la Meinecke) than did Hofmannsthal. For both,
the underlying compatibility between the two styles was nevertheless the secret of the enlightenment. At stake here is not simply an

---

Whatever springs from the very special spirit of a particular people and is therefore
inimitable is likely to make a successful universal appeal" (pp. 117–18).

ideological refashioning or cooptation of the enlightenment into a nationalistic forebear, but an earnest and not at all insensitive reading of the enlightenment as a period that can indeed be characterized by a peculiar combination of cosmopolitan and nationalistic energies. I am thus proposing a history of a dialogue rather than one of an appropriation. Before we allow our own cosmopolitan and philo-Goethean sensibilities to dismiss Mann and Hofmannsthal (at least during the First World War) as nationalist cranks, we should take a second look at the *Goethezeit* and try to find the interlocutors in this nationalist cosmopolitan dialogue that is taking place.

Cosmopolitanism as the highly valued heritage of the German enlightenment survives as a challenge to the modern interpreter in the same manner as does the Reformation discourse of toleration. The modern interpreter has to decide whether, on the one hand, to take at face value the toleration of Reuchlin and Erasmus (against the nontoleration of Luther and Eck) and the cosmopolitanism of Kant, Lessing, and Goethe (against the long trajectory of nineteenth-century nationalism from Fichte and Hegel on) as noble examples of "another Germany," or, on the other hand, to suspect that each pair of discourses—toleration and nontoleration, cosmopolitanism and nationalism—reveals substantial internal continuity.

The partial analysis of cosmopolitanism offered here takes as its model Heiko A. Oberman's recent analysis of the theory of toleration in fundamental Reformation writings, *The Roots of Anti-Semitism*. Oberman argues that in regard to the toleration of the Jews, Erasmus, Luther, and seventeen other Reformation and Counterreformation theorists were "strange bedfellows." Oberman is of course aware of the controversial character of his argument, aware that although his view might find acceptance—or might indeed have long been accepted—as far as Luther is concerned, it will seem unreasonable in its inclusion both of Erasmus, the spokesman par excellence of Christian humanism and toleration, and of Reuchlin, the defender of the Talmud. Oberman bases his inclusion of Erasmus on three points: his suspicion of a Jewish "collective conspiracy," his view of toleration not in the modern sense as a guarantor of individual rights but rather as a guarantor of Christian intellectual freedom, and his "virulent theological anti-Judaism." Oberman concludes his short chapter on Erasmus as follows: "It should no longer surprise us if the trinity of peace, harmony, and learning was conceived exclusively for application to Christian society. *Tolerance was a Christian virtue* [emphasis mine] that did not make place in society for the 'most pernicious plague and bitterest foe of the teachings of Jesus Christ,' Judaism."[3]

At stake here is of course not an evaluation or even an involvement in Oberman's analysis of sixteenth-century toleration. My purpose is rather to draw a parallel between that interpretation of toleration and an interpretation of its inheriting discourse, cosmopolitanism. If Oberman's paradoxical thesis is that "tolerance was a Christian virtue," mine is that cosmopolitanism was (held to be) a German virtue, both in the original discourse of the *Goethezeit* and in the legitimate reception of it by such thinkers as Mann and Hofmannsthal.

Toleration and cosmopolitanism were both for German thinkers intellectual vehicles of self-definition through confrontation with the outside, or with the "other." In the case of toleration, the "other," as Oberman argues, is formally non-Christian religion in general, but actually Judaism and the Jews in particular. In the case of cosmopolitanism the "other" is the West in general, France in particular. In Germany, cosmopolitanism thus served as a mode of "appreciating" other national cultures, and could be accurately renamed "occidentalism," a directional opposite but ideological cognate of the now loaded concept of "orientalism." Cosmopolitanism and toleration converge in the case of the Jews, whom non-Jewish and Jewish Germans alike have never been able adequately to categorize in terms of German nationality or extranationality.

In multinational Habsburg Austria, cosmopolitanism is a still more complicated category, as the objects of its focus, in addition to the French and the English, were the Hungarians, Czechs, Poles, etc.—in other words, non-Germans and hence from a German-Austrian perspective "foreigners" in culture and nationality, but not in political and state affiliation. Although the Austrians shared with the Germans the classification of the Jews as both "outsiders"

3. Heiko A. Oberman, *The Roots of Anti-Semitism,* trans. James I. Porter (Philadelphia, 1984), pp. 38–40.

and "insiders," the situation of multinational empire intensified the
Austrian experience of not having to look beyond state boundaries
for a test of cosmopolitan attitude. It followed that the emergence
of explicit anticosmopolitanism affected both these fronts. The two
popular political movements that rose in Austria in the 1890s, pan-
Germanism and Christian Socialism, evinced both anti-Slavism and
anti-Semitism.

The popularity of late Habsburg Austria as a topic in recent American historiography has been analyzed by several American historians with several resulting hypotheses, one of which points to the
multicultural (if not multinational) parallel between late Habsburg
Austria and the contemporary United States. Without getting into
the ramifications of that comparison, I think it appropriate to add to
the discourses of toleration and cosmopolitanism a third one which
has recently been critically appraised in the relation to American society and is equally relevant to Austria between 1867 and 1938: that of
liberal pluralism. I refer to Stuart Hall's essay "The Rediscovery of
'Ideology': Return of the Repressed in Media Studies." Hall argues
that the ideological function of the American media in the 1950s and
1960s was to create the illusion of an "achieved consensus" among
diverse cultural and economic groups. What was billed as a consensus was actually, Hall argues, the "cultural absorption of all groups
into the culture of the center."[4] Although the manifest discourse of
the media heralded a plurality of cultural forms but a necessary unity
of liberal political principles, Hall argues that the society was in actu-
ality defined in terms of culture. Thus, although the media ostensibly
served to unite the population under a liberal umbrella of shared
social and political principles, its actual program was to absorb cultural difference into the dominant, culturally defined "value consensus." Hall's analysis of *Kulturpolitik* as the foundation of an ideology
of liberal pluralism is fundamentally transferable to the Austrian discourse of liberal pluralism that bridged the collapse of the empire.
The "liberal pluralism" of Hofmannsthal, Josef Redlich, and others,
who argued for an egalitarian federation of the former component

4. Stuart Hall, "The Rediscovery of 'Ideology': Return of the Repressed in Media
Studies," in *Culture, Society, and the Media*, ed. Michael Gurevitch, Tony Bennett,
James Curran, and Janet Woollacott (London, 1982), pp. 56–90; quotation from p.
60.

nationalities of the Habsburg empire but at the same time assumed the cultural superiority of the Austro-Germans, will be discussed in the following chapter. Here my purpose is merely to introduce it as an ideological cognate of toleration and of cosmopolitanism, the latter of which I turn to now.

II

The German word for cosmopolitanism is *Weltbürgertum*; for cosmopolitan, *Weltbürger*—words rich in connotations and consequently ill served by their English cognates. (*Weltbürgertum* refers more literally to a cosmopolitan class, but it is usually used as the translation of "cosmopolitanism.") A culture or a person that is cosmopolitan in the English sense is supranational, a citizen of the world or at least of an international community and hence, according to the values inherent in the term, superior to those with nationalistic or narrowminded attitudes. Cosmopolitanism is almost universally considered a virtue. In German, the relation of cosmopolitanism to nationalism is a complicated one; they are by no means neat opposites, and therefore the meaning of the first term is a complicated matter against the straightforward meaning of the second.

Literally, the word *Weltbürger* translates as world-citizen, the epithet that Voltaire used to describe himself precisely as a supranational, as an enlightened thinker whose enlightenment lay specifically in the overcoming of nationalist prejudice. The European monarch who most admired Voltaire was Frederick the Great of Prussia, and it was probably he who translated Voltaire's self-directed epithet into the term *Weltbürger*. Frederick probably coined the term and (at least through the 1740s) set the example, but what an ambiguous example it was to become. He put the emphasis on the *Welt*; later thinkers displaced it onto the *Bürger*. For Goethe, who set the example of burgherly life that lasted well into the twentieth century— indeed perhaps into contemporary times—the loyalties of the burgher applied to a peculiar mix of local context and enlightened ideas. The solid citizen—perhaps the most accurate translation of the term *Bürger*—was loyal first to his city, his locality, and then to the larger world, the world of the nation being a vague and by no means a necessarily compelling totality for Goethe and the generation of German intellectuals that preceded the Napoleonic occupation and the Wars of Liberation. "Genuine cosmopolitanism and individualistic particularism belonged together," as a recent observer of Goethe has suggested.[5] The particularism of this most famous citizen of the free city of Frankfurt proved a powerful example, several generations later, for the most famous citizen of the Hanseatic city of Lübeck, Thomas Mann. (The story of the Buddenbrook family which made Mann famous begins in 1835 at the height of the family's prosperity and portrays them precisely as cosmopolitan particularists, as loyal citizens and senators of Lübeck who speak French and use French names.) Mann, however, unlike Goethe, became an ardent nationalist; of that more will follow shortly.

Goethe's cosmopolitanism was thus grounded in a particular realm of experience which he valued more highly than anything that lay beyond it. His particularist loyalty focused on his place of birth, the free city of Frankfurt. For example, the mature Goethe of *Dichtung und Wahrheit*, his autobiography, recalls his early childhood years during the period of peace before the outbreak of the Prussian-Austrian war of 1756 as a time of comfort and security provided by the situation of the free city: "Even if such cities rule but a small territory, they are better qualified to advance their internal prosperity; as their external relations expose them to no costly undertakings or alliances."[6] Although this particularist stance can and has been read as an avoidance of and relief from the predicaments of larger political bodies, it can also be read as a model for the prosperous life of a nation state. In both tone and content we are not far from the more explicitly nationalistic homage paid to the city of Nuremberg by Richard Wagner's Hans Sachs in 1865.[7]

5. Karl J. Weintraub, *The Value of the Individual* (Chicago, 1977), p. 339.
6. Goethe, *Dichtung und Wahrheit*, trans. John Oxenford (Chicago, 1974), I:42.
7. Hans Sachs begins the third and final act of *Die Meistersinger von Nürnberg* with a "particularist" paean to Nuremberg and ends it with a nationalistic defense of German values against the West (France in particular, although Wagner disguises his attack). The first passage reads: "Wie friedsam treuer Sitten, getrost in Tat und Werk, liegt nicht in Deutschlands Mitten mein liebes Nürenberg!" ("How peaceful and true to custom, content in deed and work, does my beloved Nuremberg lie at the center of Germany!"). Sachs makes the opera's final speech to the collected populace of the town: "Habt acht! Uns dräuen üble Streich': zerfällt erst deutsches

For this Hans Sachs, Nuremberg comes to embody German national virtues; for Goethe, Frankfurt offers not only the security of enclosure but also a symbolic center for a greater German totality. Frankfurt is the site of the coronation of the Holy Roman emperor; Goethe is proud that his grandfather had held the coronation canopy over Francis I. In the mid-eighteenth-century conflicts, however, Frankfurt had been pro-Prussian, and the old Goethe retrospectively agrees with this position, not because of loyalty to Prussia but because of sincere admiration for Frederick the Great. For the young Goethe as remembered by the old Goethe, the Prussian-Austrian polarity is curiously unimportant; each can stand as a model of a German totality, and the point of contact between citizen Goethe and that totality is the city of Frankfurt.

More than Goethe, however, the enlightenment figure that provides the ideal type of the particularist is Justus Möser (1720–1794), city administrator and historian of the bishopric of Osnabrück between the Seven Years' War and the French Revolution. The standard reading of the life of Möser, Meinecke's reading among others, is that of a pious conservative out of place in the enlightenment and consciously opposed at least to the secularizing tendencies of enlightenment thinking, and hence a forebear of the conservative, nationalistic culture and politics that will sweep postenlightenment Germany. A recent monograph disputes this reading. In his *Justus Möser and the German Enlightenment*, Jonathan Knudsen argues that Möser's "complicated, ambivalent attachment to the Enlightenment . . . was far more common to the broad center of the German enlightenment than is normally assumed." Knudsen portrays Möser as a conservative *Aufklärer*, implying portentously that this is not a contradiction in terms. Möser's politics emerge in terms of a concept of corporate or etatist enlightenment: *ständische Aufklärung*.

Volk und Reich in falscher, welscher Majestät, kein Fürst bald mehr sein Volk versteht; und welschen Dunst mit welschem Tand sie pflanzen uns in deutsches Land; was deutsch und echt wusst' keiner mehr, lebt's nicht in deutscher Meister Ehr' (Beware! Evil strikes threaten us: should the German people and realm fall to a false, Welsh [i.e. French, from the root "walisisch"] majesty, soon no prince will understand his people [i.e. Napoleon III], and Welsh vapors and Welsh kitsch will be planted in our German soil; what is German and true no one would recognize, if it did not live in the honor of German masters)." Wagner thus moves from local particularism to imperial nationalism in one operatic act.

The position contains three principles: allegiance to old-regime political institutions, survival of a moral economy and agrarian state, and resistance to imperial reform. Cosmopolitanism has a definite place in this new corporatist enlightenment. "Contact with foreigners," Möser wrote in 1770, "makes one gentler and politer, and conquers prejudices peculiar to any nation." Yet the result of this education is a resecured particularism, a state of mind that Möser defends through an attack on fashion that is at the same time an attack on France: "What would it help to have the best hatmaker if the French were to decide all of a sudden to wear hats made of oil cloth? How easily a new fashion robs the best craftsmanship of its fruits. And how far must a *state* [emphasis mine] sink if it does not anticipate [these developments] or does not change its craft?" It is surely not irresponsible to suggest that Möser's image of French fashion worn on the head may be a metaphor for French fashions worn inside the head. Expanding on Möser's ideas of education and knowledge, Knudsen suggests that "the social historian of Germany in the late eighteenth century must set aside the rhetoric of emancipation and follow Diderot's lead by exploring in what ways the emancipatory claims of education could become—and indeed did become—a powerful ideology in the service of a refurbished corporation."[8]

A similar intellectual and political disposition emerges in Kant; that his case is more complicated has to do at least in part with the fact that for Kant the category of the nation does enter the problem, if in a debatable and subtle manner, since he was not a nationalist in any conventional sense and his ethical philosophy was always grounded in the experience of the individual.

Kant's famous short essay "Idea for a universal history with a cosmopolitan purpose" ("Idee zu einer allgemeinen Weltgeschichte in weltbürgerlicher Absicht") of 1784 presents the idea of cosmopolitanism in a context that is both historically interesting and relevant to this book.[9] Kant's enlightenment language is complemented by

8. Jonathan Knudsen, *Justus Möser and the German Enlightenment* (Cambridge, 1986), pp. 149, xi, 154, 158, 53.
9. The English translation of the title is my own; I offer it as a necessary corrective to the misleading standard translation, "Idea for a universal history from a cosmopolitan point of view." Kant argues for a vision of history in which history itself proceeds

the Rousseauean idea of the development of mankind from the state of nature through his "unsocial sociability" to culture, his highest state, defined by an optimal civic constitution and morality. Society is the mediator between nature and culture; society guides the autonomous individual to culture. This is in no way a particularist or nationalist position. But at the end of the seventh thesis (out of nine), Kant makes a distinction that stands at the source of a powerful German nationalist discourse: the distinction between culture (*Kultur*) and civilization (*Zivilisierung*—the process of civilization—is Kant's term; *Zivilisation*—the state of civilization—is more common).

Kant writes: "We are to a great degree cultivated through art and science. We are civilized to the point of being burdened with every kind of social technique and propriety. But that is not nearly enough for us to consider ourselves moral. For the idea of morality still belongs to culture; but the use of this idea in the context of the resemblant morality (*das Sittenähnliche*) of the love of honor and of outward propriety, constitutes mere civilization."[10] Civilization refers to outward form, what Rousseau referred to as "amour propre." Norbert Elias, in his study of the origins and uses of the distinction between culture and civilization, traces the first appearance of the culture/civilization antithesis to Kant's essay on cosmopolitanism. He comments: "The contraposition here, where the spokesmen of the developing German bourgeoisie, the middle-class German intelligentsia, still speak in a large part 'from the point of view of a citizen of the world' [Elias's translator's translation of *weltbürgerlich*], relates only vaguely and at best secondarily to a national contrast. Its primary aspect is an internal contrast within the society, a social contrast *which nevertheless bears within itself in a significant way the germ of the national contraposition* [emphasis mine]: the contrast between the courtly nobility, predominantly French speaking and 'civilized' on the French model, and a German-speak-

---

toward a cosmopolitan goal. He is speaking of historical directionality and teleology, not of his own "point of view," as English-speaking students invariably read the phrase.

10. Kant, "Idee zu einer allgemeinen Geschichte in weltbürgerlicher Absicht," in *Kleinere Schriften zur Geschichtsphilosophie: Ethik und Politik* (Hamburg, 1959), p. 15. The translation is my own.

ing, middle-class stratum of intelligentsia recruited chiefly from the bourgeois 'servers of princes' or officials in the broadest sense, and occasionally also from the landed nobility."[11]

Thus if French was the language of the court, whose place in German political and literary life was on the decline, German was the language of the new generation of intellectuals who defined their intellectual process precisely as the forging of a new, contemporary, German language. This intelligentsia, as Elias explains, came almost invariably from the middle class and was conscious of its upward mobility. Goethe's grandfather was a tailor, Schiller's grandfather a surgeon; similar genealogies apply, in Elias's list, to Schubart, Bürger, Winckelmann, Herder, Kant, Friedrich August Wolff, Fichte, and others.[12] This generation wrote in German and posited German culture, embodied in the terms *Kultur* and *Bildung*, against the courtly society of Frederick the Great. The terms *Kultur* and *Bildung* are not abstractions, but rather must be seen as defining principles of a national perspective and ideology.

In 1780, Frederick wrote (in French) an essay entitled *De la littérature allemande* in which, notwithstanding the previous publications of Goethe, Lessing, Klopstock, and Herder, he scorned the barbarous nature of the German language.[13] Elias is no doubt correct in placing Kant's essay of 1784 within this national context, while at the same time downplaying the idea that there are any explicitly nationalistic tendencies within it. Nevertheless, if the modern German language in general and cultural discourse in particular were being formed at this time, then Kant's germinal ideas together with the terminology in which they are voiced must be taken seriously for their early position in the evolution of a "nationalist cosmopolitanism" that will rest more and more on the ideological opposition between German culture and Western civilization, whether or not this civilization appears within or outside German borders. The German intelligentsia between 1780 and 1800 did think and write, as the classical interpretation would have it, almost exclusively in cultural terms, but that does not imply a separation from any kind

11. Norbert Elias, *The History of Manners*, trans. Edmund Jephcott (New York, 1978), pp. 8–9.
12. Ibid., p. 20.
13. Ibid., p. 12.

of political conception whatsoever. On the contrary, Germany as a cultural conception generated, during the Wars of Liberation and after, the politicized nationalism that began to appear with Fichte's pivotal *Addresses to the German Nation* of 1807. Fichte "nationalized" Kant's political philosophy and his epistemology, but it is possible to find latent forms of a national position in Kant, as Elias has shown.

Kant's conception of culture and of national culture may have another and a more internal parallel—if not source—in the fundamental principles of his own critical philosophy. There is certainly much to be written about the relation between Kant's epistemology and his political philosophy, as well as on the bearing of both those categories of thought on his rejection of Hume. That Kant rejected Hume's empiricism is the first thing one learns about Kant; that he rejected Hume's politics of what might be called "transatlantic" or "enlightened" cosmopolitanism in favor of his own, German cosmopolitanism, and furthermore that this political innovation may parallel the epistemological revolution, is less clear but no less interesting. In the *Critique of Pure Reason* Kant proposes an epistemology that rests on a presentation of a priori categories of mind without which the construction of experience would not be possible. Mind and an inherent state of perspectivity therefore precede the possibility of experience. Hence the Kantian transcendental ego.[14] I would suggest here simply that a parallel exists between the epistemological construction of the transcendental ego and the cultural construction of the cosmopolitan ego [my expression], individual or collective.

German political theory beginning in the seventeenth century proposes no separation or necessary tension between the individual and the protective state. As opposed to the developing English political theory of the same period, which begins to see the individual as a bearer of rights posited against the power of the state, in German theory (seen, for example in the writings of Samuel von Pufendorf, Christian Thomasius, and Christian Wolff), the individ-

---

14. I refer to Section 2, "The a priori grounds of the possibility of experience," in the Transcendental Deduction (A), *Critique of Pure Reason*, trans. Norman Kemp Smith (New York, 1929), pp. 129–50.

ual realizes himself only as a component of the nation.[15] The nation is defined according to language. Cosmopolitanism, in the Kantian sense of the word, is therefore a transcendental principle. Just as consciousness exists and comes to know the world from the central vantage point of the individual, the nation, as a theoretically consistent extension of the individual, comes to know and to judge the world from the vantage point of its own national language and consciousness. Cosmopolitanism is therefore distinct from internationalism, which posits no a priori subject or center. What for the Germans is internationalism is cosmopolitanism for the French and the English.

III

The examples of Goethe, Möser, and Kant provide, I hope, an opening through which the early-twentieth-century vantage point on the German enlightenment can be seen to be gazing. Before going on to address its dialogue with the enlightenment according to the principles of a shared nationalist cosmopolitanism, I want to mention two figures groomed in the nineteenth century whose discourses can be seen as points of linkage between the nationalist cosmopolitanisms of the eighteenth and twentieth centuries. These figures are Heinrich Heine and Hermann Cohen. Both speak as avowed cosmopolitans in periods of highly charged nationalism, Heine in the Vormärz period and Cohen in the late Wilhelmine period, and both bring to the center of their cosmopolitan discourses the issue that Lessing had addressed: the question of Judaism and German-Jewish relations. Unlike Lessing of course, both Heine and Cohen (despite the former's baptism) speak as Jews.

As an expatriate, a Francophile, and a Jew, Heine has long been the archetype of the nineteenth-century antinationalist. If in his own time he was condemned for his antinationalism, he has in the twentieth century—and especially after 1945—been lionized for it.

---

15. Leonard Krieger has traced this principle through the course of German liberal thought in the nineteenth century in his book *The German Idea of Freedom* (Chicago, 1957).

As his biographer Jeffrey Sammons has suggested, his enemies are our enemies, and "we legitimate ourselves by Heine." Sammons nonetheless questions the heroicizing identification of Heine as cosmopolitan. First, he argues that cosmopolitanism for Heine meant a reception of French and in particular French revolutionary culture: "A substantial portion of Heine's *Weltbürgertum* is a matter of a projected alliance between the French revolutionary tradition and the implications of the inchoate achievements of the German mind; that was much, but it was not the world, not even in the first half of the nineteenth century." Sammons goes on to argue that Heine's alleged cosmopolitanism is weakened by his consistent dependence on national categories, on typological national characteristics such as the essential monarchism of Germany versus the essential republicanism of France. Sammons continues: "And I must say that despite all Heine's admiration for French brightness, sociability, and love of liberty, and his perpetual scoffing at German slowness, heaviness, and servility, there is often an undertone suggesting that, in the longer view, the Germans are the more serious, more philosophical, more sensitive, ultimately more significant people." When Heine praises Victor Hugo, "his highest praise of France's greatest writer is that he is just about as good as a German!" Sammons concludes: "Heine scholarship has not listened carefully enough to him in such matters."

For Sammons, Heine is "fundamentally a German writer; it was from this center that he perceived and interpreted the larger world." My only disagreement with Sammons is with his assumption that his "renationalization" of Heine necessarily implies an anticosmopolitanism as well. Heine is a German cosmopolitan who looks at the outside world, principally France, from the perspective of a German center.[16]

Hermann Cohen takes further the model of the cosmopolitan German Jew who wants to maintain his Germanness and his German outlook on the world. For Cohen as for Heine, the question of Germans and Jews complicated the problem of the classification of

16. Jeffrey Sammons, "Heine as Weltbürger? A Skeptical Inquiry," *Modern Language Notes* 101:3 (1986): 609–28; quotations on pp. 611, 623, 624, 626. See also Sammons, *Heinrich Heine: A Modern Biography* (Princeton, 1979), and S. S. Prawer, *Heine's Jewish Comedy* (Oxford, 1983).

and communication among insiders and outsiders that had originated in Lessing's (and Moses Mendelssohn's) corner of the German enlightenment. Cohen's desire to reconcile Jewishness with a
German national cosmopolitanism intensified during the First
World War and generated the nationalistic work *Deutschtum und
Judentum*, published in 1917. The book was a plea for the recognition
of the spiritual compatibility of Germans and Jews, and hence of
nationalism and cosmopolitanism. (The title should be translated
as "Germanness and Jewishness," since the qualities implied refer
to internal, moral identities that are "cultural" in the sense of the
culture/civilization dichotomy.)

Jürgen Habermas has analyzed this position of Cohen's in his
well-known essay "The German Idealism of the Jewish Philosophers." Habermas traces the legacy of German enlightenment
thought through Jewish neo-Kantian philosophy, and in the following excerpt discusses Hermann Cohen's German cosmopolitanism:

> He represents the liberal tradition of Jewish intellectuals who were
> inwardly connected with the German Enlightenment and supposed
> that in their spirit they might be capable of feeling at one with the
> nation in general. Immediately after the outbreak of war, Cohen deliv-
> ered before the Kant Society of Berlin a remarkable speech ('On the
> Peculiarity of the German Spirit') in which he exhibited to the imperial-
> istic Germany of Wilhelm II and his military forces the original testi-
> mony of German humanism. Indignantly he dissociated himself from
> the "insulting" distinction between the nation of poets and thinkers
> and that of fighters and state builders: "Germany is and remains in
> continuity with the eighteenth century and its cosmopolitan hu-
> manity."
>
> Less cosmopolitan is the tone of his apologia: "in us there struggles
> the originality of a nation with which no other can compare." This
> kind of loyalty to the state later delivered over those who in deluded
> pride called themselves National German Jews to the tragic irony of
> an identification with their attackers.[17]

17. Jürgen Habermas, "The German Idealism of the Jewish Philosophers," in
Philosophical-Political Profiles, trans. Frederick G. Lawrence (Cambridge, Mass., 1983),
p. 25.

Cohen was right to chart some kind of continuity between German enlightenment cosmopolitanism and the nationalism of his own day. Habermas, in contrast, is, I think, less accurate in calling Cohen's nationalism of the second paragraph "less cosmopolitan." It is still cosmopolitan, but in the German sense.

In 1915 Cohen channeled his nationalist cosmopolitanism into a project that in tone as well as in content bears on the subject of Salzburg and its ideology: a short study entitled *The Dramatic Idea in Mozart's Opera Texts*. An earlier version of the text had been written in early 1906, the hundred-and-fiftieth anniversary year of Mozart's birth, and had appeared in that time in the *Frankfurter Zeitung*. In 1914, Cohen writes in the preface, he had been asked by an unidentified "philosophical friend" to expand the study into a piece that could appear in the Mozart Festival being planned for Salzburg at that time. The war intervened. In its final form, the work's relation to Salzburg is unclear and tenuous, but its compatibility with what would later be articulated—by Hofmannsthal and others—as the Salzburg ideology is remarkable. Again from the preface: "Through the numerous forms in which the study has by now appeared, I would like to be allowed to express the wish that it be received as a triumphant message of free, pious belief in German uniqueness."[18]

IV

As I have suggested, a consideration of cosmopolitanism and the growth of nationalism in any German context evokes Friedrich

---

18. Hermann Cohen, *Die dramatische Idee in Mozarts Operntexten* (Berlin, 1915), pp. 9–10. Cohen's crusade for a reinvigorated German cosmopolitanism in the spirit of Kant was continued by his most prominent student, Ernst Cassirer, in the moving and highly ambivalent 1932 *Philosophy of the Enlightenment*. Cassirer is quite explicit in the introduction that an enlightened, humane politics presents itself as a desperate antidote to the encroaching barbarism of his own day. Cassirer's portrait of the enlightenment is on one hand a model of a multinational history in which in particular France and Germany, *philosophes* and *Aufklärer*, are presented in a dialogical structure. This remains the unique analytical value of the book. Yet on the other hand, everything culminates in Kant, and Cassirer demonstrates time and again the inclination to conceive of the multinational enlightenment tradition in terms of a teleological progression via Rousseau to Kant. Thus even Cassirer in 1932 reveals a certain retention of nationalist cosmopolitanism.

Meinecke's celebrated work of 1907, *Weltbürgertum und National-staat*. In this work Meinecke traced the development of German political ideology in the nineteenth century along what he analyzed as the nationally appropriate path *from* cosmopolitanism *to* national consciousness and nationalism. For Meinecke, then, the two world-views were opposites, and the passage from the first to the second was the hallmark of the history of nineteenth-century Germany. The cosmopolitans of the first romantic generation of Wilhelm von Humboldt, Novalis, and Friedrich Schlegel, Meinecke argued, evolved into the political romanticism of the later Humboldt and Schlegel, as well as Fichte and Adam Müller, Stein, and Gneisenau, to the age of Prussian state liberation personified by the triumvirate Hegel, Ranke, and Bismarck. The nationalist phase emerged with the unification—from Meinecke's point of view—of Prussian state and German nation, traced through the careers of Friedrich Moser, Friedrich and Heinrich von Gagern, and Bismarck, among others.

Meinecke succeeded brilliantly in maintaining the strong opposition between the two world-views exemplified in his two chief terms, while at the same time charting a smooth and indeed Hegelian evolution, through various intermediary stages, from the first to the second. The nature of that transition, and the issue of just how far cosmopolitanism and nationalism are accepted as opposites at all, pose a fascinating problem in German historiography. Other historians, before and after Meinecke, have charted a similar evolution, but have avoided defining cosmopolitanism as an opposing world-view to nationalism. I have been arguing here that this latter view is historically correct, that there existed between 1750 and 1850 a German cosmopolitanism which was distinctly different from Western cosmopolitanism (different both historically and lexico-graphically), and which was an actual generator of national ideology, not an early antagonist or even an early alternative to national ideology. (I do not, with this argument, intend to revive an obsolete monolithic historiography of Germany, but simply to propose that cosmopolitanism and nationalism are, in a large forest, branches of the same tree.)

It is the cosmopolitanism of 1920 that I am interested in, and the correct definition of that cosmopolitanism depends on an appraisal of the way thinkers of that period defined the term themselves.

Hofmannsthal defined cosmopolitanism in much the way Meinecke did; Thomas Mann defined it in the alternative manner I have proposed above. I will argue that Mann's definition was historically correct, yet nonetheless profoundly ideological, and that Hofmannsthal's was equally ideological, but disguised by his own rhetoric, which conventionally and falsely differentiated cosmopolitanism from nationalism. For Hofmannsthal, cosmopolitanism was a virtue and nationalism a vice—but an Austrian virtue fighting against a Prussian vice. Cosmopolitanism was therefore tacitly defined as a *national* virtue, and, by extension, as a nationalist ideology.

The notion that cosmopolitanism was a particularly German virtue was loudly and powerfully stated in Thomas Mann's voluminous 1918 polemic *Betrachtungen eines Unpolitischen* (*Reflections of a Nonpolitical Man*). The nonpolitical artist had been thoroughly politicized by the First World War, and in this book he summoned his own and others' political patriotism as the desperately necessary antidote to the invasion of the opportunistic political practice of the West, of France most of all. The German military, Mann held (as did Hermann Cohen), was united with the German spirit in the fight to rescue German culture from Western civilization. The antithesis of culture and civilization is the principle on which Mann's entire position rests; it is a master dichotomy underneath which a long list of oppositions flows. One of those oppositions separates cosmopolitanism, which is German, from internationalism, which is anti-German (which, in turn, almost always means French).

Mann had sketched his position in two previous, much smaller pieces, his "Thoughts in War," published in the journal *Die Neue Rundschau* in September 1914, and his celebrated essay of December 1914, "Frederick and the Great Coalition." "Thoughts in War" revealed for the first time Mann's view of Germany as the bastion of culture and spirit that must be defended against the "civilization" of the political and, a fortiori, philistine West. Germany was the land of music, metaphysics, pedagogy, subjectivism, and morality. The West was analytical, skeptical, political, social, and democratic. The German spirit was exemplified in Goethe, Schopenhauer, Nietzsche, and Wagner; the West in Zola, the Dreyfus affair (Mann scorned Dreyfusards and anti-Dreyfusards alike as political oppor-

tunists), and Mann's older brother Heinrich, an avowed franco-
phile. (In the *Reflections*, Mann added to the first list the composer
Hans Pfitzner, Tolstoy, and Dostoevsky; to the second, Flaubert,
D'Annunzio, and Barrès.)

"Frederick and the Great Coalition" followed and expanded the
tradition of the nationalist, late-romantic reevaluation of the life
and motives of the Prussian king. Frederick, according to Mann,
was still cosmopolitan, but not in Voltaire's sense. His cosmopolitanism was the attitude of a great nationalist hero, as Carlyle and
Treitschke had seen him. Mann's Frederick was the embodiment of
the Prussian-German spirit, not for his enlightened rapprochement
with France, but on the contrary for his rally and rescue of Germany
and German culture from external threat: the threat of the Habsburgs, who could reasonably be seen, at least culturally, as the
agents of "civilization" in general and French civilization in particular. The Prussian victory on the Austrian front in 1763 became the
precursor of the German struggle on the Belgian front in 1914. Both
were crucial for the survival of the nation.

The *Reflections of a Nonpolitical Man* develops these trains of
thought at great length and with great repetition; they build further
on the culture/civilization dichotomy and flesh out Mann's notion
of what I think is accurate to call nationalist cosmopolitanism. Culture is opposed to civilization as soul is opposed to society, freedom
to rights, art to literature, and cosmopolitanism to internationalism.
To the side of culture belong music, nature, and the principle of
life as something primeval, unfathomable, and unrationalizable.
Culture is the realm of the intellect or spirit (*Geist*); civilization is the
realm of politics, the opposite both of the intellect and of morality.
Politics is pure opportunism for Mann, and in attempting to sum-
mon the most powerful rhetoric he can, he reinforces the dichotomy
of intellect versus reason by means of a misguided and disastrous
application of the Kantian ideas of pure reason and practical reason.
In other words Mann appeals to all the romantic rhetoric he can
recall, right down to the image of the abyss as the metaphor for the
unfathomability of (German) culture. Germany in the struggle to
maintain this status is essentially "protestant" (the fact that adjec-
tives are not capitalized in German increases the ambiguity and the
drama of this statement).

The two outstanding qualities of the German national character, Mann proposes, are burgherly life (*Bürgerlichkeit*) and art. In a marked contrast to the theme that pervades so much of Mann's fictional work, the theme of the incompatibility between burgher and artist, here burgher and artist are entirely compatible. The German character, Mann writes, is "the middle, the medium, and the mediating one" between burgher and artist. Mann is clearly borrowing the language of Nietzsche, who in *Beyond Good and Evil* (aphorism 244) spoke of Germany as "the country of the middle." Yet Mann seems oblivious to the antinationalist Nietzsche's pun: the country of the middle is also the country of mediocrity. The attitude that for Mann embodies the compatibility of art and burgherly life is aestheticism, German *l'art pour l'art*, a point Mann attributes to Lukács's *Soul and Form*. This aestheticism, grounded in life, is the opposite of the decorative, tricksterish aestheticism of Flaubert and D'Annunzio. The art work that best exemplifies this ethic, according to Mann, is that of Wagner, whose art is not folk art, but national and cosmopolitan art.[19] (In this evaluation Mann was correcting the views of Wagner himself.)

Aestheticism thus defined is for Mann one quality of German national cosmopolitanism; the other is morality. Morality is the opposite of politics and the ultimate manifestation of politics: democracy. The political attitude of democracy is "optimistic-ameliorative," positivistic, and hence shallow. Wagner, Mann writes, recognized politics as identical to democracy and the guiding force down the path to decadence and trivialization which began with the downfall of tragedy and of the Greek state. The German resistance to this path of decadence is the key to its burgherly culture, which is moral, apolitical, and "the first purely national culture." "The deepening of the German character . . . " Mann continues, "is the work of this nonpolitical burgher culture, of this time of an everyday structure, comfortably exact and satirically cleareyed, of the time of sermons and mysticism, of Shrovetide plays, lawbooks, and *chronicles*." Burgherly culture's apogee was the world of the Hanseatic League, the age, Mann writes, that Treitschke correctly

19. Thomas Mann, *Reflections of a Nonpolitical Man*, trans. Walter D. Morris (New York, 1983), pp. 78, 72, 74, 52.

identified as "thoroughly patriotic." "And the 'cosmopolitan burgher,' " Mann goes on, "is he not also—a burgher? What else does he represent than the combination of German burgherly nature and humanistic culture? Yes, just as the German word for 'cosmopolitanism' [Weltbürgertum] includes the word and the idea of the 'burgher,' this word and idea itself also has immanent in it the cosmopolitan sense of a world without boundaries."[20]

The life of mysticism, Shrovetide plays, and religious morality which Mann eulogizes is to an astonishing degree the same life and the same morality that Hofmannsthal, writing at the same time, eulogizes as the quintessentially Austrian, explicitly anti-Prussian way of life: religious, theatrical, and cosmopolitan. Mann and Hofmannsthal use an identical language: the language of nationalistic cosmopolitanism, the opposite of "internationalism."

In December 1914, Hofmannsthal wrote a short essay that reveals startling continuities with Mann's wartime essays. Titled "Words in Memory of Prince Eugen" ("Worte zum Gedächtnis des Prinzes Eugen), the piece is a studied attempt to supply Austria's wartime imagination with an inspirational heroic image from an unquestioned historical moment. Prince Eugen (1663–1736) was the fieldmarshal who repelled the Turks from Vienna in 1683 and went on to set the eastern and southern boundaries of the Habsburg Empire which lasted by and large until 1918. Hofmannsthal states explicitly that Eugen should serve Austria in its current hour of need as Frederick the Great serves Prussia. Just as the cosmopolitan Frederick seems at first an unusual choice in Mann's nationalistic program, so is the French-born and French-educated Prince Eugen in Hofmannsthal's. There is thus a double irony in Hofmannsthal's statement that "we are able to recognize the greatness of a man and we must love him unconditionally; that is the position of today's Prussians in regard to their Frederick, that is ours in regard to the greatest Austrian, Eugen of Savoy."[21]

As Mann did with Frederick, Hofmannsthal invests Eugen with the significance of providing a mirror for the present military challenge. Hofmannsthal compares the pan-European chaos of "a

20. Ibid., pp. 15–16, 86, 80, 81.
21. Hofmannsthal, Prosa III, p. 205.

quarter of a millennium" ago to the present one, and then in an opaque use of the present tense states that "from these battles our Austria is born . . . Austria is the realm (das Reich) of peace, and it was born in battle."[22] The image of Eugen provides Austria with "inexhaustible hope" that it will always be able to defend itself. For Hofmannsthal as for Mann, the continuity of war and peace in the national character parallels the continuity between cosmopolitanism and nationalism. (As always, however, Hofmannsthal uses the opportunity to assert Austrian superiority over Prussia and reminds his reader that Eugen was "the acknowledged teacher" of Frederick himself.)

The essay on Prince Eugen is one in a series of patriotic pieces Hofmannsthal wrote during the war, a context that gave him the opportunity to participate in public affairs he had been looking for for some time. He wanted to participate as a writer, certainly not as a soldier; when in the summer of 1914 he found himself inducted into a reserve infantry company in Pisino, he successfully enlisted the help of his friend the politician and legal theorist Josef Redlich to intervene with Count Stürgkh, the prime minister, for his discharge.[23] Once back at work, he concentrated on a projected patriotic collection called the Österreichische Bibliothek, which was to be published by the Insel Verlag, with the first volume a collection of the political writings of Grillparzer. In other words, at stake was the politicization of Austrian letters.

Grillparzer played a crucial role in that process, as Hofmannsthal spelled out himself in a short essay of 1915 called "Grillparzer's Political Legacy" ("Grillparzers politisches Vermächtnis"). Grillparzer was for him "no politician, but next to Goethe and Kleist the most political spirit (der politischeste Kopf) of the modern German-language poets." This assertion serves two purposes. First, it raises politics and political consciousness up from the level of profession— what Hofmannsthal in this essay calls "a certain l'art pour l'art of politics"—to the level of the spiritual concern of poets. Second, it uses this definition of Grillparzer as poet-political thinker to imply

22. Ibid., p. 206.
23. See Werner Volke, Hugo von Hofmannsthal (Reinbek bei Hamburg, 1967), pp. 140–42.

the status of Grillparzer as Hofmannsthal's predecessor. The position Hofmannsthal seeks to share with Grillparzer is that of the provider of a national metapoetics that fuses art and politics and hence recovers an Austria that is "of a strong and deep nature, patient, wise, God-given, unartificial, and perseverant."[24]

With the help of Redlich, the Catholic playwright Max Mell, Felix Braun, Stefan Zweig, Anton Wildgans, Robert Michel, Richard von Kralik, and Paul Eisner, twenty-six volumes of the Österreichische Bibliothek appeared by the end of 1916.[25] Hofmannsthal made one solicitation on which he asked Redlich for advice. He wanted a piece from the Czech nationalist statesman Thomas Masaryk, and asked Redlich on which of two subjects to request a contribution: "either an excerpt in which he formulates the necessary annexation of the Western Slavs to Europe and not Russia, or one on a great German cultural phenomenon, Goethe for example."[26] One can clearly see Hofmannsthal's mind at work here: he envisages a statement of either literary or political pan-Germanism from the most renowned Czech nationalist.

In November 1915, Redlich wrote in his diary that "the war has noticeably influenced Hofmannsthal. He has become a realist, a political man, he wants to act in the open with results. It is really touching to me how practically he is handling his deeply inward Austrianness."[27] Of course we cannot know exactly what Redlich's evidence for this evaluation was. Nevertheless, Hofmannsthal was at that time beginning to express his evolving political thoughts in the form of short essays—of which the piece on Grillparzer is one—published in the liberal *Neue Freie Presse* and occasionally in other newspapers and periodicals (*Vossische Zeitung, Österreichische Rundschau*).

The first significant—and highly polemical—essay is addressed

---

24. Hofmannsthal's view of Grillparzer's politicality is interesting in light of the other main context in which Grillparzer was important to him—as the link in the transmission of Spanish baroque drama into the Austrian theater.

25. Werner Volke, *Hofmannsthal* (Reinbek bei Hamburg, 1967), pp. 143–44.

26. Hugo von Hofmannsthal and Josef Redlich, *Briefwechsel*, ed. Helga Fussgänger (Frankfurt am Main, 1971), letter of 24 July 1915, p. 17.

27. Redlich, *Schicksalsjahre Österreichs, 1908–1919: Das politische Tagebuch Josef Redlichs*, ed. Fritz Fellner (Graz, 1953), I:13.

to the question of the boycott of foreign languages ("Boycott fremder Sprachen?", 1914). Hofmannsthal pleads against the boycott of the languages and cultural contributions of those nations hostile to Germany and Austria. First, he evokes the somewhat tired idea of the fundamental separation of culture and politics: the land of Bismarck is that of Beethoven, that of Krupp is also that of Kant and Herder.[28] This argument is reminiscent of the pleas of apoliticality not of pacifists such as Stefan Zweig but of the "nonpolitical man," Thomas Mann. Politics is not a legitimate category by which to define and value the nation, but a cultural nation roused into political action creates a self-legitimating metapolitics.

Hofmannsthal's sympathy with Germany is based purely on cultural and not political criteria. Yet German culture, he goes on to suggest, is superior to other European cultures precisely because it is the only national culture to be possessed of a true spirit of cosmopolitanism. In other words, it is a German cultural virtue to understand foreign nations and cultures. No German would inquire, as Maurice Maeterlinck allegedly did, whether a country as beautiful as Germany had already built railroads, or worse, as an unidentified French minister allegedly did, ask the wife of a Hungarian ambassador whether her travels to the West liberated her from the constraints of the East, such as wearing veils whenever she stepped onto the street.[29] German educators, Hofmannsthal argues, must preserve the German virtue of cosmopolitanism in their students: "To isolate our children from foreign languages is precisely to make Frenchmen and Englishmen out of them." Thus for Hofmannsthal German culture unites Germany and Austria, and assures a pan-German superiority over the other European nations.

In another short piece of 1914, "The Affirmation of Austria: Thoughts on the Present Moment" ("Die Bejahung Österreichs: Gedanken zum gegenwärtigen Augenblick"), Hofmannsthal developed his metapolitics further with the comment that "politics and spirit (*Geist*) are identical."[30] The current war, he wrote, is a

28. Hofmannsthal, *Prosa III*, p. 184.
29. Ibid., p. 185.
30. Ibid., p. 190.

war of defense and hence a repetition of the final defense of Vienna against the Turks in 1683. The spirit of defense is youthful in 1914, as it was in 1683. Furthermore, the successful defense of 1683 ushered in an era of unique "national" artistic achievement; the defense of 1914 can do the same. Hofmannsthal does not attempt the impossible: the definition of "national culture" in a Habsburg context. But by the same token his notion of an Austrian national culture remains meaningless—if, that is, he is referring to anything beyond Austro-German culture.

Hofmannsthal does pay homage to the alleged unity of the Austro-Hungarian dual monarchy, and he does so by way of a fairly naive idolization of the army as a symbol-turned-reality of both political and ethical unity. In the piece called "Reconstruction, Not Demolition" ("Aufbauen, nicht Einreissen"), he suggests that the participation of Hungarian soldiers in the war reinforces Austro-Hungarian unity.[31] This hopeful image of a spiritually—to say nothing of a linguistically—unified armed forces is hardly accurate. Though German was the official language, only a very few noncommissioned officers among the Hungarian and Slavic regiments spoke it, and the result was a pidgin language dubbed "horse-German," especially predominant in the Slavic regiments.[32]

Hofmannsthal's idea of Austria, nevertheless, was German. But as the war progressed, he felt compelled to work out a political position that would defend the German political axis as well as the German cultural foundations of Austria, yet at the same time put forward an idea of new Austria politically independent from the German state. Thus he gradually evolved a political position of sympathy to the Hungarian and Slavic "minorities" as part of the Austrian realm, as well as a distinct hostility to the German state. His cultural values solidified in a manner parallel to those of Ignaz Seipel, even if Hofmannsthal never came to think in terms of practical politics. Hofmannsthal's hostility to Germany had necessarily to rest on cultural grounds alone; it eventually came to contradict the expression of cultural solidarity of the 1914 piece on the boycott of foreign languages.

31. Ibid., p. 234.
32. Arthur J. May, *The Passing of the Hapsburg Monarchy* (Philadelphia, 1966), I:490–91.

Hofmannsthal conveniently focused his cultural hostility on Prussia, as both the embodiment of German cultural values and the antithesis of Austria. "Prussians and Austrians" (1917), his well-known catalog of the differences between the two national cultures and characters (an intra-German civilization/culture dichotomy), warrants inclusion here:

PRUSSIA	AUSTRIA
As a whole	
Created, an artificial structure, a country poor by nature, all in men and by men, hence: held together by a belief in the State, more virtue, more efficiency	Grown, historical tissue, rich by nature, all from the outside; from nature and God, held together by a love of home, more piety, more humanity
Social structure	
A loose social texture, the classes divided by cultural differences; but a precise machinery. The lesser nobility sharply distinct, consistent in itself. Homogenous officialdom: embodying one spirit. 'Dominant' attitudes and customs. The people: the most easily disiplined mass, unlimited authority (army; scientific social democracy). Supreme authority of the Crown.	A dense social texture, the classes unified by culture; the mechanics of the whole imprecise. High nobility rich in types, politically inconsistent. Heterogenous officialdom: no prescribed way of thinking or feeling. The people: most independent mass, unlimited individualism. Supreme confidence in the Crown.
The individual	
Up to date in his views	Traditional in his views

(cosmopolitan around 1800, liberal around 1848, now Bismarckian, almost without a memory for past phases.)

Lacks a sense of history

Strength of abstractions.

Incomparable in orderly executions.
Acts according to instructions.
Strength of dialectic.
More skill in expression.
More consequential.

Self-reliance.
Seemingly masculine.
Makes everything functional.

Asserts and justifies himself.
Self-righteous, arrogant, hectoring.
Forces crises.
Fights for his rights.
Incapable of entering into people's thoughts.

Willed character.
Every individual bears a part of authority.
Pushing.
Preponderance of the occupational.
Extreme exaggeration.

stable almost for centuries.

Possesses an instinct for history.
Little talent for abstractions.
More quick on the uptake.

Acts according to fitness.
Rejection of dialectic.
More balance.
More ability to adapt himself to conditions.
Self-irony.
Seemingly immature.
Gives a social twist to everything.

Prefers to keep things vague.
Shamefaced, vain, witty.

Avoids crises.
Lets things go.
Enters into other people's thoughts to the point of losing his character.
Play-acting.
Every individual bears a part of all humanity.
Pleasure-seeking.
Preponderance of the private.
Irony to the point of self-destruction.[33]

33. Hofmannsthal, *Plays and Libretti*, trans. Michael Hamburger (New York, 1963), p. lxv.

The turning point in the evolution of this Prussian-Austrian dichotomy in Hofmannsthal's mind is marked by the 1915 essay
"We Austrians and Germany" (*Wir Österreicher und Deutschland*).
"Their very earnest contemporary association notwithstanding,"
the essay begins, "it must be said that among the countries of the
earth Austria is one of those least or worst understood by the
Germans."[34] Since the death of Bismarck, Hofmannsthal writes,
Germany has produced no competent observers of Austria, none
who transcend the universal error of considering Vienna a microcosm of Austria as a whole. The most inspired and significant book
about Austria, he suggests, is that of an Englishman, W. Steed.
Hofmannsthal says no more about this, but his very praise of
Steed is significant coming from an Austrian. H. Wickham Steed
was known as the shrewdest British "statesman-journalist" during
his career as a London *Times* correspondent in Berlin and Rome,
and in Vienna, where he was stationed for over a decade. In 1913,
the year he left Vienna, he published his instantly celebrated "essay" called *The Hapsburg Monarchy*.[35] The only hope for the Danube
Monarchy, Steed proposed in that work, was a new federal union
that would grant the southern Slavs equal status with Austria and
Hungary. The book was banned by the Austrian government.
Steed's anti-Habsburg rhetoric and involvement intensified during
the early years of the war, to the point where the Czech politician
Eduard Beneš referred to him as a participant in the history of
Czech liberation.[36] For Hofmannsthal, writing in 1915, to refer to
Steed in such glowing terms amounted to a distinct, if implicit,
political statement. His similar praise of R. W. Seton-Watson, who
had argued for the conversion of the dual monarchy into a triple
realm including Yugoslavia, falls into the same category.

Hofmannsthal's essay continues with the suggestions that Austria's contemporary reality is a crystalization of Germany's entire
history: the problem of the colonization of the Slavs. The Austrian
realm is a heterogenous mixture of peoples joined not by any cultural sympathies but by a shared external military threat—a mirror

34. Hofmannsthal, *Prosa III*, p. 225.
35. H. Wickham Steed, *The Hapsburg Monarchy* (London, 1913).
36. May, pp. 233ff.

of the German experience in the Thirty Years' War. "If one sees Austria in this light, as the one part of the old German empire where all the forces of German history are alive and effective . . . [one sees that] Austria is . . . an unresolved mission. . . . Austria must again and again be recognized as the *German mission in Europe*" (Hofmannsthal's italics).[37] (The implication that the Slavic national components of the empire exist solely to provide the German Austrians with a buffer against the East is a radical thought that contradicts Hofmannsthal's post-Habsburg "liberal pluralism" and federalism.) The goal of that German mission is the convergence of "the idea of Europe" and "the Austrian idea"—the titles of two essay fragments. The new Europe, Hofmannsthal writes at the end of the second one, "needs an Austria: a structure of unartificial [*ungekünstelter*] elasticity, yet a structure nonetheless, a true organism, suffused with an inner religion of its own."[38] Austria is the necessary link between Western and Eastern Europe; Hofmannsthal's "Austrian idea" is thus a distillation of his own personal idea of German culture severed from his contemporary Germany. (This idea of Austria carrying a German mission of linking East and West is of course a dominant one in post–World War II Austria, which can assume the role with all the more aplomb because a divided Germany is unable to.) Hofmannsthal's "Austrian idea" is at this point entirely unprogrammatic. He envisions a utopia that is "unartificial," a "natural utopia." Though one might argue that this is the only truly ethical and nonideological utopian idea, it is nonetheless a contradiction in terms, an ideal that defies any human action or intervention through which it might be attained. His very ethereal notion of German culture is thus combined with an essential refusal to espouse a programmatic ideology; whether that refusal was a matter of ethics or merely of apolitical temperament is hard to tell. In any case it prevents Hofmannsthal's cultural ideals from falling into the tradition of German *völkisch* ideology.

Nevertheless, imprecise as he is, Hofmannsthal does come quite close to a *völkisch* ideology in the 1915 fragment "On War and Culture" ("Über Krieg und Kultur"), an open letter sent to the

37. Hofmannsthal, *Prosa III*, p. 230.
38. Ibid., p. 406.

Svenska Dagbladet, but which never arrived. In a vein ironically close to the thought of his antagonist Karl Kraus, Hofmannsthal suggests that Austria, as a microcosm of Europe, possesses an especially keen sense of the millennial aspects of the war. "It seems to me," he writes, "that we have arrived at the end of a development whose points of departure can be precisely measured with the French Revolution and with the zenith of German spiritual life, the decades around the year 1800." The process that followed had been prophesied by "our great Austrian poet Grillparzer . . . 'from humanity through nationality to bestiality.' " Hofmannsthal thus plants his stake in what might be referred to as the Austrian prerogative: antinationalistic, or cosmopolitan nationalism. Since Austria (in the Habsburg sense) is not a nation, Austrian "nationalism" is seen to be innocent of the political or hegemonic connotations of the nationalism of any other nation-state, Germany in particular.

The second half of the fragment points to the transcendence of the present crisis of material civilization (a folkish diagnosis, compounded by the use of the loaded term *Zivilisation*, as opposed to *Kultur*): "Even this material civilization will no doubt continue to develop, but—we can at least hope—under another star, with the possibility of self-transcendence. . . . The talk must now be of the appearance of a new authority, not the authority that lies in official capacities, but rather one that will be embodied in purely psychic and spiritual forms, unanimous with the reawakening of religious meaning, so that the concept of the mass, this frightful and dangerous concept . . . might be transcended and definitively replaced with the higher concept of the *Volk*."[39]

The paradigm of this reawakened, national-religious *Volk* was to be the Salzburg Festival audience that would celebrate its own Austrian, Catholic, baroque culture, mirrored in the morality plays that Hofmannsthal devised for the occasion. Yet the result, as discussed in the previous chapter, was that ticket prices were high enough to deny access to almost all Salzburgers and to attract before anyone else the (comparatively) economically advantaged Bavarians. This audience was not prepared to participate in the

39. Ibid., p. 505.

ritual of Austrianness that Hofmannsthal, Reinhardt, and Roller had orchestrated. Thus the Salzburg *völkisch* mythology was essentially played out for an audience that had a mythology of its own and was not about to recognize any continuity between theirs and that of Salzburg. Ironically, the Salzburg Festival garnered a European-wide reputation as a place of entertainment unburdened by the sanctimonious weight of its chief competitor, Bayreuth. "Material civilization" seemed to have defeated the germ of national-religious "self-transcendence." By 1925 or 1926, Hofmannsthal himself was perspicacious enough to ride with the possibilities of material success and not to continue to beat a dead ideological horse. He did not abandon the idea of an unchanging national repertory for Salzburg, but he did give up the ambition of a spiritually and culturally homogenous audience. In 1928 he wrote two pieces on Salzburg. One reinforced the consistency of its programs; the other praised the diversity of its audiences: "paradoxical as it may sound, the atmosphere of our audience approaches that of Broadway and the Kurfürstendamm."[40] Salzburg was still to be grounded in its cosmopolitan "German national program of 1800," but the claim was no longer made that the cosmology of that national program extended beyond the footlights into the audience-as-congregation. Hofmannsthal perhaps devalued this crucial component of the festival ideology in the interest of preserving for himself the "national program" as a poetic ideal, since it was clearly inadequately mirrored in the Salzburg Festival, as indeed in the Austrian Republic itself.

40. Hofmannsthal, "Das Publikum der Salzburger Festpiele," in *Prosa IV*, p. 468; also "Zum Programm der Salzburger Festspiele 1928," *Prosa IV*, pp. 471–74.

CHAPTER 4

German Culture and
Austrian *Kulturpolitik*

I

R EADERS of the previous chapter who are used to reading Austrian history interpreted in a more linearly Austrian fashion
(the word "national" cannot accurately be used here or indeed in
any context where the intended meaning is Austria delimited by its
state borders) will have been surprised by the general German
intellectual context that I defined as "nationalist cosmopolitanism"
and into which I suggested that the Salzburg cosmology might be
placed. My reason for this broad German approach was my wish
to analyze the Austro-German intellectual heritage as it appeared
between 1914 and 1933. Austria during this period continuously
approached the intellectual and political problem of national self-
definition, always in a general German context. The agenda of
Austrian intellectuals—whether they were pro- or anti-*Anschluss*—
in the immediate post-Habsburg era was the redefinition of Austria
as a German nation. (*Deutschösterreich*, proposed as the name of the
new republic, was widely agreed upon within Austria but
disallowed by the allied powers at St. Germain in 1919.)

As far as specific Austrian political allegiances were concerned,
the various unofficial plebiscites conducted through the 1920s recorded a 70 to 90 percent pro-*Anschluss* majority. This majority was
led by the Social Democrats, a faction of the Christian Socials,
and of course the burgeoning, illegal, Austrian Nazi party. Pro-
Anschluss Christian Socials as well as Nazis had heaviest support in
the regions where German-speaking Austrians were most directly

confronted with non-German speakers: in the Burgenland and in Styria, which bordered respectively on Hungary and Yugoslavia. Salzburg, relatively insulated from the "nationalities," did not exhibit the politics of cultural chauvinism to the same extent, although, as Günter Fellner has recently shown, anti-Semitism was widespread there and crucial to political structure and action.[1] The governor of Salzburg, Franz Rehrl, as I have mentioned, was both anti-Semitic and pro-*Anschluss*, but at least expressed his motives as economic ones.[2]

The principals of the Christian Social party, the leaders of Austria from 1922 to 1938, were anti-*Anschluss*. The Catholic, conservative "Austrian idea" of chancellors Ignaz Seipel, Engelbert Dollfuss, and Kurt von Schuschnigg resembled that of Hofmannsthal and the Salzburg Festival. Anti-*Anschluss*, it was nevertheless an expression of German—Austro-German—cultural superiority. Thus, a belief in German cultural superiority constituted at least a common denominator between the anti-*Anschluss* Catholics of the 1920s and the pro-*Anschluss*, even pro-Nazi Austrian Catholics of the 1930s.

Nonetheless, two spectra figure here, and the argument for the continuity of cultural ideology is extremely complicated. One is the spectrum from cultural politics to practical politics, with Hofmannsthal on one end and Seipel, Schuschnigg, and the Austrian Nazis on the other. The second spectrum is the ideological one between, on one end, Austro-German, Catholic loyalties, and, on the other, Austrian Nazism. Although the many variations and gradations along both must be kept in mind, it will be argued here that the powerful current of German cultural ideology did create a certain continuity among the different loyalties involved. This continuity explains at least partially why it was intellectually easy—as well as politically expedient—for the Austrian bishops to declare conciliation with the German authorities when the actual *Anschluss* came. As Franz Borkenau wrote in the late spring of 1938, "Austrian political Catholicism deserves closer attention, because on its attitude depend to a certain extent the chances of the Nazis to succeed

---

1. See Günter Fellner, *Antisemitismus in Salzburg, 1918–1938* (Vienna, 1979).
2. The fact that Rehrl remained a strong anti-Nazi and spent the war in prison might suggest a lack of German cultural chauvinism in his pro-*Anschluss* politics.

in winning over the Austrians. The instance of the bishops' declaration [in support of the *Anschluss*] has opened the eyes of the world to the fact that these chances are better than may have been widely believed."[3]

This chapter, then, introduces to the Austrian political context the argument that cultural ideology, more specifically an ideology of German cultural supremacy, is at the core of political and social discourse in the First Austrian Republic and a fortiori in the intellectual history of the period. The entire range of political positions is involved. Although one might logically assume that nationalist cultural ideology would be a natural spiritual companion to a politics of "conservative revolution," one would just as logically assume that it would not enter the thought or the program of a socialist politics informed by an allegedly supranational Marxism. The surprising factor in the Austrian context is that cultural politics cannot be assumed to be the blood brother of conservatism alone, although the two certainly went hand in hand. A nationalistic view of Austro-German culture can be detected in all political viewpoints, from the left wing of the Social Democrats (the party of Adler, Bauer, and Renner) to the clerical right wing of the Christian Social party (the party of Lueger, Seipel, Dollfuss, and Schuschnigg, and, in Salzburg, Franz Rehrl).[4]

Seen in this context, the cultural program of the Salzburg Festival was definitely conservative in its view of the German cultural heritage it wished to preserve and revive as a social model. But its nationalism alone does not label it conservative according to the principles of contemporary political discourse. Although Hofmannsthal himself was by and large proclerical and pro-Christian Social, his politics, like those of Josef Redlich, his principal political confidant and mentor after the death of the industrialist Eberhard von Bodenhausen in 1918, contained a clear strand of federalism in regard to the Slavic former "nationalities," the Czechs above all. Yet

3. Franz Borkenau, *Austria and After* (London, 1938), pp. 119–20.
4. The inexorability of this national cultural politics within the ranks of the Social Democratic party, to say nothing of outside it, is fundamental to the disintegration of Austrian socialism and a factor that has, it seems to me, been overlooked in the sizable historiography on that socialism (with the exception of J. L. Talmon's book, discussed below).

his politics were not liberal in the sense of pluralistic; his federalism never encroached on his solid assumption of German (Austro-German) cultural supremacy. Geography supplies an accurate metaphor: Salzburg represented the anchoring of Austria within the bounds of German culture, and with that ballast of security Hofmannsthal could turn eastward and admit the Czechs into his political and intellectual consciousness.

II

Histories of the First Austrian Republic often speak in terms of the "tragedy of social democracy" between 1920 and 1930.[5] There is no question that Austrian Social Democratic party (SPÖ), like its German counterpart, had a difficult and violent history that culminated in the defeats of the early 1930s. The Social Democrats were the principal victims of Dollfuss's revocation of parliamentary government in 1933 as well as of the revolution of 1934. Although the Christian Socials were destroyed by the Nazis (Dollfuss murdered in 1934 and Schuschnigg ousted with the *Anschluss*), they had retained power in a smooth transition from republic to fascist state in 1933–1934.

Yet despite these substantial differences, a common strand of cultural politics joins the Social Democrats to the Christian Socials, who owned the rhetoric of the "Austrian idea." Although, as mentioned above, the plebiscites of the 1920s showed that up to 90 percent of the Austrian population was pro-*Anschluss*, the Christian Socials remained divided on the issue. The Social Democrats, on the other hand, were united in their pro-*Anschluss* position. After 1933, the so-called right wing of the Social Democratic party, led by Karl Renner, remained pro-*Anschluss*, even though Austria would have been annexed to a fascist and not to a socialist or social-democratic Germany. Renner held to his position through Hitler's actual annexation on 13 March 1938, to which he reacted with the comment "The twenty-year error of the Austrian *Volk* has now

5. See Martin Kitchen, *The Coming of Austrian Fascism* (London, 1980); and Anson Rabinbach, *The Crisis of Austrian Socialism* (Chicago, 1983).

been corrected."[6] The "left wing" of the party, led by Otto Bauer, abandoned its pro-*Anschluss* position after 1933. Bauer himself left Austria for Brno, Czechoslovakia, in February 1934; he died in Paris in 1939.

The question that this set of events and allegiances poses to the historian is how Renner could have retained his original position all the way through the 1930s. If the Social Democratic position of 1918, which desired annexation to a socialist Germany because it was socialist, was completely sincere, then Renner would not have been able to greet the actual *Anschluss* of 1938 with the high national-ist rhetoric he in fact used. The same holds for an economic argu-ment. The remaining, and I think correct, argument is that German cultural nationalism was the fundamental ingredient in the Social Democratic pro-*Anschluss* position of 1918 and remained so for Karl Renner through 1938, if not for Otto Bauer, who as a Jew was of course not presented with the choice.

The hindsight enabled by Renner's position of 1938 is not the only means of evaluating the nationalistic tenets of Austrian Social Democracy. Such tenets can be found in the early theoretical writ-ings of Adler, Bauer, and Renner at the turn of the century; for them, as for all Austrians, the question of the nationalities and their political allegiance was at the forefront of political concern. Social Democratic founder Viktor Adler had made this clear at the party conference of 1897, when he called Austria a "witches' kitchen" in which the brew of the nationalities problem was being stirred and the "laboratory (*Experimentierkammer*, with a possible pun on *Tier*— animal) of world history."[7] Adler's characterization echoes Fried-rich Hebbel's description of Austria as "the little world in which the big one holds its rehearsal": "die kleine Welt in der die grosse ihre Probe hält." Adler's challenge to the "Austrian Internationale" was to prove that socialism could overcome national difference,

6. *Illustrierte Kronenzeitung*, 3 April 1938. In a statement, originally published in English, on why he supported the *Anschluss*, Renner argued that first loyalty must be to the nation, which is long-lived, rather than to a party, which is short-lived. See Karl Renner, "Warum ich mit Ja gestimmt habe," in *Karl Renner in Dokumenten und Erinnerungen*, ed. Siegfried Naslo (Vienna, 1982), pp. 133–37.

7. J. L. Talmon, *The Myth of the Nation and the Vision of Revolution* (London, 1981), p. 133.

that "Austrian" socialism could draw strength from the proletariats of all the component nationalities.

J. L. Talmon has argued that the internal failure of Austrian socialism resulted from the degeneration of its theoretical stance from one of supranational socialism to one of "evolutionary nationalism."[8] First of all the Social Democrats' reliance on the empire's multinational status in the interest of forming a multinational proletariat turned them into de facto supporters of the imperial status quo, a condition that led Adler to speak of his own party as the "*Hofräte* [privy councillors] of the revolution." Furthermore, the insistence on one, unified socialist party was, in Talmon's words, "tantamount to taking existing German hegemony in the Social-Democratic movement for granted and natural."[9]

Renner and Bauer each followed up the 1897 conference with a major theoretical work: Renner in *State and Nation: On the Question of the Austrian Nationalities* (*Staat und Nation: Zur Österreichischen Nationalitätenfrage*), published in 1899, and Bauer in *The Nationalities Question and Social Democracy* (*Die Nationalitätenfrage und die Sozialdemokratie*), published in 1907. Bauer's work included a section in which he defined and evaluated the concept of the nation.[10] It provides an excellent description of what Talmon called "evolutionary nationalism."

Bauer begins by listing six components of a nation, which he draws from the work of "the Italian sociologists": common territory, common descent, common language, common mores and customs, common experiences and a common historical past, and finally common laws and a common religion. All these factors can be referred to, he proposes, as "a common cultural tradition." Bauer claims to present a "systematic conception." All the factors must work together to provide a "common history as the effective cause" of a nation. Once a binding common culture is formed, it can

---

8. Ibid., pp. 137–65. The basic assumption that the positions of Marx and Engels were supranational has been challenged recently in Walker Connor, *The National Question in Marxist-Leninist Theory and Strategy* (Princeton, 1984).

9. Talmon, p. 142.

10. This section can be found in Tom Bottomore and Patrick Goode, eds., *Austro-Marxism* (Oxford, 1978), pp. 102–117, from which the quotations that follow are drawn.

override discrepancies, such as a diversity of religion (as in Germany). Bauer concludes:

> Thus we arrive at a comprehensive definition of the nation. *The nation is the totality of men bound together through a common destiny into a community of character.* Through a *common destiny*: this characteristic distinguishes the nation from the international character groupings, such as an occupation, a class, or the members of a state, which rest upon a similarity, not a community, of destiny. The *totality* of the associated characters: this distinguishes them from the narrower communities of character within the nation, which never create a natural and cultural community. . . . In socialist society the nation will again be sharply defined in this way; all those who share in national education and national cultural values, whose character is therefore shaped by the destiny of the nation which determines the content of these values, will constitute the nation. [Emphases in the original]

Bauer's concept of the nation is portentous for future Social Democratic thought on two counts: its implications for the Austrian evaluation of German culture in particular, and for Austrian cultural theory and cultural planning in general. Clearly Bauer thought of Austria as a German nation; when he led the pro-*Anschluss* movement in the Social Democratic party in 1918, his fundamental desire was to unite the German nation. In 1918, cultural politics ran deeper than socialist politics. If Bauer's work is given a more general reading, as a contribution to social theory, it is clear that his thinking fits into a discourse of totality. The nation is a cultural construction that rests on an all-encompassing "community of character."[11]

It is clear that the cultural politics of 1918 had powerful indigenous roots. As Tom Bottomore has suggested, both Bauer and Renner were pro-*Anschluss* on grounds of the "cultural unity of the German speaking people which had always been an important element in their thought."[12] Yet their position had help from abroad, principally from Woodrow Wilson's Fourteen Points, which argued

---

11. Paul Sweet, in his article "Democracy and Counterrevolution in Austria" (*Journal of Modern History* 22 [1950]: 52–58), stressed the importance of the Social Democrats' German nationalism as an underexamined component of First Republic historiography. His position seems equally valid today.

12. Bottomore, p. 32.

for every nation's right to self-determination. Wilson's argument was of course aimed at the Slavic nations and their struggle for independence from Austria, but the Austro-Germans lost no time in applying it to their own situation. The Allies' prevention of the Austrian *Anschluss* with Germany was, according to the pro-*Anschluss* politicians and political theorists, logically inconsistent with the tenets of the Fourteen Points.

The socialist press as well remained staunchly pro-*Anschluss*. An editorial in the *Arbeiter Zeitung* of 19 April 1927 asserted, "all anti-*Anschluss* politics assaults both nature and culture." On 26 February 1933 the same paper claimed that the *Anschluss* had been de facto accomplished. This rhetorical convergence of nature and culture suggests a rapprochement of socialist politics with *völkisch* language, and that convergence was reinforced by Karl Renner's language, as analyzed by the Austrian historian Friedrich Heer. Renner deliberately used terms associated with a mythical German past, an age of prerational social organization: *Gau, Stamm,* and *Gemeinschaft.*[13]

III

Christian-Social *Anschluss* policy was more varied and more complicated. The *Anschluss* issue was the principal one in the election of 15 February 1919, in which all the Christian Social districts except Salzburg and the Tyrol voted for it.[14] Most party officials in Salzburg, were, like the governor, pro-*Anschluss*. An official party statement Rehrl drafted in 1918 read: "The unification of the entire German *Volk* into one state, which has been prepared through brotherhood in battle, has our support and enthusiasm."[15] By the time of the plebiscites of the 1920s, only 2 and 7 percent, respec-

---

13. Friedrich Heer, *Der Kampf um die österreichische Identität* (Vienna, 1981), p. 335. Heer comments that the word *Gau*, a Nazi favorite, was a "mythical word" which "corresponds to the German-*völkisch* ideology, but to no legal-political reality."

14. Stanley Suval, *The Anschluss Question in the Weimar Era* (Baltimore, 1974), p. 11.

15. Ernst Hanisch, "Franz Rehrl—Sein Leben," in *Franz Rehrl*, ed. Huber, p. 13.

tively, of the Salzburgers and Tyroleans supported the continued independence of Austria.

With the accession of Ignaz Seipel to the chancellorship on 31 May 1922, the Christian Social party began a national reign that continued, unstably to be sure, until the *Anschluss* of 1938. Although actual *Anschluss* politics were only academic, Seipel was faced with a tide of pro-German sentiment that posed a hindrance to whatever "Ostpolitik"—to use an anachronism—he might have wished to introduce into Foreign Minister Heinrich Mataja's already anti-German foreign policy. Thus when Seipel visited Poland in September 1923, the Christian Social journal *Volkswohl* attacked him in an article called "Germanhood Betrayed."[16]

The Christian Social government cleverly attempted to sublimate, or at least assuage, frustrated pro-*Anschluss* sentiment by way of cultural events symbolic of Austrian-German solidarity. Chief among these was a choral festival, the "Deutsche Sängerbundfest" held in July 1928. On 30 July 1928 Seipel remarked that "the only reason why I am against the *Anschluss* movements results from the character of the Austrian people." He tried to field the problem of nationalist agitation with the claim that "national consciousness . . . is neither a good German nor an Austrian conception, but rather a foreign, French, or Czech idea."[17] This is of course a return of the culture-versus-civilization argument, but its most interesting and most ironic aspect lies in its self-defeating linkage of Austrian and German ideas for the purpose of discrediting a nationalist movement whose goal was Austrian-German unification. For Seipel, who described his own political task as the drive "to maintain a counterreformation against all those tendencies that lead people away from religion and the church," had a cultural agenda for a conservative Catholic Austria which reduced even pro- and anti-*Anschluss* politics to the realm of "mere politics."[18]

The undistinguished record of the Christian Social leadership in Austria from 1922 to 1938 resulted from a narrow practical politics that did not have much room to operate according to its ideological

16. "Verrat am Deutschtum," *Volkswohl*, quoted in Heer, p. 364.
17. Heer, p. 368.
18. Rudolf Bluml, ed., *Ignaz Seipel: Mensch, Christ, Priester* (Vienna, 1933), p. 162.

tenets or pressures. The wish to remake (or even to represent) Austria as a conservative Catholic, homogenous German nation that governed Seipel's tenure, and after him those of Dollfuss and Schuschnigg, rested on a cultural ideology reduced to a directionless and despised practical politics, and had no political principles to it whatsoever. To defend Seipel as a leader who began with democratic principles but was forced slowly to abandon them for the sake of his country, so that by 1929 he presented an antidemocratic face, skirts the issue.[19] The slip into Austrofascism was certainly exacerbated by severe German pressure after 1933, but it was also prepared from within, from the lack of any internal political or institutional structures that could have presented a viable social and political system. The path to Austrofascism in 1934 and ultimately to the Nazi *Anschluss* in 1938 has at least three tributaries: first, Austrian conservative ideology and its incapacitating political effects, which I am arguing is primary; then, internal (Austrian) Nazi agitation, and finally, German Nazi agitation. No matter how historians may weigh the relative significance of these factors, the mere recognition of their existence is enough to dispel the myth of the rape of Austria and the innocence and victimization of her leaders, a myth that was fueled immediately after the *Anschluss* by Schnuschnigg and others, bought into by British and American observers sympathetic to the Austrian position, and revived after the war by an Austria eager to dissociate itself from Nazi Germany.[20] Schuschnigg's own memoirs emphasize his pro-Austrianness and his resistance to Hitler, yet he himself does not claim that an anti-Nazi position is identical to an antifascistic one. Austrofascism and Nazism, therefore, shared many ideological tenets during the period before 1938, when they represented mutually hostile political camps.

Although the cultural ideology inherent in the claim to German cultural supremacy existed in the politics of the left as well as in the dominant politics of the right, it was of course the theorists of the right who gave intellectual legitimacy to that ideology as it was interpreted by the men in power. From the Catholic conservative

19. For this argument, see Alfred Diamant, *Austrian Catholics and the First Republic* (Princeton, N.J., 1960), pp. 105–16.

20. See for example Kurt von Schuschnigg, *My Austria* (New York, 1938), including the introduction by Dorothy Thompson.

point of view, Austro-German spiritual legitimacy and superiority were garnered from Austrian, baroque Catholicism (with its two sides of religious practice and secular cultural representation and celebration) and from the church itself.

If Catholicism was the bedrock of Austrian conservatism, the question arises as to why it could not have served to move Austria toward the Catholic nationalities. To propose that Catholicism could have served to unite Austria and the former "nationalities" into a viable federation is a narrow argument that ignores the nationalities' utter mistrust of any potential federalism as a return to the imperial situation in all but name. Clearly, any allusion to the potential unifying force of Catholicism appeared to the former "nationalities" as a direct appeal to one of the instruments of Habsburg domination: the Catholic church. But it does make sense to wonder why Catholic conservatism did not *think* in that direction between 1918 and 1938. The answer must lie in the essential German nationalism of Austrian Catholicism—sacred and secular.

Alfred Diamant's survey of Catholic social and political theory in the First Austrian Republic is of great help in this context. His comparison of the various opposing branches of that theory shows an underlying compatibility and partnership of clerical, pro-German, antiliberal (if not always explicitly antidemocratic), and anti-Semitic ideology. At its foundation was a conservative reading of Pope Leo XIII's encyclical of 1891, *Rerum Novarum*, and later of its fortieth-anniversary follow-up, Pius XI's *Quadragesimo Anno* of 1931. Both encyclicals attacked socialism as a system incompatible with Catholic values and proposed instead a "corporate state" whose actual properties were left open to interpretation.

Diamant divides the Catholic theorists into two groups: the more moderate tradition of *Sozialpolitik* and the more radical one of *Sozialreform*. The *Sozialpolitik* group includes the religious hierarchy; Seipel and Dollfuss; the "realistic" lay theorists Johannes Messner, Josef Dobretsberger, Franz Zehentbauer, and Oscar Schmitz; and the "Österreichische Reform" movement. The *Sozialreform* group includes the religious socialists, led by Otto Bauer;[21] the "Vogelsang

21. This is not the Social Democratic leader Otto Bauer, but a Linz metalworker who gained reknown through his book *Ziele und Wege der religiösen Sozialisten Österreichs [Goals and directions of Austria's religious socialists]* (Vienna, 1930).

School," including Josef Eberle and Eugen Kogon; Othmar Spann; Ernst Winter; and the drafters and supporters of the "Linz Program."

The various components of this general Catholic movement share a definite ground that can be described fairly concisely. Its very existence on a spectrum of thinking that runs from Catholic-socialist reconciliation (Otto Bauer) to passionate antisocialism (Seipel and Dollfuss) suggests that that spectrum is shorter than it seems. This common ground is the essentially utopian wish to redefine society in terms of corporate *Stände* rather than in terms of class. It is thus a *völkisch* ideology. The *Stand* was a religiously (i.e., Catholic) and culturally (i.e., German) defined entity that defied social organization along lines of politics (i.e., party) and economics (i.e., class). The Austrian "politics of the unpolitical," to use Herbert Read's phrase, resulted in the actual *Ständestaat* of 1 May 1934.

Seipel argued that the *Stand* connotes a community, as in a *Gelehrtenstand*, or community of scholars.[22] With the help of the promulgation of the same argument in the *Quadragesimo Anno* encyclical, especially a quotation of Ephesians 4:16 by which the pope argued that the ideal society was one in which "the whole body being compacted and fitly joined together, by what every joint supplieth, according to the operation in the measure of every part, maketh increase of the body, into the edifying of itself in charity," Dollfuss was able decisively to politicize this conception into a national policy.[23] The result was his renowned Trabenplatz address of September 1933, in which he asserted, "We demand a social, Christian, German Austria on a corporative basis and under strong authoritarian leadership."[24]

In a similar manner, the ideas of the Österreichische Aktion faction (not unlike those of the Linzer Programm) looked back to Metternich's anti-industrial policy, since they considered liberalism and industrialization to have destroyed the empire and its values of "Heim und Haus, Stand und Beruf": home and house, social position or estate affiliation, and vocation. Although these words

22. See Diamant, pp. 189ff.
23. See Kitchen, p. 181. Kitchen argues for the parallel between this idea and the practice of Italian fascism.
24. Engelbert Dollfuss, *Dollfuss an Österreich* (Vienna, 1935).

are common (unlike, for example, the word "Gau"), their combination nonetheless generates a mythical language that recalls Renner's
(and of course the language of the German *völkisch* movement in
general). The only viable head of state was a priest, on the model
of a "paterfamilias." The goal of the Österreichische Aktion was
"deproletarianization"—*Entproletarisierung*: the reabsorption of the
worker into the social body. This is clearly a design with the goal
of systematically opposing the Marxian appeal to an increased class
consciousness, and hence conquering alienation from above,
through the total victory of ideology.[25]

The foremost contemporary theorist of the *Ständestaat* was
Othmar Spann, whose 1923 book *Der wahre Staat* (*The True State*)
was read by many in Austria, including Hofmannsthal. There is
certainly a Catholic, *völkisch* commonality between the two men,
but it is difficult and probably specious to argue for a causal link
between them. (One Austrian scholar has argued for such a link
on the grounds that Spann's name was found in Hofmannsthal's
personal address book.[26]) Spann argued for a state based on
ständische Demokratie instead of *Formaldemokratie*. This state would
be based on a principle of inequality, with some "limbs" (*Glieder*:
the organic metaphor is significant) more valuable than others.
These *Stände* would be divided into informal and formal categories. The formal would be guilds and parties (*zünftige Stände* and
politische Stände); the informal would comprise votive communities
(*Votstände*) and material and intellectual groupings (*Vollstände*).[27]

The popularity of Spann's book and thought made him into a
moderator between, on one side, conservative political and social
theorists and, on the other, literary figures, pro-*Anschluss* and anti-
Anschluss alike. The anti-*Anschluss* contingent was represented by
a cohesive group that came to be known as the "Austrian

25. See Diamant, pp. 203ff.
26. Walter Weiss, "Der Salzburger Mythos," *Zeitgeschichte* 2, no. 5 (February
1975): 114.
27. See Diamant, p. 235. See also Arnulf Rieber, *Vom Positivismus zum Universalismus: Untersuchengen z. Entwicklung v. Kritik d. Ganzheitsbegriffs von Othmar Spann*
(Berlin, 1971); and Klaus-Jörg Siegfried, *Universalismus und Faschismus. Das Gesellschaftsbild Othmar Spanns. Zur politischen Funktion seiner Gesellschaftslehre und Ständestaatskonzeption* (Vienna, 1974).

anthropologists." Among them were Hofmannsthal, Bahr, Richard von Kralik, Anton Wildgans, Richard Schaukal, Erwin Hanslick, and Richard Müller. Their loyalties were Catholic, German, monarchist, and Christian Social. The conservative pro-*Anschluss* contingent was led into the late 1930s by the literary historian Josef Nadler and the historian Heinrich von Srbik. Nadler's *Literaturgeschichte der deutschen Stämme und Landschaften* (Literary history of the German tribes and territories) asserted the spiritual unity of the "Austro-Bavarian" baroque-theatrical heritage, an argument that flattered Hofmannsthal's Salzburg pretensions.[28] Hofmannsthal's appreciation of Nadler instantiates what I think is ultimately the most important principle of First Republic political ideology: that the anti-*Anschluss* argument of Austro-German uniqueness and superiority appears more alike than dissimilar to the pro-*Anschluss* argument of pan-German or Austrian-Bavarian consanguinity and superiority. Both arguments rest on the assertion of the power of German culture as an instrument of social and political organization, and hence a rejection of any kind of pluralism.

Srbik's 1935 work *Deutsche Einheit* proposed a fairly complicated notion of German unity.[29] Although Friedrich Heer has described Srbik as "the grand master of pan-German historiography," the term Srbik used here to describe his position was not *grossdeutsch* but *gesamtdeutsch*.[30] Stanley Suval has described Srbik's work as an attempt to reevaluate the Habsburg and Hohenzollern dynasties as equal participants in German history, and hence to provide a "moral tale designed to overcome the defeatism of collapse and to serve as the restorative for German psychological wholeness."[31] Srbik's notion of German psychological wholeness enabled him to combine Austrian Catholicism with a pro-Nazi position.[32]

28. See Weiss, p. 144.
29. Heinrich von Srbik, *Deutsche Einheit: Idee und Wirklichkeit vom Heiligen Reich bis Königgrätz* (Munich, 1935).
30. Heer, p. 379; Suval, pp. 67–68, 174–75.
31. Suval, p. 68.
32. Along with Srbik, Otto Brunner and Friedrich Walter formed a triumvirate of pro-Nazi Austrian Catholic historians. Otto Brunner rationalized his position in the form of an overview of the unique anti-Western mission of Austrian historical science in "Das österreichische Institut für Geschichtsforschung und seine Stellung in der

Austrian political Catholicism, together with its corresponding cultural nationalism, attached itself to a Salzburg crusade independent of the festival that nevertheless reveals many congruities with the festival. This was the campaign for a Catholic university in Salzburg as a fully accredited German university, a campaign begun in 1917 and led through the 1920s by Archbishop Ignaz Rieder, who was also a festival supporter. The original idea was clearly a companion of a pro-*Anschluss* position; a German Catholic university in Salzburg would claim to unite the German-speaking Catholics of Austria and Bavaria. The campaign carried less weight, despite Rieder's continued support of it, once the possibility of *Anschluss* had been precluded.

Rieder himself spelled out the ideological ramifications of the university proposal in a polemic titled "Reflections on a Catholic University of the German People in Salzburg" (*Denkschrift über eine katholische Universität des deutschen Volkstums in Salzburg*). The center of reference is always German Catholicism, not Austrian Catholicism, and the allusion to the *deutsches Volkstum* in the title suggests that Rieder's argument is not only pan-German, but classically *völkisch*. "Not in politics," Rieder begins, "but in the depth of feeling itself lies the strength of the German people." The aim of a Catholic university is of course to rebuild society from the source of that depth of feeling, to serve as a social nucleus as it did in the middle ages: "In the middle ages Catholicism was the most powerful cultural factor only because it was able to create universities from its own spirit." The Catholic university project had been the ambition of the Katholische Vereine Deutschlands und Österreichs, founded in 1849, and its offshoot, the Verein zur Gründung einer katholischen Universität in Deutschland, founded in 1864. The ambition was frustrated, Rieder writes, by the war of 1866, and can now be revived.[33]

---

deutschen Geschichtswissenschaft," in *Mitteilungen des österreichischen Instituts für Geschichtsforschung*, ed. Wilhelm Bauer and Otto Brunner (Innsbruck, September 1938), pp. 385–416.

33. Ignaz Rieder, *Denkschrift über eine katholische Universität des deutschen Volkstums in Salzburg*. The copy of Rieder's piece that I consulted at the Landesarchiv, Salzburg, contained neither a date of publication nor an indication of the publisher. It is nineteen pages long and was published after 1923. Quotations on pp. 1 and 11.

The plans for a Catholic university in Salzburg also attracted the participation of Ignaz Seipel. In December 1916, Seipel wrote to Hermann Bahr of the project, which he envisaged as "a meeting ground for Germans (*Reichsdeutscher*) and Austrians."[34] It is interesting that in 1916, before the emergence of the *Anschluss* question, Seipel was eager for a Catholic university to serve as a point of mediation between Austria and Germany.

One of the most vocal opponents of this university project upon its revival in 1917 was Max Weber, who wrote a short article on the subject for the *Frankfurter Zeitung* of 10 May 1917.[35] In explaining his opposition, Weber made the issue into a paradigm of the opposition between cultural politics and science: "efforts are being made, in association with the theological faculty which exists in Salzburg, to establish a university which will have religious requirements for appointment to some of its secular professorships . . . such conditions . . . are absolutely incompatible with a selection of candidates according to strictly scientific and scholarly criteria. . . . the imperial nomination of the incumbents of no less than five of the secular professorships is to be dependent on the prior assent of the archbishop. This constitutes a *missio canonica* in every respect. Such a university would naturally not be one likely to be viewed by academic institutions as of equal standing and rights."

IV

When *Kulturpolitik* is held to be primary, it makes sense to find at least partial sources of practical political modes in the thinking and the ideological engagement of culturally significant figures outside the explicitly political arena. One group of such figures, the "Austrian anthropologists," certainly sought political participation. Two of these, Bahr and Hofmannsthal, did gain an audience: Bahr

---

34. This unpublished letter of 18 December 1916 from Seipel to Bahr is in the Bahr Nachlass, Theatersammlung, Nationalbibliothek, Vienna.

35. Max Weber, "Eine katholische Universität in Salzburg," *Frankfurter Zeitung*, 10 May 1917; reprinted in Edward Shils, ed., *Max Weber on Universities: The Power of the State and the Dignity of the Academic Calling in Imperial Germany* (Chicago, 1976), pp. 46–47.

generated a small correspondence with Seipel and Hofmannsthal wrote extensively in the press. Of particular interest is the surviving voluminous correspondence among the Christian Social Bahr and Hofmannsthal and the liberal Josef Redlich, a triangular conversation that after 1918 focuses almost exclusively on the subject of Austrian cultural reconstruction in general, and the relations between Austro-Germans and Czechs in particular. The intellectual friendship between, on one side, Bahr and Hofmannsthal, and, on the other, Redlich, represents a confrontation between Catholic conservatism and a genuine liberal pluralism, with the rhetoric of liberal pluralism controlling the language of all three men. Redlich spoke with a voice of genuine legal and political pluralism and did not emphasize the cultural questions that remained of paramount importance for Hofmannsthal and Bahr, and which prevented them from wedding their liberal rhetoric to truly pluralist attitudes. The key to the essential conservatism behind their liberal discourse is provided by the fourth man in the circle: Rudolf Pannwitz.

Redlich was a legal theorist by training, and the key to his anglophilic liberalism is probably his lifelong study of English law and political administration. In his thesis of 1901 (titled "Englische Lokalverwaltung") he had argued that local administration was the foundation for the unparalleled political maturity of the British people and the absolute presupposition of British parliamentarianism. A second work, *Recht und Technik des englischen Parlamentarismus*, established him as an authority on the British system within Great Britain as well as on the continent; the book was often cited as authoritative by Prime Minister Asquith. Redlich applied this anticentralist politics to the Austrian situation and became an ardent federalist, before and after 1918. Federalism meant an anti-*Anschluss* position, and that isolated him from the majority of the *deutschnational* "liberals."

Redlich's federalism by no means carried with it a belief in cultural equality. In his assumption of German cultural supremacy he differed neither from Hofmannsthal and Bahr nor from the traditional tenets of Austrian liberalism. Nevertheless, for Redlich, cultural superiority did not imply cultural hegemony. That is where he parted with Hofmannsthal, Bahr, and Rudolf Pannwitz, as well as with the tradition of Austrian liberalism expressed in the precept of the Austrian liberal leader of the previous generation, J. N. Berger, who had written in 1861 that "the Germans of Austria should strive not for political hegemony, but for cultural hegemony among the peoples of Austria."[36] Redlich's relative lack of cultural politics spared him from the desperate Austrian patriotism that controlled Bahr and Hofmannsthal in the 1920s. Physical absence from Austria figured as well; Redlich spent the better part of the fifteen years before his death in 1936 as a law professor in American universities.

Hermann Bahr, whom Ignaz Seipel called "an apostle of Austrian thought," was the marketing genius par excellence of Austrian letters.[37] He had an unfailing sense for intellectual, aesthetic, and political fashion, and an ability to place himself at the center of new trends without ever contributing to them. He was a champion of pan-Germanism in the 1880s, of the Secession in the 1890s, of the war effort in 1914, and of the Christian Social, anti-Anschluss "Austrian idea" in the 1920s. The pan-Germanism of the 1880s and the Christian Social politics of the 1920s lose their apparent contradiction—in the biography of Bahr and in general—when their shared tenets of German cultural superiority are brought to light.

C. E. Williams has identified in Bahr's political consciousness the constant "conviction that it was the duty of the Austro-Germans to transmit their superior culture to their less fortunate neighbours like missionaries among the heathen."[38] As Bahr wrote in his 1909 *Dalmatinische Reise* (a memoir that evokes Goethe in its title though not in its text), "is it always just a question of language, is it not rather a question of German values and our national character? Is it not more important to instill the latter in the peoples of Southern and Eastern Europe? Let the spirit of Germany gain converts for us in the outside world! Whatever language it happens to speak, what does that matter provided that the German essence gives the lead to mankind!"[39] The immediate political context of this assertion is

36. See Schorske, *Fin-de-siècle Vienna*, p. 117.

37. Seipel, letter to Bahr of 18 July 1923, Theatersammlung.

38. C. E. Williams, *The Broken Eagle: The Politics of Austrian Literature from Empire to Anschluss* (New York, 1974), p. 35.

39. Hermann Bahr, *Dalmatinische Reise* (Berlin, 1909), cited in Williams, p. 35; translation revised.

clearly the controversial 1908 Habsburg annexation of Bosnia and Herzegovina. Yet the statement reveals a mode of thought and style of expression which would be just as relevant to the politics of 1920, and just as appropriate to an anti-*Anschluss* ideology of 1920 as to a pan-German one of 1880.

Indeed, pan-Germanism and anti-*Anschluss* politics were not necessarily incompatible for Bahr (or for Hofmannsthal). The experience of the war elicited from Bahr, as from Hofmannsthal, a profound sense of common German destiny with a simultaneous adherence to the idea of an independent Austria. In September 1914, Bahr wrote to Hofmannsthal of his stay in Bayreuth the previous month (where his wife, Anna Bahr-Mildenburg, was singing at the Wagner festival), and his encounter there with the German mobilization. "I have never seen a greater sight," he wrote, "nor so purely sensed the German spirit."[40] Yet in a June 1916 letter to Hofmannsthal he wrote the following: "I fear that you do not see the terrible danger that threatens Austria. It [Austria] is presently in the hands of traitors, who are methodically delivering it to the German Reich. The form of the Habsburgs, as long as they themselves last, will remain, but we will have become something on the order of Serbia. Help can only come from our Slavs and from the church, both of which will try to resist this devastation to their last breath. In Austria today, any politics that is not Slavic or Catholic is un-Austrian."[41] Bahr's German cultural ideology and Slav-oriented politics converge to form the same position that determined Hofmannsthal's view of the Slavic world: German culture provides the ballast that enables the "liberal" attention to, even appreciation of, the former "nationalities."

Bahr's 1912 move from Vienna to Salzburg, his installation there as the resident intellectual and voice of the true Austria, and his purchase of the Schloss Arenberg reinforced his position as the city's cultural aristocrat. The move to Salzburg itself was a cultural pilgrimage, foreshadowing the cultural symbolism of the festival, which Bahr helped promote. (Once the festival had begun, how-

40. Letter of Bahr to Hofmannsthal, 13 September 1914, Box 38, Bahr Nachlass, Theatersammlung.
41. Letter of Bahr to Hofmannsthal, 16 June 1916, Box 38, Theatersammlung.

ever, Bahr vacillated between his initial position of festival supporter and *Theatermensch* and his adopted position of conservative
citizen of Salzburg. On the one hand, he helped mediate the negotiations between Hofmannsthal and Reinhardt and Archbishop Rieder concerning the use of the Kollegienkirche for the *Welttheater*;
on the other, he wrote in August 1920 that the atmosphere in
Salzburg is "horrible" and that the city "will breathe again when
Jedermann is over!"[42])

Bahr's conviction of the necessity of a Slavic politics in the interest
of Austrian autonomy was not lost on Hofmannsthal. In June 1917,
Hofmannsthal made a well-publicized week-long trip to Prague.
He intended it as a cultural mission, and it was perceived that way
by his circle of friends.[43] Hofmannsthal thus made personal contact
with several people he had been corresponding with since the
beginning of the war. Prominent among these were Jaroslav Kvapil,
a fellow opera librettist and the director of the Czech National
Theater (and an acquaintance of Bahr's), and Paul Eisner, a poet
and translator from German into Czech (later the translator of Kafka
and Thomas Mann).[44]

Contact with Kvapil resulted from a volume of collected photographs that Hofmannsthal was planning, a volume that would
include images and descriptions of Czechoslovakia, but whose title
would be "Ehrenstätten Österreichs" (Noble sites of Austria). The
title was of course planned before the Habsburg dissolution, but it
is still revealing for its, so to speak, Austrocentrism. Kvapil's letters
to Hofmannsthal were always highly respectful, but indicative of
enough intellectual and political disagreement to cause some
friction.

In his first letter to Hofmannsthal, Kvapil wrote: "I must briefly

---

42. Letter to Josef Redlich of 14 August 1920, in Fritz Fellner, ed., *Dichter und
Gelehrter: Herman Bahr und Josef Redlich in ihren Briefen, 1896–1934* (Salzburg, 1980),
p. 421.

43. For a detailed chart of Hofmannsthal's itinerary, see Heinz Lunzer, *Hofmannsthals politische Tätigkeit in den Jahren 1914–1917* (Frankfurt am Main, 1981), pp. 240–
54.

44. Hofmannsthal's contact and correspondence with Kvapil and Eisner as well
as Franz Spina and Ottokar Winicky have been documented in a three-part article
by Martin Stern in the *Hofmannsthal Blätter* (Frankfurt), Heft 1 (1968), Heft 2 (1969),
Heft 3 (1969). These will henceforth be referred to as Stern 1, Stern 2, and Stern 3.

repeat to you what I have just written to Bahr: the most beautiful and noble of what our past has to offer has very seldom been seen as such by Austria, and the other way around things are even worse. Most of what my people have lost in terms of political, national, and religious independence, it lost through Austria and to Austria. . . . These are not the words of an insane patriot."[45] In a letter of January 1915, Kvapil commented on Hofmannsthal's recently published polemic "Bejahung Österreichs" (Affirmation of Austria):

> From the very outset we disagree fundamentally, as your point of view—I refer not so much to your letter as to the article which I recently read in the *Schaubühne*—rests on an intense belief in Austria— and this belief I do not have nor can I gain it from recent events. . . . In this article you write impressively of the Austrian artistic blossom that lasted from 1683 until the death of Joseph II. Well, these hundred years signify for my nation in Austria the greatest cultural, national, and economic debasement. . . . How we suffered in that century at the hands of Vienna and Rome (and from Rome via Vienna). . . . Then the question was religious; today it is the national question. And what we have become in the last hundred years, we have become without Austria, despite Austria—and at times even against Austria.[46]

In his penultimate letter, Kvapil suggested to Hofmannsthal that "what is referred to as the 'Austrian problem' we will never see with the same eyes."[47] Kvapil thus resigned from the "Ehrenstätten Österreichs" project, which Hofmannsthal himself soon abandoned.

In 1917 Hofmannsthal embarked on a successor project to be called the "Czech Library" and to serve as a companion series to the "Austrian Library" series on which he was working. Paul Eisner was to translate Czech poetry into German. Eisner requested the participation of Bahr and Pannwitz, "who have earned it for their uncovering of the Czech essence," as well as that of both brothers Mann, Rilke, Hesse, and the Prague-born Franz Werfel.[48] Eisner's perspective was clearly German, and thus essentially different from Kvapil's.

45. Kvapil, letter of 19 November 1914: Stern 1, p. 13.
46. Kvapil, letter of 11 January 1915: Stern 1, pp. 19–21.
47. Kvapil, letter of 9 February 1918: Stern 1, pp. 25–26.
48. Eisner, letter of 9 January 1918: Stern 3, pp. 198–200.

This was true even more of Franz Spina, a German scholar at the University of Prague whom Eisner recruited for the Czech Library project. For Spina, the continued unity of Austrians and Czechs was essential. In a letter to Hofmannsthal of January 1918, Spina praised the latter's recent essays on Prince Eugen and Grillparzer for having reaffirmed faith in the

> God-givenness and indestructable unity, the inner necessity of Austria so clearly recognized by the realistic Austro-Slavic Czech politicians (Havlíček and Palacký), now under the ruinous effect of the evil half-concept of self-determination, a dangerous relapse into a political romanticism which no Czech will want anything to do with. . . . The one genuinely Slavic feature of this inwardly Germanized people is the immoderation of its goals, the overestimation of the achievable and of one's own strength, and an incorrigibility through history and reality. The development of this psychosis since the return of [Karel] Kramár [a leader of the Czech independence movement], the politician of misery, points to a *purposeful* isolation of the people, to a radical separation of Czech culture from the German element, a situation that is thoroughly inorganic and—in terms of real politics—simply impossible."[49]

Hofmannsthal's own writing was never quite so impassioned, but he approved of such rhetoric from the pens of others. The case of Spina is one example; that of Rudolf Pannwitz is perhaps the strongest. Hofmannsthal's trip to Prague coincided with his discovery and patronage of Pannwitz and his book *The Crisis of European Culture*. He immediately sent copies of the book to Bahr and to Redlich, who were both impressed, and he asked Pannwitz to send copies to Jaroslav Kvapil and to Paul Eisner.[50]

In a September 1917 letter which Hofmannsthal received with great pleasure, Pannwitz outlined a cultural theory that he planned to apply to a group of essays about the Czechs. (Those essays appeared in 1918 in the Viennese journal *Der Friede*.) His theory revolved around a central distinction between a world-culture (*Welt-*

49. Spina, letter of 26 January 1918: Stern 3, pp. 202–4.
50. Hofmannsthal, letter to Pannwitz of 17 September 1917: Deutsches Literaturarchiv, Marbach.

kultur) and a national culture or "small" culture. He applied his terms in the following way: "Austria-Hungary bases its empire on the German world-culture. One must demand of the Germans in Austria that they perceive themselves as a world-culture and above all not as a national culture. . . . One must demand of the Czechs that, as a national culture, they subordinate themselves to a world-culture, in other words that they not fight for recognition as a historical fact, but rather that they enrich and rejuvenate themselves through their rising national strength."[51]

Pannwitz at this point planned to write a book called *Österreischiche Kulturpolitik*, a work in two sections: "Austria's Potential," and "The Spirit of the Czechs." As a German-born Austrophile, Pannwitz had decided that Austria had earned the right to be the legitimate bearer of German culture, and this book was to be a blueprint for that eventuality.[52] Hofmannsthal reacted with the urgent advice that Pannwitz travel to Prague, as he himself had done several months before: "In my opinion you absolutely must see and speak with the Czechs, breathe their air, before you write about the 'spirit of the Czechs,' for otherwise everything hangs in mid-air, and nuances are false, no matter how clever and profound one's thoughts or how sensible and gifted one's guesses."[53] Pannwitz went to Prague in early December 1917, and upon returning to Vienna wrote to Hofmannsthal: "I now see that the Czechs are the strongest contrast to the Austrian Germans, and yet are deeply related to them and that 'the Austrian' is the truest type." And: "I found everything different from what I had expected and come back with an uncontrollably excited belief in Austria and in an Austrian Europe."[54]

In this same letter Pannwitz wrote that he was eager to meet Max Mell, Redlich, and all of Hofmannsthal's "society." Through Hofmannsthal, Pannwitz established contacts with Paul Eisner in Prague, Redlich in Vienna, and Bahr in Salzburg. He introduced

51. Pannwitz, letter of 24 September 1917: Marbach.
52. Pannwitz, letter of Hofmannsthal of 9 November 1917: Marbach.
53. Hofmannsthal, letter to Pannwitz of 12 November 1917: Marbach. This letter was written three days after the letter cited directly above; therefore it can probably not be assumed that Hofmannsthal was answering the 9 November letter.
54. Pannwitz, letter to Hofmannsthal of 16 December 1917: Marbach.

himself to Bahr in writing in October 1917, expressed the wish to meet with Bahr but warned him that he would "find in me no less than a revolutionary.[55] In a long letter to Bahr written three days later, Pannwitz discussed the compatibility of his and Bahr's political thought. The reconstruction of Austria, he argued, must proceed on a superorganic (*überorganisch*) model, as opposed to a mechanical one.[56] In this second October letter, Pannwitz mentioned the necessary "synthesis" of the new Austria; he spelled out that notion a bit more in a letter written seven months later. The Catholic church, he stated, must serve as the symbol of the new synthesis, but not the reality; the church is limited by its institutional trappings, which will be transcended by the new synthesis.[57] A year later, in this same context, Pannwitz offered an interpretation of Bahr's Catholicism, which he respected. Bahr's was "the absolute opposite of current Catholic culture . . . a kind of Protestantism against Protestantism."[58] None of this is coherent, and there is no evidence that Bahr answered these letters, but Pannwitz's religious notions are interesting for their indication of the mythic universe in which he was operating. Himself a German, he claimed to have found his true German identity in Austria and in Hofmannsthal's "Austrian idea" (as he himself confessed to Bahr), and his vision of a new German cultural synthesis based on Austria thus had a foreignness that served his psychological disposition.

Pannwitz's friendships with all these figures, including Hofmannsthal, broke off decisively in 1920. For one thing, he seems to have owed them all money. But the crucial final episode came in a bizarre letter that Pannwitz wrote to Redlich in January 1920, declaring a complete rupture of their friendship and personally insulting Redlich. In a paranoid outburst, Pannwitz accused Redlich of reacting duplicitously to his *Deutsche Lehre*, and betraying his friendship: "I consider you incapable even of understanding what I hold against you. . . . You are a pitiful liberal, a small man

55. Pannwitz, letter to Bahr of 26 October 1917: Theatersammlung.
56. Pannwitz, letter to Bahr of 29 October 1917: Theatersammlung.
57. Pannwitz, letter to Bahr of 31 May 1918: Theatersammlung.
58. Pannwitz, letter to Bahr of 26 May 1919: Theatersammlung.

and a little Jew."[59] Redlich wrote Hermann Bahr about this episode, suggesting that his recent refusal to finance a trip to Italy for Pann-witz and several female companions ("the new Mohammed and his four wives," as he put it) had incurred Pannwitz's rage. He had not acknowledged Pannwitz's letter, Redlich wrote to Bahr, as he was not in the habit of "corresponding with lunatics."[60] One can only speculate whether there were deeper, intellectual causes for Pann-witz's outburst; in any case his reference to Redlich as a "pitiful liberal" reveals something about his true political convictions, on which was built a cultural theory that for a short time influenced so many leading Austrian intellectuals.

Although Pannwitz then disappeared from the scene, his mode of perceiving cultural questions in general and the role of Austro-German culture in Europe in particular clearly retained a spot in the thinking of Hofmannsthal and Bahr, if not of Redlich, whose liberalism really did separate him from the others. Pannwitz's thought was not original, and he wrote in an opaque, pseudo-Nietzschean garble, a "Zarathustra-tone that is hard for me to take even in Nietzsche," as Redlich commented.[61] Yet in his cultural criticism he did provide a vocabulary that placed the Austrian-Czech question in the context of what I have referred to as German "nationalist cosmopolitanism." The Czechs, as a "national culture" were to be appreciated by the Austro-German "world-culture."

"Appreciation" is no doubt the right word to describe Hof-mannsthal's relationship to Czech culture. The theme was certainly important to him, and he used it as the pivot of the last opera libretto he wrote for Richard Strauss, *Arabella*, which will be discussed in the next chapter. But although *Arabella* was about the marriage of Austrian and Czech culture (as represented by the heroine Arabella and the hero Mandryka), it was formally a German opera. It never

59. Pannwitz, letter to Redlich of 21 January 1920: Marbach. Redlich seems never to have mentioned this episode to Hofmannsthal. There is no mention of it in the Redlich-Hofmannsthal correspondence (*Briefwechsel*, ed. Helga Fussgänger [Frank-furt, 1971]). Having come into contact with Pannwitz through Hofmannsthal, Red-lich may not have wanted to upset the latter with this event.
60. Redlich, letter to Bahr of 31 January 1920, no. 493 in Fellner, ed., *Dichter und Gelehrter*, pp. 395–97.
61. Ibid. In his published works, Pannwitz wrote without any punctuation or capitalizations.

occurred to Hofmannsthal to stage a Czech opera at the Salzburg Festival (such as Dvorák's *Rusalka*, which had a libretto by Jaroslav Kvapil). Czech culture remained an object to be seen and appreciated through a German lens.

CHAPTER 5

Allegory and Authority in the Work of Hugo von Hofmannsthal

I

THERE is a convergence between the Salzburg Festival as an ideological cultural program and the intellectual biography of its principal intellectual founder, Hugo von Hofmannsthal. Although my method in this book is not a biographical one, but rather one that takes biography as a subset of culturally shared patterns of ideas and ideologies, a more considered portrait of Hofmannsthal himself is still needed: a sketch of those strands in his career that are most relevant to the problematic of the Salzburg Festival. Like the other three chapters that attempt to define and connect the festival's ideological origins, this one also works in two directions. By explicating origins, it attempts to point to implications as well. It argues for a dialectic between Hofmannsthal's political ideology and his creative work, between the emergence of a conservative model of national authority and the turn to a model of cognitive and literary authority that constituted, for Hofmannsthal, allegorical practice.

As a leading poet of his generation as well as a product and diagnostician of widespread cultural malaise, Hofmannsthal has received fairly constant scholarly attention since his death in 1929. Literary scholars who have continued to stress Hofmannsthal's importance have tended to concentrate on the early period of his career, the decade of the 1890s, when as a teenager he became a matinée idol among Viennese literati. Hofmannsthal himself periodized his own career, and analysts have tended to follow that periodization. The lyric poetry period ends in 1900, with the publication of the famous "Letter of Lord Chandos," a manifesto rejecting poetry and language itself as insincere and unsuccessful vehicles for the understanding and expression of human experience. Hofmannsthal's middle period can be said to last from 1900 to 1914, a period of Greek dramas and opera librettos which extended the problem of the breakdown of language, communication, and rationality into an apocalyptic vision realized through the form of tragedy (*Elektra, Oedipus and the Sphinx*). Hofmannsthal never committed himself completely to a tragic tone, however, and during this period he wrote comedies as well, comedies that despite their continued treatment of these serious themes pointed to some positive resolution (*Ariadne auf Naxos, Der Rosenkavalier*).

Hofmannsthal's apocalyptic writings, then, chronologically preceded the actual political apocalypse of 1918. The next period of Hofmannsthal's work, one of reconstruction through conservative revolution, indeed began with the onset of war in 1914. When Hofmannsthal was drawn to politics, he was drawn to an ideology of reconstruction which entered his poetic and dramatic works just as it pervaded his political and critical writings. The dramatic works of this late period include the wartime operatic parable *Die Frau ohne Schatten, Arabella*, and the plays *The Difficult Man* and *The Tower*. The last of these was a project that Hofmannsthal wrote and rewrote over a quarter of century, and it was the closest to him of all his works; its final form retains a pessimistic tone that is not in keeping with the reconstructive posture of his late period. Rounding out his late works is the set of Catholic morality plays, *Jedermann* and *Das Salzburger grosse Welttheater*.

With the possible exception of *The Tower*, these parables of reconstruction reveal a path into ideology and a corresponding aesthetic decline. Perhaps the most inferior work, *Das Salzburger grosse Welttheater*, is both the most allegorical and the most programmatic. Like many other thinkers of his time, Lukács and Benjamin among them, Hofmannsthal revalorized allegory as a form of discourse capable of understanding modernity. Yet he did so from the perspective of his most (formalistically and politically) conservative perspectives. Allegory became for him a mode of discourse that inherited and applied the *authority* of religious models and projections, an authority that combined as its principle of power both cultural control and the control over meaning and representation. Symbolic discourse for Hofmannsthal retained an indeterminate referentiality; allegory explained the cosmos.

In this mode, Hofmannsthal never ceased to think in terms of totalities. During his "apocalyptic period," if that locution is not too awkward, he treated political apocalypse as a subcategory of metaphysical apocalypse: the breakdown of language and understanding carried with it the breakdown of political structures of communication. When the theme changed to programmatic reconstruction, with conservative revolution and Catholicism as the components of the program, Hofmannsthal had to ignore the metaphysical and epistemological aspects of his early cosmology. (That they are not ignored in *The Tower* accounts for its incompleteness, as well as for his actual inability to finish it.)

This passage from a cosmology of metaphysical and political apocalypse to one of ideological reconstruction can be charted according to what may be called the devaluation of the symbolic. Hofmannsthal's poetic and dramatic work was throughout his career grounded in the use of symbolism. His early lyric poetry reflects the symbolist poetry of the French as well as of Yeats, and the use of symbols as a basic formal principle carries through his writing. However, the meaning of those symbols was devalued, I think, from the status of metaphor to that of a restricted form of allegory. In Hofmannsthal's late, ideological practice of allegory, imaginary constructions achieve social and political relevance through determined and definite structures of reference. Jedermann becomes Austria, and Austria becomes an end in itself—aesthetically as well as politically. Thus baroque allegorical practice (in a general sense as well as in a specifically Austrian one) is impoverished as the relationship between symbol and symbolized is made rigid. Indeed, the nineteenth-century transformation of the idea of the nation into the ultimate symbolized entity (the signified) rather than a further level of symbol (or sign) can be said to define much nationalist ideology. Hofmannsthal's baroque, Austrian ideology thus takes shape in literary practice through a process of allegorization that speaks to one side of Walter Benjamin's well-known definition:

For allegory is both: convention and expression; and both are inherently contradictory. However, just as baroque teaching conceives of history as created events, allegory in particular, although a convention like every kind of writing, is regarded as created, like holy scripture. The allegory of the seventeenth century is not convention of expression, but expression of convention. At the same time expression of authority, which is secret in accordance with the dignity of its origin, but public in accordance with the extent of its validity.[1]

II

The early symbolic universe of Hofmannsthal's lyric poetry and its connections with his youthful life and his social and political milieu have been masterfully analyzed by Hermann Broch. My purpose here is to restate some of the principal elements of Broch's portrait and to extend it beyond the analysis of Hofmannsthal's lyric poetry and literary prose writings (the work Broch covers) to examine some of the middle and late period drama. Broch's own study, *Hofmannsthal und seine Zeit*, as he himself stated, shows "how a highly talented man, who out of weakness succumbed too much to the conditions of his time, became a bad poet."[2]

Broch begins his biography with a short history of four generations of the Hofmannsthal family, a "history of an assimilation," in his words. The poet's great-grandfather, Isaak Löw Hofmann, had come to Vienna in 1788 as a young man, one among the thousands of Moravian and Bohemian Jews who migrated to Vienna after the declaration of the Josephinian Patent of Toleration of 1781. For his contributions to the Austrian textile industry, the profession with which he had arrived in Vienna, Isaak Hofmann was honored in 1835 by Emperor Ferdinand with the conferral of a patent of nobility and the title "Edler von Hofmannsthal." Along with the Rothschild family, Isaak Hofmann was a founding member of the Viennese Jewish community (*Israelitische Kultusgemeinde*),

---

1. Walter Benjamin, *The Origin of German Tragic Drama*, trans. John Osborne (London, 1977), p. 175.
2. See Michael P. Steinberg, Introduction to Broch, *Hofmannsthal and His Time*, p. 4.

whose synagogue on the Seitenstättengasse he helped finance. Hofmann's son August began the path of assimilation to which Broch refers. He married the daughter of a Milanese Catholic patrician and brought up their son (Hugo, Sr.) as a Catholic. Their grandson, the poet Hofmannsthal, was therefore the first in the line born of two Catholic parents, but the second to be brought up in the religion.

He retained an equivocal attitude to his religious constitution. As an adult he was not observant, but was an honorary member of a Franciscan order, and as a young man he expressed a wish that he be buried in Franciscan garb. This wish was respected at his death in 1929, though his literary executor, the scholar Rudolf Hirsch, has suggested that he had privately long abandoned it.[3]

As an aesthetic principle, however, Catholicism remained a fundamental ingredient of Hofmannsthal's world-view. For Hofmannsthal, Catholicism was essential as a principle of cultural and aesthetic style, and, as his career and political concern developed, his own inhabitation of that style intensified into a political and social program. He associated this Catholic style with Viennese theater, most importantly with the Burgtheater. Broch identifies the evenings in the Burgtheater as the formative experiences of Hofmannsthal the poet, and he identifies the Burgtheater as the bastion of Habsburg baroque, secular Catholicism, a role paralleled by the Comédie Française in Paris, but he does not put those two points together to identify the Burgtheater as a Catholic principle in the formation of Hofmannsthal's poetics. This step has to be taken.[4]

Hofmannsthal was educated at the Wiener Akademisches Gymnasium, a secular institution, but his principal education, a sentimental education, was the code of *Bildung* he absorbed from his father. Broch describes this code as "the development of those abilities through which the leisure hours of the burgher class were being transformed to 'noble enjoyment,' to the enjoyment of art in winter, nature in summer."[5] Carl Schorske has set Hofmannsthal's aesthetic education within the context of the depoliticization of the Austrian middle classes after the economic crash of 1873 and the

3. Rudolf Hirsch—personal communication.
4. Broch, pp. 38, 61–63, 101–4.
5. Ibid., p. 88.

subsequent decline of liberalism, a situation felt particularly acutely by the Viennese Jews.[6] Insofar as the liberal crisis entailed a crisis of toleration and assimilation for Jews, a combination of factors that would certainly have been relevant for Hugo von Hofmannsthal senior, born of a Jewish father, then the cult of *Bildung* in which he in turn raised his son must be seen to be informed by the assimilation crisis. Thus in the 1870s—in a nationalist context in Germany and a "postliberal" one in Austria—the ethic of *Bildung* appears as an increasingly illusory belief in the possibility of assimilation through language. It also reveals the liberalism of the 1860s to have been a much thinner layer of political behavior than Schorske sees it. By the time of Hofmannsthal's birth in 1874, the assimilation of his family was complete, but his childhood absorption of baroque culture speaks to the continuing dominance and power of this cultural mode, which has nothing liberal about it.

That the Burgtheater became for Hofmannsthal a dreamworld in which he lived and which structured his imagination has been suggested in Chapter 2, in the context of the ultimate parity of his theatrical vision with that of Max Reinhardt. Broch describes the nature of that dreamworld in the following way:

There is no doubt that for father Hofmannsthal and his son the visits to the Burgtheater—before that to the "Prater" and its Kasperle-Theater—formed the high points of the aesthetic-aestheticizing game of education in which and with which, naturally predisposed to one another, they built and made lasting their relationship. Yet this paternal influence in no way diminishes the discriminating capacity the boy added on his own. That so young a person would prove unable to extricate himself from the decoration- and beautification-filled epoch was only to be expected; that he nevertheless succeeded in discovering perhaps the single truly fruitful elements in it, namely the high performing art practiced in the Burgtheater (that of the Comédie Française was as yet unknown to him), and hence the element in which the decorative artistic practice of the time had transcended itself and had grown into the genuine, the "re-genuine," reflected an extraordinary instinct in a boy; it was an achievement that was bound to have further effect.[7]

6. Schorske, "Politics and the Psyche: Schnitzler and Hofmannsthal," in *Fin-de-siècle Vienna: Politics and Culture*, pp. 3–23.

7. Broch, pp. 101–2.

From the Burgtheater, Broch proposes, came the "compromise with the stage that Hofmannsthal seized upon too enthusiastically." The result became the underlying stylistic principle of Hofmannsthal's work, no matter the genre: "The world becomes a beautiful theater . . . that the artist must present to the very same world, he, its ideal observer and hence its ideal illustrator, so that sitting in his orchestra seat within the crowd . . . he too can wander into the seclusion and solitude of the stage."[8] Broch traces this principle through the lyric poetry to the transitional lyric dramas, which conclude the early period. The theater thus carries Hofmannsthal's childhood *Bildung* into the manifestations of his mature career and remains the vehicle for cognitive, aesthetic, and ethical engagement with the social world. Yet the baroque origins of his theatrical cosmos do not impose an unchanging ideology, as the middle period shows.

III

Hofmannsthal's middle period begins with the "language crisis" of the "Letter of Lord Chandos" and the subsequent renunciation of lyric poetry. In the form of a letter written to Lord Chancellor Francis Bacon, an imaginary Lord Chandos expresses the anguish born of the discovery that all language has lost meaning, that words and objects are no longer connected, and that writing and words have become useless and insincere instruments by which to understand human experience. Michael Hamburger has argued that Hofmannsthal in effect never left his "Lord Chandos period," that the self-consciousness about words and the thematic importance of communication and its problems remained crucial for him throughout his mature career.[9] Hamburger quotes from one of Hofmannsthal's earliest prose pieces, written in 1891, which can indeed serve as an explication for his life-long concerns: "We have no generally valid tone in conversation because we have no society and no

8. Ibid., p. 100.
9. See Michael Hamburger, Introduction to Hofmannsthal, *Plays and Libretti*, pp. ix–lxxii.

conversation, just as we have no style and no culture."[10] Broch does not question the prevalence of this theme in Hofmannsthal's post-Chandos writings, but he does question its depth. He argues that the very stylistic choice of framing the Chandos manifesto within a context of Elizabethan propriety reveals an essential conservatism that undermines its apocalyptic message. Ultimately, Broch argues, the Chandos letter cannot escape the irony that it is a body of words written to express the futility of words and writing.[11] More specifically, it is quite literally a baroque document that undermines the baroque. There is security in irony.

The same ironies (intended and unintended) may be said to inhabit Hofmannsthal's major dramatic piece of this middle period, *Elektra*, a parable about the shattering of rational and political order, both symbolized by the rule of the Mycenean king Agamemnon, murdered by his wife Klytemnestra and her lover Aegisthus. Elektra, Agamemnon's daughter, is a half-demented creature who has in effect given up her humanity and her rationality as a means of refusing to give up the old world. She longs for the appropriate revenge, the matricide to be committed by her brother Orestes. But the ultimate purpose of that revenge, the restoration of order, is impossible, so that the return of Orestes and his actual murder of both Klytemnestra and Aegisthus—the drama's climax—are ultimately meaningless.

"Language crisis" and noncommunication prevail in *Elektra* on all levels. The drama is a series of conversations in which communication fails—Hofmannsthal's 1891 statement, quoted above, is relevant here. The opening scene sets the atmosphere of decay: five serving maids from the palace discuss, in a rather panicked manner, the fact that the princess Elektra, forced to live among the animals and now herself degenerated to a subhuman level, appears nightly at the same hour and howls after her dead father "like a wild cat."[12]

10. Ibid., p. xv.
11. Broch, pp. 121–25.
12. Hofmannsthal, *Elektra*, in *Plays and Libretti*, p. 5. The standard complete German edition of the Hofmannsthal dramas is Hugo von Hofmannsthal, *Gesammelte Werke in Einzelausgaben*, ed. Herbert Steiner (Frankfurt, 1945–55). A new, critical edition of the complete works is currently being prepared by the Hugo von Hofmannsthal Gesellschaft in Frankfurt, in association with the Fischer Verlag, but it is as yet incomplete.

Elektra does appear, and in a soliloquy that begins as a lament and ends as a battle cry, she imagines the bloody revenge that will occur when Orestes returns.

The following scene, between Elektra and her sister Chryso-themis, establishes a juxtaposition of two female "ideal types" that Hofmannsthal was to retain throughout his playwriting career. Elektra is the past-obsessed, heroic figure, both subhuman and goddesslike, who has abdicated her position in the world. (Other representatives of this type are more manifestly goddesslike, Ari-adne, for example.) Chrysothemis, on the contrary, wants to forget the past and live an anonymous life directed toward marriage and motherhood. This juxtaposition of two women contains the overall juxtaposition of apocalypse and reconstruction that is essential to Hofmannsthal's work. At this early stage, his focus and sympathy are on the apocalyptic mentality of Elektra.

After the arrival of a rumor that Orestes has been killed, Elektra decides that she and Chrysothemis must carry out the revenge themselves. Chrysothemis refuses, and Elektra curses her. The rumor, however, has actually been planted by Orestes himself, in preparation for his return. Orestes arrives as Elektra is digging for the ax that had murdered her father and that she had hidden in anticipation of a perfect revenge. Neither one recognizes the other, and their nervous dialogue becomes deeply ironic as Elektra curses the stranger for surviving her brother, whose life was worth "a thousand times" his. They finally reveal their identities to each other, and Orestes carries out the double revenge. The palace is exultant, but Elektra refuses to join the general celebration. She begins a ritual dance, and her last words to the crowd are the command "Be silent and dance," as she falls dead.

The metaphorical victory of dance over language is clearly at the symbolic and thematic core of the work. That language has lost its power of communication and rationality is shown in every dia-logue, but especially in the one between Elektra and Orestes, the alleged restorer of order and rationality. Elektra's dance is an uncon-trolled frenzy, a metaphor for the power of the irrational and the destructive and in her sense of the world the only valid communica-tive system.

Elektra, first staged in 1903, was a box-office success, thanks at least in part to Gertrud Eysoldt's performance. Yet Hofmannsthal remained dissatisfied with it as a complete work and considered it, so to speak, formally self-contradictory. He decided that its theme of the undermining of rational order and communication through language and the accompanying surge of violent instinct could ultimately not be served through the medium of the theater, whose principal instrument is the spoken word. The "Lord Chandos" problematic remained. Hofmannsthal thus offered the play to Richard Strauss as an opera libretto, in the thought that music would provide the foundation capable of incorporating the irrational, metalinguistic element. Strauss's compositional style was ripe for the assignment; the portrayal of frenzied dancing was his forte. (His previous opera had been *Salome*, with its score built around the Dance of the Seven Veils, and even if the atmosphere of that opera was governed by a heavy sensuality completely irrelevant to *Elektra*, the importance of the dance music created a significant stylistic precedent.) Strauss's accomplished dance music gained metaphoric value through Hofmannsthal's thematic context.[13]

There is thus a direct link between the "language crisis" of the "Letter of Lord Chandos" and the decision to transform *Elektra*, with its parallel thematic, into a libretto. A completely sincere treatment of the theme of linguistic impotence necessitated a move beyond the formal—that is, linguistic—nature of drama. Thus in the case of Hofmannsthal, writing for the opera was an action that enabled the further exploration of the "Lord Chandos" theme. It can thus be argued, I think, that Hofmannsthal's libretti are superior to the contemporaneous theater pieces because they incorporate, so to speak, the awareness that they do not stand alone as linguistic documents. The crux of the original language crisis was the assertion that language as a symbolic system had lost its power of signification, that it had lost its grasp on the objects to which it referred. The signifier had lost the signified. By grounding dramatic content

13. For the chronicle of the Hofmannsthal-Strauss collaboration, see *The Correspondence between Richard Strauss and Hugo von Hofmannsthal* (Cambridge, 1980). See also Michael P. Steinberg, "Metaphor of the Dance: The Meaning of the Waltzes in *Elektra* and *Der Rosenkavalier*," *Opera News*, January 1980. For a short discussion of the juxtaposition of female "ideal types" in *Elektra* and *Ariadne auf Naxos*, see Michael P. Steinberg, "Death or Transfiguration," *Opera News*, March 1979.

within the symbolic system of music, a system that absolutely lacks the object-world to which language refers (a musical note or phrase being describable as a signifier without a signified), Hofmannsthal preserved the undefinability of the referent which is necessary for a true metaphor. The texts refer to the unavailability of a true linguistic and rational order; the dimension of the music, to which that object-world is by definition unavailable, legitimates the very project. This fact helps explain why Hofmannsthal's nonoperatic texts, especially those with the cosmological pretensions of *Jedermann* and *Das Salzburger grosse Welttheater*, descend from the level of metaphor to the level of allegory, to the level where the object-world is argued to be available and definable, in other words to the level of ideology.[14]

IV

Much intellectual distance separates *Elektra* from *Die Frau ohne Schatten*, Hofmannsthal's massive wartime parable, finished in 1916 but first staged in 1919. It is the fourth work in the collaboration with Strauss (*Der Rosenkavalier* and the two versions of *Ariadne auf Naxos* come in between), and it is arguably the transitional work into the late Hofmannsthal's politically conscious, socially directed oeuvre. If in *Elektra* Hofmannsthal used a Greek model for a discussion of a modern condition, here—less obviously, to be sure—he invoked imagery from German enlightenment theater, *Faust* and *The Magic Flute* above all. *Elektra* portrayed an anguished

14. By suggesting this model of the meaning of the word-music relationship in the Hofmannsthal-Strauss operas, I by no means intend to imply that this is a necessary relationship in opera generally. It is a relationship specific to the Hofmannsthal libretti, whose general problematic is the very weakness of words. Arnold Schönberg, for example, addressed the problem with diametrically opposite results in his opera *Moses und Aron* (1930–32), which will be discussed in Chapter 6. Invoking a biblical idea of the word as truth, Schönberg made the role of Moses a nonsinging role. Moses's brother Aron, the ideologist who builds the golden calf, sings melodiously. With this juxtaposition, Schönberg suggests that music (or perhaps, from his point of view, conservative music) is a cloak of falsehood that hides and blocks the power of a word—a conclusion directly opposed to the tacit working principle of Hofmannsthal and Strauss.

state without proposing any antidotes; *Die Frau ohne Schatten* begins to take a reconstructive attitude. Its prescriptions are vaguely stated, and the operatic genre, I would continue to argue, prevents the text from descending to the level of allegory, but the psychology of its characters and the general turn of its plot suggest as its essential theme the moral necessity of a postapocalyptic reconstructive mission for the poet.

The reconstructive mission of Hofmannsthal the poet can be traced to the birth of his political and national consciousness at the outbreak of war in 1914, as I mentioned in the first chapter. Hofmannsthal's decision to enter political discourse and the barrage of political writings that followed were greeted by Josef Redlich as a sign of a "second puberty."[15] Yet when one observes the results of this political reorientation in Hofmannsthal's creative work, one is forced to question the extent of the transformation as Redlich interpreted it. Hofmannsthal once again seems to be rejecting the poetic for the political, the life of art for that of social action. In a way this seems like an extension of the "Lord Chandos" crisis and the rejection of the aestheticist tradition of the 1890s. Hofmannsthal rejected the life of the aesthete in 1901, and again in 1914. Ultimately, however, these two shifts in his consciousness represent a transformation rather than a rejection of the aestheticism that from his early education remained at the core of his consciousness.

Until 1914, this crisis of aestheticism versus social action remained a theme *within* Hofmannsthal's creative work. The solipsistic existence of the aesthete, the entrapment within the temple of art, as Carl Schorske has phrased it, is certainly a component in the antisocial withdrawal of Elektra.[16] The Elektra/Chrysothemis conflict is regenerated in the confrontation between Ariadne and Zerbinetta in *Ariadne auf Naxos*, a comic opera that conceals another treatment of Hofmannsthal's most constant problematic.

Ariadne auf Naxos sets up the confrontation between the two female archetypes by way of a plot in which operatic convention,

15. Letter of Redlich to Hermann Bahr, 13 July 1918, in *Dichter und Gelehrter*, ed. Fritz Fellner, p. 353.

16. See Schorske, p. 16: "From the very beginning, the aesthetic attitude was problematic for Hofmannsthal. The dweller in the temple of art, he knew, was condemned to seek the significance of life purely within his own psyche."

in effect, talks about itself. The scene is set in the *Stadtpalais* of an eighteenth-century Viennese nobleman, who has commissioned an *opera seria*, *Ariadne auf Naxos*, to be performed that evening. A commedia dell'arte troupe, led by the comedienne Zerbinetta, is to perform following the opera. In the interest of time, however, the nobleman orders that both works be performed simultaneously. The result (the second act of the actual opera) is the confrontation of Ariadne, as soliloquizer in her own opera, with Zerbinetta, who interrupts the princess to tell her to stop lamenting her fate (she has been abandoned on the island of Naxos by her lover Theseus), and find another man. Zerbinetta argues for a pragmatic approach to life in an imperfect world, while Ariadne holds on to her obsession with the past and her withdrawal from life. At the end of her impassioned plea to an unbending Ariadne, Zerbinetta sighs, "The lady and I speak different languages." Hofmannsthal's theatrical legerdemain is revealed at the opera's conclusion, as the apparently extraneous intervention of Zerbinetta in the *opera seria* actually changes the latter's outcome: the god Bacchus arrives to claim Ariadne, but instead of sinking into a *Tristan*-like love-death, Ariadne is swept into a new romance. The scene that was supposed to echo *Tristan und Isolde* becomes a parody of the final scene of *Siegfried*.

In *Ariadne auf Naxos*, then, Hofmannsthal makes a choice as to which of his female archetypes holds the more viable world-view, and it is the opposite choice from the one he had made in *Elektra*. He never endorses Elektra's solipsism and withdrawal, but he makes it clear that her position is the true one in the apocalyptic world she inhabits. This is not the case with Ariadne. The noble solipsism of Elektra has, through its incarnation in her mythological kinswoman, Ariadne, become two-dimensional and artificial—a pose, intensified by the fact that Ariadne is actually portrayed as an actress acting in a play. Hofmannsthal's sympathies are clearly with Zerbinetta and her ethic of social integration.

Thus the transformation of Hofmannsthal's sympathies from one side of the female dichotomy to the other, from the side of Elektra and Ariadne to that of Chrysothemis and Zerbinetta, coincides with the reconstructive posture he took as actual apocalypse seemed to appear in the form of the First World War. The "second puberty" he showed in his wartime pamphlets and actual political endeavors is thus complemented contrapuntally by the thematic changes in his creative work.

This transformation was a conscious one, and Hofmannsthal developed his own vocabulary for it. He expressed the two basic principles of the newly formed ethic with the terms "the social" (a fairly flat translation of the unusual locution "das Soziale") and the principle of attention to the "other," a principle he described with the equally exotic expression "the allomatic" ("das Allomatische").

Manfred Hoppe has analyzed the roots of this ethic in Hofmannsthal's early work. Hoppe argues for chronological as well as thematic continuity in Hofmannsthal's creative work, against the more conventional model—indeed against Hofmannsthal's own self-interpretation—of strict periodizations. In this respect Hoppe and Schorske uphold a similar point from opposite directions: Schorske argues that the aestheticist attitude was problematic for Hofmannsthal before one might have suspected (i.e., already during the decade of the lyric poetry and lyric dramas), while Hoppe argues that the aestheticist attitude remained prominent into the middle and late periods, altered but not dissipated. A synthesis of Hoppe and Schorske's interpretations reveals a constantly self-conscious Hofmannsthal followed throughout his career by the problematic of aestheticism. Hoppe argues that the vocabulary and conceptual structure to which Hofmannsthal appealed during the formation of this other-oriented ("allomatic") ethic reveal that in effect he never made the choice between the inner-directed and the outer-directed, or between psychology and politics (or indeed that he never defined these two as polar). What he arrived at was ultimately not a rejection of aestheticism but the extension of aestheticism into worldly—more specifically, political—life. The entry into politics becomes a psychological necessity. Thus Hoppe cites the surprising congruence between two ostensibly different prose pieces: the autobiographical sketch *Ad me ipsum* (1916) and the later manifesto (discussed in Chapter 2) of "conservative revolution," "Das Schriftum als geistiger Raum der Nation" (1927). Hoppe places both pieces within the context of "conservative revolution," which he defines as the revitalization of the present through the adoption of the living strengths of the past.[17]

The passage from apocalypse to reconstruction thus combines a psychological ethic with a political one. In the Catholic morality plays this ethic is rationalized into a programmatic metapolitics; in the operas a psychopolitics is developed which remains unprogrammatic and hence unideological. Conceived in this crucial period of the war, *Die Frau ohne Schatten* takes the form of a psychopolitical parable of social reconstruction. There is no reconstructive policy, but rather a study of the psychological transformations necessary for the individual to orient himself to the task of social reconstruction. This transformation remains on the level of the individual, and for Hofmannsthal it is an autobiographically motivated idea.

The plot is original but derived from standard fairy-tale plots as well as standard German classics (*Faust* and *The Magic Flute*). A fairy princess falls in love with and marries a mortal emperor, but stands under her father's curse: if she does not carry a child within twelve months, she must return to the realm of the spirits and her husband will turn to stone. Fertility, sexuality, and humanity are associated and represented through the symbol of the shadow: her casting a shadow will be the sign that the empress has gained three-dimensionality, the state where light will no longer pass through her glassy form. The opera opens in the twelfth month of the empress's marriage; the emperor leaves for a hunt while a spirit-messenger from the empress's father waits to take her back with him. Desperate to obtain a shadow, the empress and her duplicitous nurse (in a Faust-Mephistopheles contract) descend to the lowest level of humanity, the household of the dyer Barak and his frigid wife, in the hope that the dyer's wife will consent to sell her shadow—in other words her fertility, sexuality, and humanity. Barak's household is a paradigm of social collapse. He supports his brothers: the One-eyed, the One-armed, and the Hunchback. Clearer emblems of a war-torn society would be hard to imagine. The brothers constantly evoke the prosperity and security of a prior—prewar, so to

17. Manfred Hoppe, *Literatentum, Magie und Mystik im Frühwerk Hugo von Hofmannsthals* (Berlin, 1968), p. 2.

speak—generation, and talk of their father's house, where there were ten other brothers, riches, and food. The disgust of the dyer's wife with her surroundings is exacerbated by the dyer's complacency and good-natured optimism; both will undergo psychological trials before their fates are happily resolved.

The meeting of the two worlds represented by the empress and the dyer's wife—and the eventual goodness produced by that meeting—is itself symbolically charged. The morally necessary descent into the squalid world of the dyer clearly represents, on one level, the decision of the poet to descend from a two-dimensional, aestheticized reality into the squalor of political and social reality. Hans Mayer has called the work a "parable about the overcoming of the egocentric world of the artist with the help of other human beings."[18] The story's conclusion reveals the two worlds bettered by the communication with each other, but they never converge. The level of the emperor and empress and that of the dyer and his wife remain separated: the double quest of the four protagonists of *The Magic Flute* (the noble Tamino and Pamina, the earthy Papageno and Papagena) is explicitly evoked.[19]

As the empress and her nurse begin the task of persuading the dyer's wife to part with her shadow, the empress observes the new surroundings with deepening empathy. The dyer's wife consents to sacrifice her shadow, but the transaction will be complete only when the empress seals it by drinking from a fountain of life. Faced with the misery that the decision of the dyer's wife has brought on her husband as well as on herself, the empress refuses to drink. For her generosity and self-sacrifice, she is awarded her own shadow by unidentified cosmic forces. Both couples are reunited happily, serenaded by the chorus of their unborn children. (This last feature

18. Hans Mayer, "Die Frau ohne Schatten," in *Versuche über die Oper* (Frankfurt, 1981), p. 139. Mayer identifies the roots of the problematic of "the solitude of the individual artistic life" in Hofmannsthal's early (1897) lyric drama *Der Kaiser und die Hexe*—p. 137. It may not be entirely whimsical to suggest that the descent from the imperial realm to the dyer's very earthly household might be taken as a reference to Hofmannsthal's professional descent into collaboration with the tone-poet (i.e., colorist) Richard Strauss. In any case, *Die Frau ohne Schatten* as well as the other works examined in this chapter clearly shows Hofmannsthal's proclivity to infuse female characters with autobiographical meaning.

19. For a consideration of this comparison, see Mayer, pp. 127–29.

has elicited discomfort and parody from many, beginning with
Strauss himself, but Hofmannsthal insisted on its symbolic importance.) Hans Mayer has interpreted the empress's action as an
example of a Kantian rejection of instrumental reason, the principle
that "no human being may be handled as a mere means."[20]

Fertility and the moral duty to reproduce serve as metaphors for
this reconstruction; the woman without a shadow is the infertile
woman who in effect gains fertility as she matures emotionally and
morally to the point where she sees its significance. Reproduction
and ethical humaneness are inseparable as principles of social reconstruction. The fairy-tale empress who realizes her humanity
in this fashion continues the problematic of Elektra and Ariadne,
Chrysothemis and Zerbinetta. She is in effect the bridge between
the two types: the ahuman, asocial figure whose moral imperative
(a change in tone from earlier operas) is to achieve humanity and
social life.

                                    V

Die Frau ohne Schatten represents Hofmannsthal's largest-scaled
effort to infuse a creative work with his growing social consciousness as well as with a reflection of the roots of that social consciousness in his life. This combination is repeated (on a far smaller scale)
in the 1921 comedy of manners Der Schwierige. The "difficult man"
of the title, Count Hans Karl Bühl, is a self-portrait based partly in
self-analysis and partly in wish-fulfillment. For his attractive quality
of dignity and honesty without a claim to innocence, Count Karl is
a kind of male Marschallin (but one who ultimately does not opt
for romantic self-sacrifice). He is also a war hero, an identity to
which Hofmannsthal would have liked to have an honest claim.

Count Karl's delicate code of honor rises from his desire to maintain both his romantic flirtations and the respectability of his inherited seat in the upper house of parliament. His code of silence
brings him ultimate romantic success once he finds a woman who
shares it. But although he gives a speech to parliament during the

20. Mayer, p. 152.

course of the play, his own disbelief in the communicative power of speech precludes any meaningful political participation. His attitude is revealed in the pivotal scene with Helen Altenwyl, his nephew's fiancée: "For everything in the world is set a-going by words. It's rather ridiculous, I admit, for a man to imagine that by stringing words together skillfully he can exert God knows how great an influence in this life of ours, where in the long run everything depends on what is essentially inexpressible. Speech is based on an indecent excess of self-esteem."[21]

For his code of silence about his own and other people's behavior and his desire for a style of personal communication without words or gesture, Count Karl has been called the most Wittgensteinian of Hofmannsthal's characters.[22] Whether or not Wittgenstein can legitimately be evoked, there is no doubt that Count Karl's code of silence carries forward Hofmannsthal's Lord Chandos language crisis. In any case, here is a theater piece in which Hofmannsthal was able to maintain a critical treatment of the theme of language and modern society; he did so by working these into the plot.

In *Arabella*, (1928, premiered 1933) the spirit of domestic comedy is continued, with clearer political symbolism. Where Count Karl achieved private but not political fulfillment, the romantic heroes of *Arabella* achieve personal happiness that itself serves as a metaphor for political fulfillment, but does not amount to it. The simple plot is reminiscent of *Der Rosenkavalier*, but set a century later and a social class down. As Baron Ochs auf Lerchenau of *Der Rosenkavalier* endeavored to marry the daughter of a wealthy parvenu to replenish the finances of the rural aristocracy, the impoverished Count Waldner (his title a result of military honor) plots to marry his daughter Arabella to a Czech landed farmer, Mandryka, who blithely gives cash advances as an incentive for the betrothal. Arabella happens to be in love with Mandryka, and the happy ending is only delayed by several misunderstandings due to confused identities.

As in *Ariadne auf Naxos*, there are unexpected ghosts of Wagner

---

21. Hofmannsthal, *The Difficult Man*, trans. Willa Muir, in *Plays and Libretti*, p. 759.

22. See William Johnston, *The Austrian Mind* (Berkeley, Calif., 1972), pp. 212–13.

at work, in this case from *The Flying Dutchman*. The key to the character of Mandryka is his foreignness. The Flying Dutchman offered gold treasures to the fisherman Daland in exchange for his daughter; Mandryka offers cash. Before the transaction was struck, Daland's daughter Senta had been staring neurotically at a portrait of a seaman mystically resembling the Dutchman; Waldner's daughter Arabella has been staring at the "mysterious stranger" who has been seen around the Vienna hotel in which the Waldners have been staying.

Unlike Senta, however, Arabella has a healthy psyche and her marriage to the exotic Mandryka will be successful, if one is to judge by the mood of the final curtain. The romance is never explored or portrayed psychologically, but exists rather as a social and political metaphor. The tired, decadent, impoverished urban Austria finds renewal and purification through a partnership with the rural vitality of Czechoslovakia. The action is set in 1860, a tired period for Austria but also the decade of the "compromise" that conjoined Austria with Hungary. Mandryka, however, is Czech, and Arabella fits chronologically and thematically into Hofmannsthal's flirtations with Austro-Czech politics described in Chapter 4. Hofmannsthal laced Mandryka's speech patterns with long quotations from Slavic folksongs lifted from an anthology called "Folksongs of the Slavs," compiled by Paul Eisner.[23]

The marriage of Arabella and Mandryka represents the wished-for partnership of Austria and the Slavic world in general, Czechoslovakia in particular, but the delicate tone of this comedy of manners never approaches any programmatic allegory. Thus Hofmannsthal's flirtation with liberal pluralism is paralleled by his retention of symbolic rather than an allegorical style. He had always had the gift for the invented, indeterminate symbol (the silver rose), and in *Arabella* he achieves theatrical and intellectual elegance with the invention of the betrothal symbol of the glass of water. The glass of water is in the context of the plot an invented Czech symbol with which Arabella (read Hofmannsthal) offers her loyalty to

---

23. See Rudolf Hirsch, "Paul Eisners *Volkslieder der Slawen,* Eine Quelle für *Arabella,*" *Hofmannsthal Blätter* 4 (1970): 287–88. It is standard practice for the baritone taking the role of Mandryka in *Arabella* to adopt a faintly Slavic speech intonation.

her Czech fiancé. Yet the symbol is also a symbol of symbolic indeterminacy: clear, transparent, absorbable.

Marriage as a symbol of the idealized union of two nationalities or cultures has precedents in Hofmannsthal's instrumentarium of symbols. The symbol of the sacred betrothal (*die heilige Vermählung*) has been explored by Manfred Hoppe in his study of Hofmannsthal's sketches for the ballet suite *Die Ruinen von Athen*. In this context, the sacred marriage is that between Germany and Greece, with all the rich connotations of German romantic classicism. *Die Ruinen von Athen* was a play by the German romantic poet Kotzebue, written during the height of German philhellenism; Beethoven had written an incidental overture for it. In 1919 Hofmannsthal and Strauss, the latter as director of the Vienna Opera, decided to combine Beethoven's overtures for *The Ruins of Athens* and *The Creatures of Prometheus* into a new ballet score, with a new scenario by Hofmannsthal. Manfred Hoppe has observed that Hofmannsthal consistently referred to this work as a "festival" (*Festspiel*), a term which through its connotations of a sacred celebration of linkage with a past, mythologized culture implied an ideology of conservative revolution—in the context of *Die Ruinen von Athen* as well as in that of the Salzburg Festival.[24]

The mythologized past that Hofmannsthal was celebrating here was not an Austrian one but a German one. It was the poetic union of Germany and Greece as heralded by the romantics from Winckelmann through Hölderlin and Goethe. Nietzsche had perpetuated this German attention to Greece, but with a completely different tone. By 1919, however, Hofmannsthal had read Ernst Bertram's *Nietzsche: Versuch einer Mythologie*, which interpreted Nietzsche's discussion of Greece as a plea for the reinvigoration of modern culture through the appropriation of the aesthetic unity of Attic culture. Hofmannsthal accepted Bertram's interpretation of Nietzsche and in *Die Ruinen von Athen* he treated the problem of returning Germany to the ideals of Greece. His scenario depicted a wandering artist on the model of Goethe roaming through the ruins of Athens.

24. Manfred Hoppe, "Hofmannsthal's 'Ruinen von Athen': Das Festspiel als 'konservative Revolution,' " *Jahrbuch der deutschen Schillergesellschaft* 26 (1982): 325–56, esp. p. 335.

Nietzsche had described the Germans as distinct from the Latins for their fundamentally Hegelian ("even if there had never been a Hegel") loyality to the concept of becoming (*Werden*) or development (*Entwicklung*), as opposed to the Latin sense of being (*Sein*).[25] Bertram had misinterpreted Nietzsche's essential acceptance of this historicist spirit for a rejection of it, and spoke of Nietzsche's "longing for the South" (*Südweh*) as a "homesickness for Being."[26] In Hofmannsthal's *Ruinen von Athen*, as Hoppe has observed, "the Wanderer, accompanied by the shadows of Hölderlin and Nietzsche, slowly becomes form. . . . to become form (*Gestaltwerden*) means to wring from the constant state of becoming a lasting shape."[27] Thus, for Hofmannsthal, via Bertram's Nietzsche and a twice-removed interpretation of German romantic hellenism, the holy betrothal between Germany and Greece was a sublimation of the "becoming" of the north into the "being" of the south, of history into myth, flux into permanence. As Hoppe observes, this attraction to myth is at the heart of Hofmannsthal's sense of "festival" in general as well as of his ideology of conservative revolution.

Ultimately, however, Nietzsche has the last laugh. He never advocated a return to a static, mythologized past, as Bertram and subsequently Hofmannsthal read him as saying. He viewed culture as historical and dynamic, and discussed music as the cultural form that best revealed and embodied that movement. Thus his innovations in the field of classicism (innovations that alienated him from the scholarly community of the 1870s, led by Wilamowitz) lay in his theory of "the birth of tragedy from the spirit of music," the title of a work that juxtaposed the musical, dynamic, "Dionysian" principle of Greek culture against the visual, plastic, formal, or "Apollonian." As a self-proclaimed Nietzschean, Richard Strauss based his compositional style on the principle of Dionysian movement. Hence, if in Hofmannsthal's anti-ideological period, the period of his "language crisis," the form of music in general added an anti-ideological dimension to his work, in his late, ideological period, the music of Strauss in particular sustained a spirit of move-

25. Nietzsche, *Die fröhliche Wissenschaft*, as quoted in ibid., p. 336.
26. Bertram, *Nietzsche*, p. 79, quoted in ibid., p. 337.
27. Ibid., p. 337.

ment and history that acted as an antidote to Hofmannsthal's intensifying ideology of fixed cultural ideals and myths. Where there was no music, as in the Catholic morality plays, the path toward allegory and ideology was cleared.

CHAPTER 6

The Catholic Culture of
the Austrian Jews, 1890–1938

I

THE performance of *Jedermann* that inaugurated the Salzburg Festival in August 1920 met with some unexpected protest. During the hours preceding the play's opening, a group of students from the Borromeum—the local Catholic boarding school—assembled, carrying trumpets. Their intention was to interrupt the performance—which was to take place on the cathedral square—by blowing the trumpets from the adjoining square. Their plan was foiled by the police and went unreported in the press. Although it is impossible to say who inspired or organized this episode, the witness who told me of it reported that the desire to heckle the play came from the objection to the "Jewish" element that underscored the Catholic pretensions of the Salzburg Festival in general and the *Jedermann* performances in particular.[1] Similarly motivated protests did gain circulation in the Austrian press during the days following the premiere. A general account of press reactions to the Salzburg *Jedermann* will appear in the next chapter. Here I will concentrate on one aspect of the negative reception of the play and the festival itself: the anti-Semitic rejection of the entire enterprise as the allegedly insincere, entrepreneurial Catholicism of Jews. I will continue with a discussion of the intellectual and ideological patterns of assimilationist and anti-

1. I have not been able to corroborate this account, told to me by a Salzburg-born eye-witness to the 1920 festival whom I met in Austria in 1983. I would appreciate any corroboration or refutation.

assimilationist culture into which much of the Salzburg enterprise plays.

Günter Fellner has investigated the anti-Semitic press response to the festival as a basic component of what he argues to be the fundamental anti-Semitic character of Christian Social Salzburg in the early 1920s. As it had been in Vienna in the 1890s, anti-Semitism in Salzburg in the 1920s emerged as the common denominator between Christian Social and pan-German parties. Between 1897 and 1918, Vienna had been a Christian Social, or "black" city. After the war and the proclamation of the republic, Vienna became the center and haven of Austrian Social Democracy, and hence a "red" city. Yet since the majority of the non-Viennese Austrians were Christian Socials, Austria's second and third cities—Salzburg and Graz—became increasingly important bastions of Catholic conservatism, antisocialism, and anti-Semitism. Anti-Semitism and antisocialism became more and more symbiotic as the perception grew that the Social Democratic party was led by Jews. The Social Democratic government that administered Vienna in the 1920s was commonly referred to as the "Judenregierung in Wien." When the Salzburg-reared Ignaz Seipel became chancellor in 1922, the black/red, Christian Social/Social Democratic, Salzburg/Vienna polarization became for many synonymous with the opposition of (the true) Austria (or Salzburg qua Austria) to Vienna, which in turn incorporated the opposition of tradition to decadence, Catholicism to Judaism. Salzburg had had no Jewish inhabitants at all before 1867, when the town was legally forced to renounce the anti-Semitic laws that had forbidden Jews from remaining for more than an hour within city limits. In 1869 there were 47 Jewish citizens, 199 in 1900, 285 in 1910, 239 in 1934. Pan-German anti-Semitism in Salzburg emerged in the 1880s and inspired the establishment of several antiliberal, anti-Semitic organizations, among them the "Deutsche Schulverein," the "Salzburger Turnverein," the "Salzburger Liedertafel," and the "Deutsche und österreichische Alpenverein."[2] In 1888 the pan-German weekly Der Kyffhäuser spoke of the fight against the "Hebrew superpower" ("hebräische Grossmacht") and the problem of a "Jewry that multiplies like rabbits"

---

2. Günter Fellner, Antisemitismus in Salzburg, 1918–1938 (Vienna, 1979), pp. 78, 58, 61.

("das sich kaninchenartig vermehrende Judentum"). The Christian Social *Salzburger Chronik*, which in 1891 had referred to clericalism as "the ideal anti-Semitism," stated in 1906 that "it can make no difference to Christendom whether the Jews strive for world domination in one way or the other; the main thing is that they strive for it and must be prevented from doing so."[3]

In December 1918 the Salzburg Christian Social party called in its election program for the "sharpest defensive battle against the Jewish danger." The preceding May the *Salzburger Chronik* had roused its followers "to the battle against the 'Jews,' against this semitic vampire." In September 1920, one month after the premiere of *Jedermann*, the Salzburg pan-German People's party (Grossdeutsche Volkspartei) convened and formulated its "Salzburg Program." The program contained several pages on the "Judenfrage" and stated that the Jews were a "foreign body" ("Fremdenkörper") and a parasite in their relation to the *Volksgemeinschaft*.[4]

The same references to the Jews as foreign invaders of the *Volksgemeinschaft* appeared in the polemics against the Salzburg Festival, with both Hofmannsthal and Reinhardt and their audiences depicted as "jüdische Sommerfrischler": Jewish vacationeers. In February 1923 the *Salzburger Chronik* reported that the district meeting (*Gautagung*) of the Salzburg Antisemitenbund had proposed "defensive measures" against the "invasion of Jewish vacationeers," and "the sharpest possible protest against the return of the Jews Max Reinhart [*sic*] and [Alexander] Moissi (the star of *Jedermann*) with the poetry of the Jew Hofmannstal [*sic*] to this year's festival." A year later the same paper printed an article under the heading "Jewish Summer Guests Unwanted," the decision made by the Christian Socials and pan-Germans of the market town of Oberndorf. In 1921 the pan-German *Salzburger Volksblatt* encouraged the making of "assiduous propaganda to attract Aryan travelers, so that there will be no room left for the Jews."[5]

With regard to the performance of *Jedermann* itself, the National-Socialist *Deutscher Volksruf* printed an article called "The Reinhardt

3. *Der Kyffhäuser*, 12 August 1888, and *Salzburger Chronik*, 8 October 1906, quoted in ibid., p. 63.

4. Ibid., pp. 72–73. *Salzburger Chronik*, 28 May 1918, quoted in ibid., p. 83.

5. *Salzburg Chronik*, 4/5 February 1923; *Salzburger Chronik*, 25 April 1924; *Salzburger Volksblatt*, 23 March 1921; all quoted in ibid., pp. 101–3.

Circus," which condemned "the falsification of German art through Jewish dilettantes." The same paper's review of the *Salzburger grosses Welttheater* in August 1922 stated that "the content of this work falls totally within the racial context of its author, everything is dragged into the mud. . . . The idea of class conflict is dragged in. . . . The Festspielhausgemeinde should never have permitted such an act of homage to the International or such support for international Jewry." The *Freie Salzburger Bauernstimme*, the organ of the local government, wondered how "a Jew could write a Catholic mystery play." And *Der Eiserne Besern*, the organ of the Antisemitenbund, suggested that a poor reception be accorded to Reinhardt, "who prefers to present his Jewish artistic products on cathedral squares and in Christian houses of worship." In 1924 an article in this same paper stated: "Smoking Jewesses inside our Christian houses of God, collected by the Semites Max Reinhardt, Moissi, and Hoffmannstal [*sic*], as was the case two years ago, will no longer be tolerated."[6]

Yet although the anti-Semitic motivation of such assaults on the festival aesthetic is clear and dismissable, they did not represent the only charges of false representation. The poet Else Lasker-Schüler had a similarly negative, if obviously differently motivated, reaction to *Jedermann*: "The performance of *Jedermann* is an unartistic act, a shameful one. . . . Life and death, sin and judgment, Heaven and Hell—all are degraded to a spectacle, like those elephants and Arab horses decorated with ribbons and trinkets, yet not even for the delight of children in that case, but for the edification of a rich, sensation-hungry public."[7]

For Reinhardt, the Catholic morality play was indeed a vehicle for sensational theatrical spectacles. His participation in the stagings of *Jedermann* and *Das Salzburger grosse Welttheater* carried none of Hofmannsthal's ambitions of cultural reformation. Hofmannsthal was sincere in his wish to represent Austrian Catholic values, but for Reinhardt representation and theater were themselves the

---

6. *Deutscher Volksruf*, 19 March 1921; *Deutscher Volksruf*, 26 August 1922; *Freie Salzburger Bauernstimme*, 17 August 1922; *Der Eiserne Besen*, 10 September 1923; *Der Eiserne Besen*, 22 March 1924; quoted in ibid., pp. 103–4.

7. Else Lasker-Schüler, letter to Herwarth Walden, editor of *Die Aktion*, quoted in Michael Hamburger, Introduction to Hofmannsthal, *Plays and Libretti*, pp. xlii–xliii.

highest values. Such a judgment is not contradicted by evidence from his tenure in Berlin. He had gone there not to escape Austria or Austrian theatricality, but to bring it to Berlin. This is not to say that he strove simply to transplant the conservatism of the Burgtheater. In his choices of repertory and in his production styles, Reinhardt was an innovator. His first production at the Berlin Kammerspiele was Ibsen's *Ghosts*, with scenic designs by Edvard Munch. He never respected the conventional boundaries of proscenium theater and consistently strove to involve his audiences, both spatially and emotionally, in his productions. Yet he did transplant the essential qualities of Austrian baroque theatricality: the belief in the theater of the world—in the power of representation—and the belief in the aesthetic validity of the dreamworld, conceived as a coherent set of imaginative tableaux. This approach applied to his productions of symbolist and expressionist drama as well as to the fairy tale into which he rendered *A Midsummer Night's Dream*. The mannerist gestures he elicited from his actors further confirmed his retention of the Burgtheater's baroque style. Alexander Moissi's *Jedermann* was perhaps among most celebrated of these mannerist performances.

But if Reinhardt left no effect untapped, he never seems to have gone as far in Salzburg as he did in his production of the morality pantomime *The Miracle* in New York in 1924, for which he transformed the Century Theater into a cathedral, with "soaring columns and groined arches filling the stage and masking the interior of the house as far back as the balcony," completing the effect with "the sounds of sacred music as the audience came in and ushers in nuns' wimples showed them to their pews in a dim religious light."[8]

Hofmannsthal's commitment to baroque ideology was deeper than Reinhardt's, entirely sincere, but also more complicated. In making manifest this ideology through the Salzburg morality plays, he clearly did not expect the most vociferous opposition to come from Catholic conservatives. Those critics attacked as insincere the element that Hofmannsthal considered to be the most genuinely tied to the baroque tradition he wished to restore: the theatricality of the *Jedermann* production (and, in 1922, that of the *Welttheater* as well). Thus the Catholic-conservative rejection of the Salzburg Festival

8. Styan, *Max Reinhardt*, p. 101.

emerges as an interesting case in cultural psychology: it could be argued that that the rejection came from a recognition of the artificiality of the cultural pretensions of the festival, which were exactly the pretensions of the Austrian Catholic conservatives. As far as the attackers themselves were concerned, however, their opposition was clearly the zealous unmasking of a fraud. The enemy was not directly or explicitly the Jew, but rather the Catholic culture of the Jew and that culture's claim to authenticity. The most surprising element in this anti-Semitic onslaught is the fact that Hofmannsthal himself, despite the deeprootedness of his assimilation into Austrian Catholic culture, should have been a target of this kind of attack along with the more clearly Jewish Reinhardt. As an assimilated but unconverted Jew and a theatrical personality known more as a Berliner than as an Austrian, Reinhardt was mistrusted on two counts. Characteristically, his attackers tended to refer to him by the name to which he was born, Max Goldmann. (He had taken the name Reinhardt at the beginning of his acting career in 1890; beyond this gesture there is no evidence that he ever took any formal steps to distance himself from his Jewish background.)

The anti-Semitic attacks on Reinhardt and Hofmannsthal are thus historically significant and indicative of a crucial level of meaning as far as the Salzburg Festival in general is concerned. Even if one were to disregard the thorny question of the Jewish identity of Hofmannsthal, Reinhardt, and others, one must recognize first that the baroque style of the Salzburg morality plays speaks from within a long and powerful tradition of assimilated culture in Austria, and, second, that it comes at the end of the period of assimilated culture. A crucial difference between the anti-Semitism of the 1890s and that of the 1920s is the difference in attitude toward the assimilated and converted Jew. The anti-Semitism of Lueger's Vienna encouraged assimilation and conversion; the anti-Semitism of the pre-*Anschluss* era rejected both as further evidence of the polluting of the dominant culture.

One of the facets of meaning of the Salzburg Festival is therefore its position as a late manifestation of the Catholic culture of the Austrian Jews. To explore the festival as a manifestation of assimilation is not to trivialize or reduce it, just as to explore the assimilation culture of the previous generation—of Mahler, for example—is neither trivializing nor reductive. The drive toward assimilation—or the drive away from it—in Austrian fin-de-siècle culture cannot be interpreted merely as an issue of social expedience, but must be seen, far more important, as a decision of whether or not to participate in the dominant *secular* culture. Baroque culture controlled the representation of Austria as a totality and thus became itself a cultural language in which Jews as well as others for whom the totality of Austria was important strove to participate. For many, assimilation and conversion were not merely instrumental gestures taken cynically with the sole purpose of opening doors, but profound intellectual reorientations. Conversion to Catholicism was thus a cultural decision more than a social or religious one, and it was therefore for many intellectuals a decision based on the desire to participate in public forms of meaning, to adapt their minds, intellectually and spiritually, to the dominant culture, rather than on the wish to join a faith or—as has more often been thought—on the wish to participate socially or politically in the dominant, Catholic world. Social and political considerations were there, but in the lives of many intellectuals they were secondary to cultural and intellectual criteria. Thus Freud, who during the 1880s and 1890s wanted desperately to obtain a professorship that was informally unavailable to him as a Jew, never considered converting to Catholicism, because such a decision was foreign to his overall intellectual orientation. Mahler, faced with a similar situation, did convert, and did so a little over a year after the completion of his *Resurrection* Symphony, a work that revealed the spiritual momentum of his decision to convert.

Thus the problem of the Jew in the Austrian Catholic world ran parallel to and reinforced the problem of the critical intellectual in the world. It was one dimension in the overdetermined dialectic of Jew/Catholic, outsider/insider, mute/expressive (the Lord Chandos problematic), barrenness/decoration (Loos against historicist architecture). None of these dimensions stands for or symbolizes another; they are all equally and interdependently significant dialectics in Austrian—and especially Viennese—intellectual life at the turn of the century. The Salzburg Festival, like most of Hofmannsthal's late work, is a result of the conscious conversion from one side of the dialectic to the other, from muteness in the style of

Chandos to expressivity, from outsider to insider (more in his own mind than in the eyes of his public), from political recluse to (at least in sentiment) political participant, from avant-gardist to decorative artist. Conversion from Judaism to Catholicism is of course not relevant in the case of Hofmannsthal. But it is directly relevant to other intellectuals who operate in this context and therefore one element of the cultural problems that concern us here.

II

The Jewish intellectuals who worked in the world of the Austrian fin-de-siècle clearly inhabited an increasingly anti-Semitic social and cultural context. Austrian anti-Semitism in the second half of the nineteenth century and the first third of the twentieth was more informal than formal, more social than political. But the decrease in political and legal anti-Semitism that took place between the revolts of 1848 and the ratification of Karl Lueger as mayor of Vienna in 1897 was countered—and indeed perhaps motivated—by the grave intensification of social and cultural anti-Semitism. Official tolerance was balanced by unofficial intolerance; anti-Semitism was a question of attitude rather than of policy. The attitude was powerful enough to require informally assimilation and often conversion from Jews who sought participation in the dominant Catholic culture. As Hermann Broch observed, "Tolerance is intolerant and demands assimilation."[9]

The years following the events of 1848 were actually marked by an increase in anti-Semitism on the part of those who objected to the large numbers of Jews who had lined the barricades, especially doctors and medical students. Thus, although the Austrian Jews won complete legal emancipation in 1859 and profited from the so-called liberal period which lasted till the crash of 1873, they were never free of informal anti-Semitism. After 1873 and the founding of the Christian Social party, and the emergence in 1875 of Karl Vogelsang as editor of the Catholic-conservative, anti-Semitic journal *Vaterland*, pressure mounted. In 1879 Prime Minister Eduard

9. Broch, *Hofmannsthal and His Time*, p. 83.

von Taaffe placed quotas on Jewish access to schools and universities, making them the only institutions with formal anti-Semitic restrictions, and they became hotbeds of popular anti-Semitism. In the theater, anti-Semitism was informal, but grew in power, so that a year after Lueger's first election as mayor in 1895 (the emperor refused to ratify him), Gustav Mahler was told that he would never be able to assume the directorship of the Vienna Opera unless he converted to Catholicism.[10]

In discussing Austrian intellectual culture between 1890 and 1938 we need to identify two intersecting spectra: the spectrum from the critical, avant-garde, or revolutionary to the conservative, and the cultural and religious spectrum with Jewishness as the position least integrated into mainstream society, Protestantness as the middle position, and Catholicity as the most integrated position. The awkwardness of these neologisms is deliberate. Every possible combination of points along these two spectra exists with prominent figures to represent it. A list of Jewish critical intellectuals would include Freud, Herzl, Schnitzler, Kraus, Mahler, Schönberg, Broch, Viktor Adler, Max Adler, Otto Bauer, and many others—and this is perhaps the most frequently evoked roster of Austrian intellectuals. But out of these ten figures, five converted, three to Catholicism, two to Protestantism. To complicate the picture further, one of the Catholic converts—Kraus—left the Catholic church (his disgust at the Catholic pretensions of the Salzburg Festival was the catalyst) and one of the Protestant ones—Schönberg—formally reconverted to Judaism. But it is of course incorrect and irresponsible to call Viennese critical culture Jewish culture; one cannot neglect Mach and Musil, Otto Wagner, Josef Hoffmann, Loos, Schiele, Klimt, Berg, and Webern. There is also Jewish cultural conservatism—the bond that unites Max Reinhardt, Richard Beer-Hofmann, Stefan Zweig, and perhaps Josef Redlich. Christian conservatism is easily represented by Christian Social politics and culture. And there are a few figures so changeable and elusive as to be completely impossible to classify: Hofmannsthal, for example, who may be the ultimate Austrian for his total cultural liminality. Is he Jewish or Catholic, revolutionary or conservative? He has been credited with or accused of being all or none of these. It is nearly impossible to know when he found out about his Jewish identity and what effect this discovery had on a child raised in a Catholic home with a Catholic education. The same holds, on the Protestant side, for Wittgenstein, although Judaism was more relevant to his family and he referred to himself as a Jew.[11]

The role of Jewish identity in the lives of intellectuals and in the culture in general is thus both crucial and ambiguous. An analysis of the phenomenon must therefore respect both these qualities and avoid two related and all-too-common methodological traps: the argument that the intellectual agenda or production of either a single individual or, worse, an entire cultural style or period ("fin-de-siècle Vienna") is determined by a certain fixed cultural or religious identity. In other words, a model is necessary that can interpret the relations of ambiguous but intense patterns of cultural identity to equally ambiguous and intense patterns of intellectual and cultural production by stressing questions of meaning and avoiding assumptions of deterministic causality.

There are many Jews and much Jewishness at the center of Austrian modernism, but it is methodologically false and politically pernicious to label Austrian modernism a Jewish phenomenon, whether from antimodernist and anti-Semitic or whether from pro-modernist and philo-Semitic perspectives. If we attempt to "explain" the twelve-tone system in terms of Schönberg's Judaism, we cannot understand Berg; if we do the same with Broch's fragmented authorial voice, we cannot understand Musil. Aside from the logical problems of imposing a causational model on intricate patterns of cultural and intellectual production, the conflation of critical and Jewish culture places the historian in a posture of reifying Jewish culture, of reasserting the primacy of a "Jewish problem"—only reversed now into a "Jewish phenomenon." In other words, this posture reimposes onto Jewish culture a false homogeneity and two-dimensionality and renders Jewish culture into a potentially fixed set of properties, easily understood and easily separated from

11. See Wittgenstein, *Vermischte Bemerkungen* (Frankfurt, 1977), translated by Peter Winch as *Culture and Value* (Oxford, 1980), passim.

Christian—or indeed from "Austrian"—culture. There thus emerges a logical and methodological parallel—a shared fallacy—between a sincerely philo-Semitic historiography that wants to celebrate "Jewish contributions" to modern culture and the older, anti-Semitic historiography that wishes to delegitimate forms of modernism by identifying them as Jewish and hence inauthentic and external. Both create historical reconstructions that reduce cultural production and variation to uniformity and problems of meaning to formulations of deterministic causation.[12] Jewishness in Austrian culture is a question of meaning, not cause.

Beyond the simple definition of these alternatives, it seems to me unproductive to try to discuss the complicated question of the connection between personal cultural orientation and intellectual work according to the values of groups. To select a series of individual cases make more sense, and the possibility of arbitrariness strikes me as a lesser danger than the probability of forcing intricate lives into flat patterns. I shall thus briefly discuss four major figures for whom revolutionary innovations in intellectual and artistic discourses implied reevaluations of cultural and religious identity: Herzl, Freud, Mahler, and Schönberg. For all these figures, Jewish, Catholic, and Protestant identities were not absolute, and Jewishness, Protestantness, and Catholicity became profound intellectual choices: one component, crucial to be sure, in the changing self-definition of the critical intellectual. Just as important, these intellectuals' engagement of the issue of their personal cultural and intellectual identities—issues of personal context—developed symbiotically with their innovative engagements within the formal

---

12. There are many examples of both positions. The position of anti-Semitic anti-modernism is expressed, for example, in Ernest Ansermet's *Les fondements de la musique dans la conscience humaine* (Neuchâtel, 1961). In the desire to reject twentieth-century music from Schönberg on, Ansermet asserted that atonal music rejected the natural order on which all Western music had been built; Schönberg, the source of this aberration, fell "into the confusion of the abstract and the concrete—this Jewish quirk that is also the quirk of the intellectuals" (I:512). For Ansermet, cultural "abstraction" was the Jewish predicament that Schönberg shared with Spinoza, Marx, Freud, and Einstein (I:516,26). The philo-Semitic argument, with specific reference to fin-de-siècle Viennese culture, has been championed by George Steiner, who has argued often that the Talmudic predisposition toward rationalism, language skepticism, and antirepresentationalism generated and hence defines Austrian modernism. See Steiner, "Le langage et l'inhumain," in *Revue d'esthétique* 9 (1985): 65–70.

dynamics of their particular intellectual (scientific, artistic, and political) discourses.

In the case of Freud, for example, the *choice* of Jewishness was
unproblematic. Thus although Freud's identity as a Jew is a highly
complicated question, his choice to remain a Jew and to characterize
himself as such is not problematic and remains an integral component in his intellectual self-definition. Theodor Herzl's prognosis of
the problem of the Jews, on the other hand, despite its radicalization
in the form of Zionism, never lost the element of baroque theatricality to which Herzl remained attracted, and to which he had
appealed in his original proposal for a mass conversion of the Jews.
In the cases of artists for whom issues of representation, totality,
and closure were the organizing principles of the forms in which
they worked, the aesthetic spectrum of totality versus fragmentation became connected to a personal identity struggle that mani-
fested itself in patterns of agonized conversions. Mahler and
Schönberg are two celebrated cases in point. I shall introduce the
discussion with a brief section on Hofmannsthal, who sheds much
light on this Austrian problem, notwithstanding the remoteness of
his own Jewish ancestry.

III

The case of Hofmannsthal is among the most complicated, because of both the intricacy of his Jewish/Catholic heritage and the
opacity of his sensibility when it came to what his heritage meant
to him. Hermann Broch is the one critic to have taken seriously
Hofmannsthal's Jewish background as a potential factor in his
intellectual development, but even he could only hint at the meaning of the connections. In charting Hofmannsthal's adult development as an artist (in other words as a producer, rather than as an
appreciator, or passive aesthete), Broch organized his study under
the rubric "the second assimilation."[13] He argued that Hofmannsthal's artistic path revealed a growing desire for assimilation of the
artist into a sentimental vision of a noble, Austrian society rather than

---

13. Broch, *Hofmannsthal and His Time*, pp. 102–8.

a bourgeois one. Broch's argument is profound, and it is unsatisfactory only in its vagueness as to the concrete nature of Hofmannsthal's program of "assimilation"—a program that can be traced through his late work and through the Salzburg Festival program.

The "first assimilation" to which Broch implicitly refers is that of Hofmannsthal's Jewish grandfather (August von Hofmannsthal) into Catholic society. This was a double assimilation: into Catholicism and into the burgher class from the aristocracy into which August's father, Isaak Löw Hofmann von Hofmannsthal, had been ennobled. The poet Hofmannsthal's assimilation amounted to the drive to reenter the nobility through art and "the artist's claim to nobility," and hence in some manner to vindicate the values of the founding Hofmannsthal, his great-grandfather. Broch writes:

> For in destroying the Jewish-feudal purposes of their ancestors and taking the turn toward the Christian-burgher camp, both father and grandfather had burdened themselves with guilt. And so this new defection, in which the bourgeois was abandoned in favor of the artistic, made its amends only through the revival of the entire assimilation process, together with its feudal goal, which had gone wrong with the grandfather's Catholic marriage. The psyche's calculations are of unparalleled intricacy. In the end, not as a Jew—although he was the first Hofmannsthal in three generations to enter into a Jewish marriage—but as an artist and with the artist's claim to nobility, Hugo von Hofmannsthal renewed the mission of assimilation. The spirit of his great-grandfather, embodied in the mystically potent image of the tablets of the law in the family crest, received a brilliant post facto apology, if not the kind of brilliance he might have dreamed of for his great-grandchildren.[14]

Broch thus argues that, through this "second assimilation" into the role of the artist, Hofmannsthal somehow reassimilated some of the values of the founding great-grandfather, but that he did so not as a Jew but as an artist. The artist and the Jew run somehow parallel, but there is no suggestion of any conscious—or indeed of any unconscious—connection in Hofmannsthal's mind between the identity of the artist and that of the (partial) Jew. The parallel

14. Ibid., p. 105.

that Broch argues for, as well as the "second assimilation," remains in the realm of poetic justice.

It is very difficult to transcend this kind of argument based on poetic parallel when it comes to Hofmannsthal as intellectual and Hofmannsthal as partial Jew. In this kind of context, some sort of psychobiographical insights would perhaps be useful, if the evidence to support them existed. All the same, I would suggest that in a crucial text of the period of the First World War, the story and then the libretto *Die Frau ohne Schatten*, Hofmannsthal drew into the orbit of ethical drama the problem of his Jewish ancestry. I make this suggestion with deliberate reference to and in spite of the arguments of the previous chapter. Despite the ideological and formal decline described there, Hofmannsthal retained in some of his most profound writings the power of the mysterious symbol, as Arabella's glass of water instantiates. The symbolic jungle of *Die Frau ohne Schatten* suggests a confrontation with issues he may never have intended to engage.

Within the plot of this thick fairy tale, the locus of power and source of magic are held by the absent father of the empress, Keikobad. The empress's ethical path is the spine of the work, and her absolute refusal to drink from a fountain that would provide her with happiness at the expense of others becomes the moment of her ethical transformation, her humanization, and the source of her magical reward. This moment, which occurs well into the third act of the opera, is the work's dramatic climax, for its process of tension building and total resolution (a process masterfully set by Strauss). The moment builds as the empress addresses her absent but present father:

> Vater, bist dus?
> Drohest du mir
> aus dem Dunkel her?
> Hier siehe dein Kind!
> Mich hinzugeben,
> hab' ich gelernt,
> aber Schatten
> hab' ich keinen
> mir erhandelt.

Father, is it you?
Do you threaten me from the darkness?
Behold here your child!
I have learned to sacrifice myself,
but I have not traded for a shadow.

This is the empress's darkest moment, and it accompanies an overdetermined symbolic discourse that is utterly incompatible with the brilliant, *Magic Flute*-like finale. The invocation of the father recalls Elektra's invocation of the dead Agamemnon ("Vater! Agamemnon! Hast du nicht die Kraft, dein Angesicht herauf zu mir zu schleppen? / Father! Agamemnon! Have you not the strength to drag your countenance here before me?"), and the few lines cited above incorporate the transformation of the address to the mythic absent father of the Greek myth into the invocation of the present and benevolent Christian father. The transformation from Greek myth to Christian allegory is joined by the transformation from Jewish father to Christian father. The punitive Keikobad (he has turned the emperor into stone) also evokes Jehovah, who is now transformed into a loving father through the ethical transformation of the child. That Hofmannsthal saw himself in the empress is clear, and the transformation of the empress's fate and world becomes a fantasied Christianization and allegorization of the dark symbolic world inhabited by Greek and Hebrew mythic processes. The scene continues with a burst of water that the empress refuses to drink because there is blood in it. Just as Barak's refusal to eat the fish from which the audience hears the voices of unborn children certifies their symbolic content in a Christian frame, the empress's ethical stance cleanses the water of its Mosaic allusions (the bloody Nile that threatens the Pharaoh) and transforms it into its Christian incarnation, holy water. The symbolic continuity of uneaten fish to undrunk water is reinforced by the inclusion of the voices of the unborn children in the resplendent ensemble finale that occurs instantly as the empress makes possible the magical, happy resolution of the fates of all four protagonists.

Hermann Broch suggested that *Die Frau ohne Schatten* stood at the pinnacle of Hofmannsthal's "voyage of discovery into the primal forest of symbols." But he went on: "Hofmannsthal enters the jungle, but proves that it is not that of the primal forest; no, it is a symbolic garden."[15] Hofmannsthal resolves the irresolvable conflict between symbolic indeterminacy and programmatic social renewal through the reaffirmation of baroque theatricality and the overcoming, on the way, of Jewish ancestral symbolism. The symbolic world of *Die Frau ohne Schatten* approaches the richness and impenetrability of that of *Elektra*, but the happy ending is Hofmannsthal's fantasied escape from symbolic indeterminacy, from the jungle to the garden.

IV

The power of the baroque was always present in the political projections of Theodor Herzl, even though his late work was guided by a process of radicalization just as much as Hofmannsthal's was guided by one of conservatism. Although it is tempting to see the final development of the Zionist position as the result of a recognition of unresolvable conflict and hence secession, aspects of Herzl's construction of the Zionist alternative reveal striking continuities with formulations from his assimilationist early years.

Herzl's initial strategy for solving the problem of the Jews had been to mount a series of duels against leaders of anti-Semitism— Schönerer, Lueger, and Prince Alois von Liechtenstein.[16] The second strategy was yet more theatrical. In 1893, Herzl dreamed of a conversion pact with the Vatican. He composed an imaginary letter to the pope in his diary: "If you help us against the anti-Semites, I shall lead a great movement for the free and decent conversion of the Jews to Christianity. . . . In the clear light of day, at high noon, in solemn procession [and] to the tolling of bells, the conversion shall take place in St. Stephen's Cathedral. With a proud countenance, [the Jews would enter the church]—not ashamed like the individual convert heretofore . . . whose conversion has appeared either as cowardice or climbing."[17]

15. Ibid., p. 151.
16. See Schorske, "Politics in a New Key," in *Fin-de-siècle Vienna*, p. 160.
17. Herzl, *Tagebücher*, I:8; quoted in Schorske, p. 161.

In both these anti-Semitic strategies, the overcoming of prejudice and isolation was equated with entry in to a world defined and governed by theatricality. The first strategy contained drama—in another word, conflict. After fighting a series of duels, the Jew would gain honor and respect. (In university dueling societies at this time, a Jew was not *satisfaktionsfähig*, worthy of satisfaction.) Conversion played no part in this scenario. The second strategy contained only theater, the pageantry of a newly harmonized totality. Herzl understood clearly the cosmological pretensions of the secular Catholic Austrian theater.

The fact that Herzl never relinquished his sense of theatricality must be seen as informing both the content and the style of his developing Zionist position. Although it is well known that the writing of *The Jewish State* in 1895 was somehow inspired or at least energized by a reaction to a performance of Wagner's *Tannhäuser*, the actual connections between his reception of the opera and the formation of the Zionist positions of the book remain to be charted. Bernard Avishai suggests that *Tannhäuser* proved to Herzl how ingrown and hence ultimately unavailable to Jews the traditions, pieties, and promises of German culture really were, as expressed in the plot-terms of redemption of sin through Germanic and Christian piety.[18] But the very quality of theater and theatricality must also be seen as a connective principle. The character Tannhäuser achieves redemption and peace as his rebellious passions are diffused not through his initial appeal for papal intervention (corresponding to Herzl's proposal for resolving the Jewish problem), but through the pious self-sacrifice of the Christian heroine, Elisabeth. The artistic revolutionary (himself cut from the same block as his predecessor, the Flying Dutchman, whose Jewish mythical burden is heavy) is redeemed by the asexual mother figure who herself, mediated perhaps by the suggestion of her namesake the Empress Elisabeth, can be seen to have represented the accepting, forgiving Mother Austria of Herzl's fantasies. Clearly the opera *Tannhäuser* presents a theatrical resolution of an assimilationist fantasy. Theatricality, in the Viennese baroque fashion that Herzl himself assimilated, presents and represents a totality that is able to resolve conflict.

18. Bernard Avishai, *The Tragedy of Zionism* (New York, 1985), pp. 38–39.

Well after the formation of Herzl's Zionism, and made clear within the utopian adumbration of the future Jewish state in the 1902 novel *Altneuland*, the Zionist vision retains a large measure of harmonizing theatricality. The social structure of the projected Zionist state is called *gemeinschaftlich*, and the potential Arab problem is dismissed via the figure of Reshid Bey, "the Moslem character in the novel," according to Avishai, "who quickly adapted to the New Society's operas and salons." What is presented is an orientalistic program of the acculturation of the non-Western native toward a cultural model that is more Austrian than Jewish. The Jewish state would allow Austrian Jews to be good Austrians.

V

There is no evidence that Freud ever considered religious conversion, even though his career would have benefited from it. Any consideration of conversion would have compromised the Hannibal fantasy, the perception of psychoanalysis as the victory of the Semitic general against the forces of Rome: in Freud's context, Austrian clericalism and Catholicism.[19] But I want to make two points. First, I think that Freud considered psychoanalysis to be the true achievement, rather than a displaced achievement, of the Hannibal fantasy. His sense of drama (not theater) thus required that Vienna and Austria remain the focus of his psychoanalytic activity. Freud/Hannibal had to remain in the clutches of Rome qua Catholic anti-Semitism: the relevant counter-context. That Freud considered Viennese society the right field in which to pursue his research is made clear by his lifelong loyalty to a city he basically disliked. Late in his life he confided to Ernest Jones that he became depressed every time he returned to Vienna from a trip. Yet he never left, despite sporadic opportunities to emigrate to England and to Holland. Freud's view of Vienna is a cogent reminder to the historian

---

19. The centrality of the Hannibal fantasy has been shown by Carl Schorske. See "Politics and Patricide," in *Fin-de-siècle Vienna*. William McGrath, in his recent book *Freud's Discovery of Psychoanalysis* (Ithaca, 1986), works within the Schorskean paradigm of the Hannibal fantasy but restores the Jewish dimension to a more dominant position.

that from the perspective of an innovator, fin-de-siècle Vienna was not a crucible of innovation but a provincial city. "I have lived here for fifty years," Freud told Jones, "and have never come across a new idea here."[20]

Second, the psychoanalytic process in both its therapeutic and social-philosophical contexts operates in terms of a management of conflict, both psychic and social, rather than projecting a resolution of conflict. In this sense it is truly a political as well as a dramatic process. Freud's ability, even desire, to retain a large measure of conflict and irresolvability in his psychological and social models accounts for the scientific as well as the political style and legitimacy of his positions, as opposed to those, for example, of Wilhelm Fliess and Otto Weininger. The opposition of drama to theater, of conflict management to the presentation of an illusory totality, holds here.

Freud's conviction that thinking is acting emerges in an episode recounted by his son Martin and pertaining to the living out of the Hannibal fantasy. In an article written for a volume called *The Jews of Austria*, Martin Freud attempted to portray his father from the point of view of his Judaism. He begins by quoting a letter his father had written to a B'nai B'rith lodge which was celebrating his seventieth birthday in 1926: "as a Jew, I was prepared to be in the opposition," Freud had commented on his career. The article continues with quotations from letters Freud had written to Martha Bernays during their long engagement in the 1880s. Through these quotations, Martin Freud attempts to portray his father as a "fighting Jew."[21]

In the longest of the letters quoted, Freud describes to his fiancée an incident that emerges as a structural opposite to the story of Jakob Freud's humiliation in a Freiberg street.[22] He writes of a skirmish in a train in which he was called a dirty Jew for insisting

20. Ernest Jones, *The Life and Work of Sigmund Freud* (New York, 1953), I:293.

21. Martin Freud, "Who Was Freud?", in *The Jews of Austria: Essays on Their Life, History, and Destruction,* ed. Joseph Fraenkel, (London, 1967), pp. 197–212, 198.

22. Ernest Jones and Carl Schorske have both argued that the childhood episode in which Freud heard this story from his father did much to generate the Hannibal fantasy. "Freud-Hannibal as 'Semitic general,' " in Schorske's formulation, "would avenge his feeble father against Rome, a Rome that symbolized 'the organization of the Catholic Church' and the Habsburg regime that supported it." See Schorske, "Politics and Patricide," in *Fin-de-siècle Vienna*, p. 191; Jones, I:22.

on keeping a window open. Freud reports that he stood his ground in the face of a growing, hostile "mob," who, he concludes, "must have noticed that I wasn't afraid, and I did not allow this experience to dampen my spirits."[23] The anecdote itself ends with the arrival of the train conductor who closes the window, but Freud's narrative is the narrative of a victory. The victory of the spirit is the one that counts, and it is a true victory as far as Freud is concerned.

Yet these claims of independence and spiritual impenetrability notwithstanding, was Freud the intellectual pariah truly intellectually immune to the cultural prejudice of which he was victim? Clearly the intersections of his work with that of Wilhelm Fliess and Otto Weininger between 1895 and 1903, intersections long dismissed but recently rechartered (by William McGrath and others) were determined at least in part by an assimilation anxiety to which his increasingly anti-Semitic surroundings did not permit him to be totally immune.

If psychoanalysis as social critique set Freud permanently against Austrian society and resolved the Hannibal fantasy at least insofar as it defined the opposing positions in the conflict, the origins of psychoanalysis can and should be seen in the context of the assimilation crisis between 1895 and 1897, the years of Karl Lueger's election and ultimate ratification as mayor of Vienna. When Freud smoked a cigar to celebrate the emperor's initial refusal to ratify Lueger's election, he in effect enacted through this archbourgeois gesture the overcoming of what he himself enthusiastically described as a neurotic symptom: recurrent nasal infections. Fliess had operated on his nose twice, the second time in the summer of 1895, a few months after the disastrous, now infamous, operation on Emma Eckstein in March.[24] Although Freud suspected that his nasal infections, as well as his recurring heart palpitations (arhythmia), were organically determined, he implored both Fliess and his mentor Josef Breuer not to hide from him their potential belief that his symptoms might be neurotically determined. Jones has no difficulty in assuming that they were neurotic and asserts that if the heart palpitations had been organic, Freud would not have been

23. Martin Freud, p. 201.
24. Jones, I:309.

able to "climb the Rax mountain in three and a half hours." On the suspicion that his symptoms might be organic and aggravated by his smoking, however, Freud had, with great difficulty, abstained from cigar smoking in early 1895, only to break down for the sake of a theatrical political gesture.[25]

Only a limited sense of Jewish as well as of anti-Semitic folklore is necessary to understand that the nose is itself a significant referent for assimilationist anxiety. Fliess's nasal-genital theories are superfluous here. I would guess that Freud was well aware of this symbolism and that he engaged it playfully, a foretaste of the method of coy engagement with his own psychic patterns that would generate the narrative of the *Interpretation of Dreams* in the coming five years. In this case, a courting of his own allegedly neurotic symptoms served to demonstrate the scope of his psychosocial positions.

Such intellectual—to say nothing of diagnostic—playfulness was out of the question for Fliess and Weininger. Once Lueger was in and anti-Semitism was on the rise, Freud's neurotic symptoms, if they were indeed neurotic symptoms, were transcended by the psychoanalytic theory that developed between 1896 and 1900. The symbiosis of psychic and social conflict management continued. The scientific—or pseudoscientific—models of Fliess and Weininger differed from Freud's in their refusal to accept unresolvable conflict, psychic or political. Without trying to rehearse or to solve the coordinates in the work of the three men with regard to the shared theory of bisexuality, one can be sure that the sexual and politicosocial ramifications of the theory worked out differently for Freud than they did for the other two. Weininger mapped onto the masculine-feminine axis the categories of Aryan and Jew. Aryanness-masculinity denoted strength; Judaism-femininity, weakness. Weininger's despairing perception of himself as Jewish and (on the grounds of his homosexuality) feminine contributed to his conversion to Protestantism, and, a year later, to his suicide. Thus, the state of mind that drew both Weininger's thought and his life into collapse was not his conflation of psychosexual and cultural-social categories (categories that Freud also conjoined), but the ironhand-

25. Ibid., p. 311.

edness with which he superimposed his categories onto each other with the necessary result becoming a negative judgment of himself. His positions demanded absolute resolution of psychological and cultural-social conflict. Thus on every ground on which Freud was able to accept the persistence of conflict, Weininger was unable to do so. For Weininger, theatricality prevailed on every level, as the well-known suicide scenario (in a Vienna residence used by Beethoven) only confirmed.

VI

Those thinkers who worked within art forms that depended on representation by means of coherent and unified formal systems did not have the ready intellectual tools with which to incorporate a disunited view of the social and cultural world into their discourses. Thus, I suggest that for them the very nature of aesthetic discourses precluded the kind of intellectual productivity based on a perception of conflict of the type seen in Freud and—after 1893—in Herzl. This is not to imply that there were no assimilationist scientists and no pariah literary figures—Weininger in science and Schnitzler in literature would immediately disprove so rash a hypothesis. More modestly, however, I am arguing that aesthetic modes of representation tended logically and structurally to a symbiosis with a normative view of the social and cultural world as a totality.

In Austria, theater led the art forms that tended to represent the world as a unified totality. Neither writing for the theater (to say nothing of staging) nor other forms of literature grappled seriously with the problem of representation. In its relation to language, Austrian literature did not confront contemporary and co-national innovations in linguistic philosophy. The philosophy of Wittgenstein and of the more indigenous Vienna School had no real followers or counterparts in literature. There was no Austrian Joyce, as Hermann Broch observed, though he himself probably came closest. Although Hofmannsthal questioned the relation of language to meaning in his work between 1895 and 1905, he never did so with the revolutionary intransigence of Joyce, and after 1905 (probably after *Elektra*), he abandoned that line of questioning alto-

gether. A similar sympathy for reform without reform itself domi-
nated the Café Grienstiedl group that formed a significant part of
Hofmannsthal's literary company after 1891. It included Hermann
Bahr, Schnitzler, Richard Beer-Hofmann, Peter Altenberg, Felix
Salten, Felix Dörmann, and, peripherally, Stefan Zweig.

If the theater, language itself, or even the visual arts offered the
possibility of revolution in any way comparable to the musical
revolution of Schönberg, none took root in Austria. Music, on
the contrary, became the art form that provided the most drastic
alternatives, enabling Schönberg to reject the claims to formal coherence and natural legitimacy of all preceding musical language,
and to form a new system. The two remaining figures I examine
in this chapter both operated on the dual axes of representation/
nonrepresentation, assimilation/nonassimilation. They are Mahler,
who converted to Catholicism, and Schönberg, who converted to
Protestantism in 1898 and back to Judaism in 1933.

Mahler's official conversion to Catholicism in Hamburg in February 1897 was clearly tied to his anticipation of being appointed
conductor at the Vienna Hofoper. Brahms and Karl Goldmark had
recommended his appointment, which carried the implication that
he would soon replace Wilhelm Jahn, the current *Hofoperndirektor*.
Mahler's initial appointment required the approval of the *Obersthof-
meister*, Prince Rudolf Liechtenstein. Mahler's biographer Henry
Louis de la Grange states that Mahler was told (he does not say
who the speaker was) that "under the present circumstances, it is
impossible to engage a Jew for Vienna." As to Mahler's conversion,
de la Grange suggests that "he embraced the Catholic religion
because he knew that his native Judaism would prove an insur-
mountable obstacle to his appointment." Mahler himself commented, "I do not hide the truth . . . when I say that this action,
which I took from an instinct of self-preservation and which I was
fully disposed to take, cost me a great deal."[26]

Mahler's own comment reveals that his relation both to Judaism
and to Catholicism was more complicated that the picture his wife
tried to present in describing him as "a Christian Jew" ("ein Christ-

26. Henry Louis de la Grange, *Mahler* (Garden City, N.Y., 1973), I:390, 411, 412.

gläubiger Jude").[27] Two points are clear: first, the conversion involved spiritual and intellectual conflict, and, second, although social expedience was a factor, the character of that social expedience needs to be redefined. For Mahler his return to Vienna was not only a question of professional advancement but an intellectual and spiritual reintegration into the culture to which he felt he belonged. The work he had most recently completed while the question of Vienna and conversion took form was the Second Symphony, and Mahler's own ambivalent attitude toward the program he devised for it—which gave it the name *Resurrection* Symphony—is an eloquent indication of the state of his mind at a pivotal point in his life.

Mahler had begun the immense first movement of the Second Symphony toward the end of 1888 in the form of a death march for the vaguely portrayed hero of the First Symphony (the "Titan"). In this early phase of its composition, Mahler was uncertain how to continue it, uncertain as to what kind of program—if any at all—would suitably follow a solemn requiem (*Totenfeier*). The circumstances that, almost six years later, inspired the resurrection theme and the use of Klopstock's poem "Resurrection" ("Aufersteh'n") are well known: the latter was sung at Hans von Bülow's funeral in Hamburg in 1894. Mahler's friend the Czech composer Josef Förster recounted that the Klopstock poem came as a powerful inspiration for Mahler that suddenly pointed the way toward the resolution of the symphony and thus solved a problem that Mahler had been unable to solve for two years.[28] To Klopstock's two verses Mahler added five more, and he prefaced this final movement with a short song called the "Urlicht," or "Primal Light." The words of the two movements read as follows:

Urlicht

    O Röschen rot!
    Der Mensch liegt in grösster Not!

---

27. Ibid., I:414.
28. See Donald Mitchell, *Gustav Mahler: The Wunderhorn Years* (Boulder, Colo., 1975), pp. 168ff.

Der Mensch liegt in grösster Pein!
Je lieber möcht' ich im Himmel sein!
Da kam ich auf einen breiten Weg;
Da kam ein Engelein und wollt' mich abweisen!
Ach nein! Ich liess mich nicht abweisen:
Ich bin von Gott, ich will wieder zu Gott!
Der liebe Gott wird mir ein Lichtchen geben,
Wird leuchten mir bis in das ewig selig Leben!

Aufersteh'n (Klopstock)
Aufersteh'n, ja aufersteh'n wirst du,
Mein Staub nach kurzer Ruh!
Unsterblich Leben! Unsterblich Leben
Will der dich rief dir geben.

Wieder aufzublühn wirst du gesät!
Der Herr der Ernte geht
Und sammelt Garben
Uns ein, die starben!

(Mahler's verses)
O glaube, mein Herz, O glaube,
Es geht dir nichts verloren!
Dein ist, was du gesehnt,
Dein, was du gelebt,
Was du gestritten!
O glaube,
Du warst nicht umsonst geboren!
Hast nicht umsonst gelebt,

Gelitten!
Was entstanden ist,
Das muss vergehen!
Was vergangen, aufersteh'n!
Hör auf zu beben!
Bereite dich zu leben! . . .

Aufersteh'n, ja aufersteh'n
Wirst du, mein Herz, in einem Nu!
Was du geschlagen,
Zu Gott wird es dich tragen!

Primal Light

O rosebud red!
Man lies in greatest despair!
Man lies in greatest pain!
I would much rather be in Heaven!
There I came to a wide road;
There came a little angel and wanted to reject me!
Ah no! I did not let myself be rejected;
I am from God, I want to return to God!
Dear God will give me a little light,
Will lighten my way into eternal joyous life!

Resurrection (Klopstock)

Resurrected, yes, you will be resurrected,
My dust, after a short rest!
Immortal life! Immortal life
Will you be given by him who called you.
You are sown to bloom again!
The Lord of the harvest goes
And gathers up us sheaves, who died!

(Mahler's verses)

O believe, my heart, O believe,
You are not lost!
Yours is what you have longed for,
Yours, what you
have lived,
What you have striven!
O believe,
You were not born in vain,
Have not lived in vain,

Suffered!
Everything that is must die!
What has died must be resurrected!
Stop your trembling!
Prepare yourself to live! . . .

Resurrected, yes, resurrected

Will you be, my heart, in a twinkling!
Your labors will carry you to God![29]

Is this Tannhäuser talking? The content of these lines is one-dimensional and clear, and the lines that Mahler added himself repeat rather than deepen Klopstock's message of resurrection. The accompanying musical structure is equally one-dimensional, especially when contrasted with the complicated opening movement of the symphony. Thus, in its musical structure and in the relationship of the program text to the music, the Second Symphony's treatment of the theme of death and resurrection is much simpler than that of the later symphonies, especially the Third, Fifth, Eighth, and Ninth.[30] The words seem to simplify rather than elaborate the subject matter.

Leon Botstein has suggested that the formal simplicity of the last movement of the *Resurrection* Symphony may be a conscious evocation of the ethic of simplicity in Anton Bruckner's music. This view seems to strengthen the patterns of association between simplicity and totality in the representation of Austrian-Catholic ethical truth.[31]

The Third Symphony (composed in the summers of 1895 and 1896) offers an immediate contrast to the Second. Its texts are the "Drunken Song" from Nietzsche's *Also sprach Zarathustra* and a poem from the *Des Knaben Wunderhorn* anthology describing Christ at the Last Supper. The latter takes shape in the form of the lightest and shortest movement and ultimately disappears between the previous movement—the ponderous setting of the Nietzsche song that is the musical pivot of the symphony—and the immense final one, which contains no text at all. In this final movement Mahler seems to declare the need to transcend the text, to let music speak in a formal realm that transcends representation. Hence, the Second Symphony's double allegiance to representation per se and to the representation of Christian themes in particular has become much

29. I have omitted one of Mahler's own verses, as indicated; the translation is my own.
30. See David B. Greene, *Mahler: Consciousness and Temporality* (New York, 1984), pp. 127, 249, 274.
31. Leon Botstein, personal communication.

more problematic for him—and is indeed at least partially rejected—in the Third Symphony. Kurt Blaukopf has suggested that
in its choral finale the Second Symphony pays homage to Beethoven's Ninth Symphony; the Third Symphony seems to move in the
opposite direction, with a short choral episode followed by a long
and solemn orchestral final movement that reexplores and reinte-
grates the work's main musical ideas into a strictly formal, nonrep-
resentational structure.[32]

In the conclusion of the Second Symphony, Mahler declares
adherence to two principles, one pertaining to content, the other
to form. The first principle is the belief in the representability of the
idea of resurrection; the second is the confidence, derived from
Beethoven, in a symphony that combines words and music. But
just as his later treatment of these principles became much more
uncertain, so did his own opinion of the program of the Second
Symphony. At a performance of the work in Munich in 1900, he
refused to let the text be distributed to the audience, stating that
"the music must speak for itself."[33]

The Vienna premiere had been in 1899, and the press reaction
may have contributed to Mahler's reduced confidence in the legitimacy of the text. The *Neue Freie Presse* called it a "piece of imaginary
theater." The anti-Semitic press, predictably, was harsher. From its
point of view, the *Resurrection* Symphony was the insincere Catholic
language of a Jew. Thus Maximilian Muntz of the *Deutsche Zeitung*
called the work "pompous sham," and called Mahler the "incarnation of Jewish musical decadence, ignoring all measure, all regard,

32. See Kurt Blaukopf, *Gustav Mahler, oder der Zeitgenosse der Zukunft* (Vienna,
1969), pp. 114–19. For a detailed discussion of the Third Symphony see William J.
McGrath, *Dionysian Art and Populist Politics in Austria* (New Haven, Conn., 1974),
pp. 120–62. (McGrath gives more relative weight to the fifth movement and its
imagery than I do.) It seems to me that if Beethoven and his turn to the use of words
in the last movement of the Ninth Symphony constituted a model for Mahler in the
last movement of the *Resurrection* Symphony, Brahms was the relevant model in the
Mahler Third. (The opening bars of the Mahler Third seem to quote the main
theme of the fourth movement of the Brahms First Symphony.) Alternatively, the
Beethoven Ninth can be seen as a negative model for the Mahler Third, which
embraces and then rejects a text. Indeed, "taking back" Beethoven's Ninth in this
very way is the final aesthetic agenda of Thomas Mann's fictitious composer Adrian
Leverkühn, who has much Mahler in him.
33. De la Grange, I:596.

all restraint in the pursuit of his goal.[34] The Catholic theater of Hofmannsthal and Reinhardt elicited similar responses twenty years later.

Although the Vienna-born Arnold Schönberg began his compositional career by setting the poems of the Viennese poets Richard Dehmel and Peter Altenberg, he felt at home neither in Vienna per se nor in its Catholic culture. If Schönberg, who converted to Protestantism in 1898 and moved to Berlin in 1911 (he also lived there between 1903 and 1905), does not fit into a discussion of the Catholic culture of the Austrian Jews in any direct sense, he fits profoundly into the parallel discussion of the continuity between personal cultural conviction and the problem of aesthetic representation. As the one unquestionable aesthetic revolutionary in the pantheon of fin-de-siècle Vienna, Schönberg organized his creative path on the rejection of conventional systems of representation, and his personal cultural and religious allegiances followed closely on the development of his aesthetic program.

Schönberg's early compositions integrated the formal innovations of both Brahms and Wagner. Schönberg realized that the polarization of the two composers was the result of the disputes of epigones rather than the outcome of essential aesthetic differences. Thus although the 1899 *Verklärte Nacht* was a program piece and hence Wagnerian, its setting for a string sextet was in the style of Brahms. Similarly, as H. H. Stuckenschmidt has argued, in the 1899 songs—like *Verklärte Nacht* set to poems of Richard Dehmel—"the chromaticism of *Tristan* is married to the classic symphonic procedure which Brahms had brought into the field of song."[35]

The importance of Brahms as aesthetic model increased as Schönberg's music moved further away from tonality and representation. Although he continued to set texts (as had Brahms), the musical systems that combined with those texts were not referential in the sense of program music. Rather than shaping the music into an image of the text, Schönberg seems to be discussing, through

---

34. Ibid., p. 507.
35. H. H. Stuckenschmidt, *Schoenberg: His Life, World, and Work*, trans. Humphrey Searle (New York, 1978), pp. 39–40.

music, the very problem of the relation of music to text. In a sense, the "program pieces" of the period 1908–1912, including *Erwartung, Die glückliche Hand,* and *Pierrot Lunaire,* are about the problem of musical representation. For example, in the eighteenth of the pieces that form *Pierrot Lunaire,* the section called "Moonspot" ("Mondfleck"), Pierrot discovers a white spot on his back, which he unsuccessfully tries to rub off. The idea of a man seeing his own back as in a mirror fascinated Schönberg, and he wrote the accompanying music for this scene in the form of a canon first played forward and then backward (the retrograde). The piece therefore goes through a mirror and is then seen from the other side; the moment where the music goes through the mirror comes as the phrase "a white spot" is mentioned in the text.[36] This kind of musical self-consciousness culminated in the "discovery" of the twelve-tone system, where the emphasis on formal logic is taken to new heights.

Brahms was more than the aesthetic model in this intricate process. Schönberg opened his renowned 1947 essay "Brahms the Progressive" with a description of Brahms's position in Vienna that echoed his own position in the musical world. He described Brahms as an intentionally isolated figure, with a "method of surrounding himself with a protective wall of stiffness as a defence against certain types of people, against the obtrusiveness of oily bombast, moist flattery, or honeyed impertinence."[37] Brahms the prophet, as opposed to Wagner the priest, was Schönberg's personal model.

I think it is legitimate to argue that it was this constellation of principles—intellectual isolation and even a prophetic stance, as well as a growing self-consciousness about the meaning of aesthetic representation—that informed *both* of Schönberg's conversions. The 1898 conversion to Protestantism took place a year after Brahms's death; I would argue that homage to Brahms and to the antitheatrical principles he represented played a part in Schönberg's turn to Protestantism. In his conversion, Schönberg chose a path

36. See ibid., p. 199.
37. Arnold Schönberg, "Brahms the Progressive," in *Style and Idea* (Berkeley, Calif., 1984), p. 398.

away from representation. The reconversion to Judaism, which took place in Paris in 1933, was unquestionably an expression of political solidarity with the Jews, but it carried intellectual weight as well, coming as it did after the completion of the opera *Moses und Aron*, a massive reconsideration of the problem of representation as a moral and religious issue.

Schönberg wrote the score of the first two acts of *Moses und Aron* to his own libretto between 1930 and 1932 (he never set the third act). The plot is built on the biblical episode of the golden calf; the confrontation of Moses and Aaron becomes the confrontation of idea versus image, truth versus representation, word versus music. The role of Moses is set for a bass singing in *Sprechstimme;* Aaron is a bel canto tenor role. The second act ends with Moses's cry of despair "O Wort, du Wort, das mir fehlt!" ("Oh word, thou word that I lack!"); this cry for silence in the face of the falseness of all representation almost necessarily precluded the possibility of a musical third act.

Schönberg's elevation of Brahmsian nonrepresentation to a moral position with biblical underpinnings had a precedent in a smaller work, the second of the four songs that comprise the Four Pieces for Mixed Chorus, written in 1926. Schönberg's own words ran as follows:

> Du sollst dir kein Bild machen!
> Denn ein Bild schränkt ein, begrenzt, fasst,
> was unbegrenzt und unvorstellbar bleiben soll.
> Ein Bild will Namen haben:
> Du kannst ihn nur vom Kleinen nehmen;
> du sollst das Kleine nicht verehren!
> Du musst an den Geist glauben!
> Unmittelbar, gefühllos, und selbstlos.
> Du musst, Ausserwählter, musst, musst—
> willst du's bleiben!

> You must make no image for yourself!
> For an image limits, sets bounds, encompasses
> What must remain unbounded and unrepresented.
> An image wants a name:
> You will be able to name it after only small things;

you must not pay homage to what is small!
You must believe in the spirit!
Unmediated, without feeling and without self.
You must, Chosen One, must, must—
will you remain thus![38]

38. Schönberg, "Vier Stücke für Gemischten Chor," in *Sämtliche Werke, Chorwerke I* (Mainz, 1980), pp. 42–43. The translation is my own.

CHAPTER 7

Festival Repertory and
Its Contexts, 1920–1943

I

THIS chapter offers a "history of reception" on two levels. It seeks first to analyze the reception of festival repertory, in its specific context, by the Salzburg and Vienna public and press, and second to examine further the process of interpretation that went into the choice (and in the case of *Das Salzburger grosse Welttheater* the creation) of that repertory.

The Salzburg repertory included orchestral concerts, theater, and opera.[1] Opera meant, almost exclusively, Mozart. The fact that his operas at first retained a stylistic and ideological independence from the dominant stagings of the Salzburg theater pieces resulted more from logistical circumstances than anything else. Hofmannsthal saw *Don Giovanni*, for example, as a morality play that would stand beside *Jedermann* and offer the same spiritual message. But when the first *Don Giovanni* came to Salzburg in 1922, it came in a traveling production from the Vienna Opera (directed by Hans Breuer with scenery by Roller) which was not altered for the sake of Salzburg spiritual pretensions. Nor was any change evident when these Mozart operas were given in indigenous Salzburg productions, starting with *The Marriage of Figaro* and *Don Giovanni* in 1927. Profound associations with Vienna remained: the Vienna Philharmonic and opera chorus were retained, and the stage directors were familiar Vienna figures. Most fundamental, however, is the fact that

1. A complete list of the repertory from 1920 to 1944 can be found in the Appendix.

these productions bore the stamp of their conductors, and Mozart in Salzburg in the 1920s was dominated by the Vienna-based Franz Schalk and the Munich-based Bruno Walter. Opera in Salzburg never lost—indeed has still not lost—its imported flavor.

The opposite is the case with the theater pieces. It is commonly forgotten that *Jedermann* had its premiere in Berlin in 1911 and that *Das Salzburger grosse Welttheater* was presented in the Burgtheater in Vienna in 1931. (The latter was performed during only two Salzburg seasons—1922 and 1925.) *Jedermann* had lasted only sixteen performances in its original Berlin engagement, but was, in Reinhardt's words, a "smash hit" in Salzburg.[2] Perhaps the most powerful case is that of Goethe's *Faust*. Reinhardt's 1933 production, with its construction of the naturalistic "Faust-city" in the Felsenreitschule, easily became the most famous production of the play in this century, and every subsequent production has inevitably been compared to it, even in the post-World War II period. These three plays—a recently written morality play, an especially commissioned morality play, and a classic reinterpreted as a morality play—formed a trio that became the theatrical core of the Salzburg Festival.

As a German classic, *Faust* clearly had and retained a life of its own; Hofmannsthal's two morality plays remained tied almost exclusively to the festival. Their success in Salzburg was a function of their efficiency as vehicles of festival ideology; as dramas they are inferior works. Cynthia Walk has suggested that the success of *Jedermann* in Salzburg came from the magnificence of the "natural" setting and the ingenious way Reinhardt used it.[3] Hermann Broch interpreted its success in terms of an allegorization motivated by the collective psychological needs of a postapocalyptic audience: "As death approaches, Everyman has found the way back to his Christian youth. This was the 'great consolation' that should have fallen to the Austrian people in its state's hour of death. But this death proved so full of terror, was so war-bloodied and so apocalyptic, that the earnest-humorous death consolation of *Everyman* was

2. See Cynthia Walk, *Hofmannsthals "Grosses Welttheater": Drama und Theater* (Heidelberg, 1980), p. 26.
3. Ibid.

trivial in the face of it, and the World Theater theme had to be taken up again; it became the *Salzburg Great Theater of the World*, a conjuring up of the spirit of Calderón, in the hope that a collapsed Austria and a collapsed world might regain an ethical bearing from its Christianity." Hofmannsthal's Everyman is saved by the personifications of Works and Faith, a wish-fulfillment that follows Christian formula and was certainly applicable to the hopes of an Austrian audience. Broch suggests that the aesthetic and ethical failure of these plays lay in their illusions of a restored Christian community, symbolized in turn by the alleged fluidity between actors and audience: "In reality [the plays] were transformed into Reinhardtian spectacles. . . . It was all handled as if the medieval relation to the public could be restored, instead of conceding that what was at hand was a costume play."[4]

All these elements contributed to the complicated and varied reception of the Salzburg premiere of *Jedermann* (and hence of the inauguration of the Salzburg Festival itself) on 22 August 1920. The liberal Viennese *Neue Freie Presse* reported the opening of *Jedermann* in the middle of the paper on 26 August. It recorded the sold-out premiere and its international audience and suggested that "the city which Hermann Bahr, Stefan Zweig, Andreas Latzko, and Franz Karl Ginzkey among other citizens have chosen has raised itself into a new position as an art-city." A "feuilleton," which appeared in its traditional place "below the line" ("unter dem Strich") on the front page the following morning, was written by the paper's regular theater critic, Raoul Auernheimer, and was a good deal more cynical. Auernheimer suggested first that the main point of the production from Reinhardt's perspective was to prove that he had contact with living authors. (This appears to be a lame criticism, since Reinhardt had been staging Hofmannsthal's plays for almost twenty years; contemporaneity by no means precluded conservatism.) Auernheimer suggested that Reinhardt directed with the naive spectator in mind, an attitude expressed by his staging of the pivotal cries of "Jedermann!" from the rooftops around the cathedral square. This view Auernheimer defended with the comment, "every true spectator is naive." His doubts

4. Broch, *Hugo von Hofmannsthal and His Time*, p. 177.

concerned the religious pretensions of the play. The theater-church symbiosis it preached, he wrote, "goes too far": "That we must die concerns us all without exception, it is absolutely the human tragedy; but that we must all die in a Catholic manner is, at least for the non-Catholic spectators, not a foregone conclusion."

The Salzburg papers of course covered the event more thoroughly. The German-nationalist (*deutschnational*) and later pro-Nazi *Salzburger Volksblatt* published a "preview" of the *Jedermann* performances on 5 August, an article of high moral and religious pretensions. "The name of 'Everyman,' " it began, "is deeply symbolic," and the judgment that forms the dramatic core of the play pertains not only to "a rich man, a 'Capitalist,' the way in which it is presented in the play for reasons of greater effect and comprehensibility," but to everyone. The *Volksblatt's* reviewer of the play on 23 August instinctively absorbed the morality play's baroque ideology of the transcendence of the worldly and claimed that the performance was "no longer theater; it raised itself far beyond the worldliness of the modern stage." The review spoke as well to two essential elements of contemporary German conservative rhetoric: sacredness—the achievement of true aesthetic and cultural representation—and the transcendence of the modern.

On 1 August the Christian-Social *Salzburger Chronik* announced the upcoming performances of "a play of the death of a rich man, from the middle ages, as it was performed in German market-places by traveling actors." An English play had swiftly become a German one. The *Chronik* was not as enthusiastic about Reinhardt as the *Volksblatt* was. In an article of 13 August called "The Retirement of Max Reinhardt" the paper suggested that Reinhardt was waiting for sufficient funds and for the political air to clear before moving permanently to America. He and his brother and associate Edmund, it suggested, had inherited a dairy farm in Sweden and were waiting for visas to emigrate to the United States from there. Yet the *Chronik's* 24 August review was glowing, and lavish in its praise of Reinhardt himself. A week later, the author of that review, Franz Donat, wrote a second article in which he attempted to discredit the various objections to *Jedermann,* objections that had ranged from complaints about the bad weather and the high prices, to the "proletarian-middle class and anti-Semitic hostility" to the performances themselves. "The people (*das Volk*)," Donat wrote, certainly implying that the objections were widespread, "found the Jewish influence, like the Jewish immigration, too strong. When seen objectively, even this does not come from a spirit of anti-Semitism. In any case this perception contrasted sharply with another one, which claimed to see in *Jedermann* yet another brand of hidden clericalism. As one can see, every faction, from one end of the spectrum to the other, has had a chance to strike." Donat was especially critical of what he called the "pseudoclerical" indignation of an article in the *Reichspost*, which will be discussed below.

The Social-Democratic *Salzburger Wacht*, very much as the *Neue Freie Presse* had done, divided its coverage of the festival opening into fairly positive reportage and a fairly critical review. A preview article on 18 August recorded a fact that went curiously unnoticed in the rest of the press: that the Salzburger Festspielhausgemeinde had decided to donate the proceeds of these opening performances to charitable causes, including veterans, widows and orphans of war-dead, the transport home of Austrian prisoners of war, and American childrens' charities. The article concluded, "In such a way the festival serves Salzburg not only as an 'artistic act' but also as a 'good work' in the spirit of *Jedermann*." Yet in a review of 23 August, the *Wacht* criticized *Jedermann* itself for not speaking to the proletariat. "The banal consolation," it argued, "that death spares no one, and that nasty Mammon faithlessly abandons its possessor on his journey into the eternal beyond . . . , flattered the moral pretensions of the rich." "Every contemporary proletarian," it continued, "who reads the consoling story of Everyman's fortune and death, will have no choice but to reject decisively the moralizing purpose of the mystery drama; such morality and its rewards can gain the approval only of the well-sated bourgeoisie." But the article concluded with the contradictory wish that a special performance of *Jedermann* be put on for the workers. In a second review article, signed "A," five days later, the *Wacht* suggested that the play would come off better in a plain market-place, instead of the cathedral square with its excess of "theatricality and artifice."

The unequivocally negative press reactions took several tacks. An article in *Der Merker* of 1 September set the example of pointing out the incongruity between an alleged folk festival and exorbitant ticket prices. "All the morality," it suggested, "was borne with zeal. But whether the morals of the spectators were thus caused to take a new turn is doubtful. . . . The people [*das Volk*] on the other hand . . . yes, the people! Five hundred who couldn't afford tickets watched from behind cordons."

The *Deutsche Tageszeitung* offered more trenchant criticism: "Salzburg wishes to develop into a festival city, into an Austrian Bayreuth, into a central European [*mitteleuropäisch*] cultural center, and the *Jedermann* performances on the cathedral square were the first artistic life-sign of this bold undertaking, the completion of which according to the architect Poelzig's plans would demand a minimum capital base of a hundred million kronen. . . . In any case as an artistic program the *Jedermann* performances under Max Reinhardt's direction were a bad sign, for the odd mix of Catholicism and Americanism at work on the cathedral square directly contradicted the festival idea, which, as everyone had thought, was to let blossom in Salzburg the spirit of Mozart and the music of the surrounding landscape." That "Americanism" was simply a euphemism for "Judaism" became clear two paragraphs later, when Reinhardt was referred to by his original name of Max Goldmann. The article cited a current joke, "of profound significance," which described Reinhardt as a "Hungarian communist" from Pressburg who had "broken into Salzburg and taken over the cathedral" in a kind of "putsch."[5]

But the most vehement condemnation—vehement enough to cause a minor scandal—came from an article called "The Salzburg Cathedral and *Jedermann*," which appeared in the conservative Catholic Viennese paper *Die Reichspost* on 26 August. It was written by an unknown Salzburg privatdozent named Dr. Otto Drinkwelder, who became for a few weeks a celebrated figure in the Austrian press. Reinhardt was again the villain, and the production of *Jedermann* was for Drinkwelder a desecration of the cathedral and of Catholicism on religious and aesthetic grounds.

5. "Salzburger Festspieltage," *Deutsche Tageszeitung,* 25 August 1920. Reinhardt was born in Baden (outside of Vienna) but spent his childhood in Pressburg, the former Hungarian capital that became the Czech city of Bratislava after 1918. He did have Hungarian citizenship until 1918, as did his son Gottfried (Gottfried Reinhardt, *Der Liebhaber: Erinnerungen an Max Reinhardt* [Munich, 1973], p. 26).

Although the scenery was there for Reinhardt, he wrote, the costumes were borrowed from theaters in Berlin and Vienna and incompatible one with the next. The use of the organ and the cathedral bells for the performance was sacrilegious. Most offensive to Drinkwelder, however, was the use of the cathedral interior as theater wings and dressing rooms, and of the main cathedral door as the entrance to the stage. He imagined "an actress standing in front of the sacrament alter, completing her toilet in front of a mirror, held by a servant." Drinkwelder concluded with the call "Katholisches Volk, wo bleibst du?"—"Catholic people, where are you?"

Four days after the publication of Drinkwelder's article, the *Salzburger Volksblatt* published a response by Erwin Rainalter called "*Jedermann*, the Salzburg Cathedral, and Herr Privatdozent." Rainalter defended *Jedermann* as a "pious German play which received the highest consecration from its [cathedral] background." Drinkwelder's argument, he wrote, was "pharisaic and jesuitical." He concluded, echoing Drinkwelder, "Catholic people, will you allow an instigator and a curious fanatic, more pious than the pope, to destroy a beautiful and pious play? . . . The privatdozent would enlist the Catholic people in his fight against Reinhardt and Hofmannsthal. It seems to me more necessary for the Catholic people to beware of such hysterical preachers, who with their uncontrollable, stuttering rage compromise only their faith and their vocation."

The *Salzburger Volksblatt* then attempted, two days later, on 1 September, either to close or to heighten the controversy by publishing a ten-line poem in rhyming couplets by an anonymous "Salzburg child," which extolled the appreciation of beauty, art, and God over the "screaming of bad men."

The second festival year's production of *Jedermann* received more advance press coverage than the first, but, understandably, fewer reviews. The great majority of the audience came by car from Bavaria.[6] The church bells were not rung during the performance. Erwin Rainalter reviewed the opening night and criticized that

6. *Neue Freie Presse*, 18 August 1921.

A scene from the 1922 production of *Das Salzburger grosse Welttheater* in the Kollegienkirche. Courtesy of the Max Reinhardt Archive, State University of New York, Binghamton, New York.

audience for "consisting mainly of people who sat there only to prove that they were able to sit there, despite the enormously high ticket prices."[7]

II

The negotiations that led Archbishop Ignaz Rieder to permit *Das Salzburger grosse Welttheater* to be performed in the Kollegienkirche

---

` 7. *Salzburger Volksblatt*, 16 August 1921.

were discussed in Chapter 2. Its premiere on 13 August 1922 represented a new height in the Salzburg morality plays' claims to sacredness. To perform a morality play at the altar of a church was clearly
a more intense gesture than to perform one in front of a church. With
Jedermann, Hofmannsthal, Reinhardt, and Roller (who had devised
the banquet scene) had collectively asked for their theater to be taken
as gospel; with the *Welttheater*, they clearly considered it to have
reached that status.[8]

It is difficult and perhaps unwarranted to trace this elevation
in sacred pretension to any one member of the trio. It resulted
more from the dynamics of their interaction. Hofmannsthal
clearly intended and strove to write a sacred play, but for him
sacredness was more a question of text than of performance.
According to Rudolf Hirsch, he originally wanted the play
performed in the Felsenreitschule, and not in the Kollegienkirche.[9]
It was Reinhardt who wanted the church setting, both for the
theatricality of its baroque splendor and for its audience capacity,
which exceeded that of other indoor spaces. This dynamic is
confirmed in a letter of Hofmannsthal's to Georg von Franckenstein, written in March 1922: "*Welttheater will* probably be given
in the place that Reinhardt called the right place—the Collegiate
Church. The deciding factor was probably the good Archbishop's
liking for the play and his warm, simple, downright way of
saying so—and also his hope and trust that the receipts, combined
with the little the State can do, may save the beautiful church
(one of the finest of eighteenth-century monuments) from the
serious dangers that threaten it."[10] As with so many facets of the
Salzburg Festival, the baroque associations of secular pomp,

8. Rudolf Hirsch suggested to me that the banquet setting for *Jedermann* had been
Roller's and not Reinhardt's idea. This device provided the audience with a consistent,
static image of the dramatis personae and in addition clearly reinforced the parallel between the fate of Jedermann and that of Don Giovanni, who also meets his fate at a
banquet.

9. Rudolf Hirsch, personal communication. In September 1922 Hofmannsthal
expressed the wish that when the play was performed in Vienna, it would be
performed in a "profane space": Letter to Helene Thimig, 3 September 1922, quoted
in Walk, pp. 126–27.

10. Hofmannsthal, letter of 10 March 1922, quoted in Franckenstein, *Facts and
Features of My Life*, p. 242.

with its connotations of historical glory, and religious pretension converged into a unified style.

Hermann Broch was right to see the *Welttheater* as a repetition of *Jedermann* with higher stakes. The scenario is again a Catholic judgment scene: instead of a man being judged, it is the world itself. Hofmannsthal's ambitions seem to be raised to the level of world redemption through theater, and in that context one recalls Nietzsche's account of Wagner as a perennial redeemer who raises the object of his redemption with every opera, from an "interesting sinner" (*Tannhäuser*), to the Wandering Jew (*The Flying Dutchman*) to "the old God" (the *Ring*).[11]

In general the 1922 festival received relatively little press coverage. Perhaps the most celebrated reaction to the premiere of the *Welttheater* was one of the few unequivocally negative ones: Karl Kraus's article in his journal *Die Fackel* "Of the Great World Theater Swindle," in which he dubbed the spirit of the new play "Herr, gib uns unser täglich Barock"—"Lord, give to us our daily Baroque." He called the trio of Hofmannsthal, Reinhardt, and the actor Alexander Moissi the "holy trinity" and the "tribus parvis impostoribus."[12]

A preview article in the *Neue Freie Presse* recounted the issue of performing a play inside the Kollegienkirche and reported that the rehearsals in progress were making it clear that the content of the new play was "not unworthy" of its sacred surroundings. A second preview "feuilleton" article by the young theater scholar Josef Gregor celebrated the new play by placing it within a historical trajectory. The tradition of the world-theater, he wrote, passes through the "world-pictures" of Homer, Dante, Shakespeare, and Goethe. He concluded: "An age of new, strong religious life had to come that could ignite this *World-Theater*, and form an ordered work of art from very powerful but blurred nonsentences. This unparalleled accomplishment of reuniting theater and religion for the first time since Aeschylus lies in the drama of the Spanish baroque." For Gregor, Hofmannsthal's

11. See Nietzsche, *The Case of Wagner*, Aphorism 3.
12. Kraus, "Vom grossen Welttheaterschwindel," *Die Fackel*, nos. 601–7 (November 1922):2.

Welttheater, in the spirit of Calderón and the Spanish baroque, reunited stage and altar.[13]

The *Neue Freie Presse* review on 14 August praised the play as "a specific conception of Calderón's evolved into a timeless form, a very moving drama relevant to the problems of our time." Equal praise went to Reinhardt's contributions, especially the "grandiose, climaxing, unforgettably impressive dance of death." Five days later the *Reichspost* printed a glowing review with no echo of Otto Drinkwelder's anti-*Jedermann* polemics. Franz Donat wrote a review for the *Salzburger Chronik* on August 15, praising the "pure religious" quality of the play and the appropriateness of its being performed in church. Erwin Rainalter wrote in the *Salzburger Volksblatt* (14 August) that "the festival has surpassed itself: Hofmannsthal's *Welttheater* is behind us!" In the same issue, the *Volksblatt* published a second article by Josef Gregor, called "The Idea of the World Theater." It asserted: "We human beings of today want once again to seize what our forebears possessed—true religiosity."

In sum, the Austrian press stressed the religious content of the piece and extolled Hofmannsthal for it, while at the same time tolerating Reinhardt's direction. An interesting foil is to be found in some of the foreign press reactions—the festival had become of international interest by 1922—which held none of the pieties associated with the representation of new religious Austrian national consciousness. W. J. Turner in the *London Mercury* wrote that "the sheer power of the performance was such that one could

13. Article of Th. Mayrhofer, *Neue Freie Presse,* 4 August 1922. Josef Gregor, "Welttheater," *Neue Freie Presse,* 1 August 1922, pp. 1–3. Gregor (1888–1960, remembered mostly for service as Richard Strauss's librettist after the Nazi regime prevented him from working with Stefan Zweig in 1933) ultimately provided another example—like that of Heinz Kindermann—of a Catholic-conservative theater scholar and ideologue who easily made the transition to pro-Nazism after 1938. He served as director of the Austrian National Library's Theater Collection (*Theatersammlung*) during the Second World War. In 1943 he published *Das Theater des Volkes* (Vienna, 1943), which he dedicated to Baldur von Schirach, the leader of the Hitler youth and himself the son of a Weimar theater producer. The sequence of chapter titles indicates the ideological path of his sense of the theater as well as of his own intellectual biography: "The Theater of the Germanic Mythos"; "The Theater of the Christian Mythos"; "The Popular Theater [*Volkstheater*] of Austria [*Ostmark,* the Nazi term for Austria] as World-Theater [*Welttheater*]"; "The Viennese Rise of Austrian Popular Theater" [same terms]; "Transformations of Popular Theater and the Return to the Nation."

not help being gripped, although the play from an intellectual or poetical standpoint is absolute piffle." And Maurice Sterne in *Theatre Arts:* "It was neither the play nor the acting that . . . thousands of visitors . . . went to see. It was Reinhardt's production."[14]

Despite the generally positive and calm Austrian reception of the *Welttheater,* one controversy did make its way into the press. It concerned the role Hofmannsthal assigned to the beggar, the one element that Archbishop Rieder had originally considered sacrilegious. In the prologue of the play, as the various roles are being distributed among the "actors" assembled to perform the morality play-within-the-play, the actor assigned the role of the beggar (among the other roles of master, angel, second angel, world, curiosity, death, nay-sayer, bodiless souls, king, beauty, wisdom, rich man, and peasant) refuses to play his part, claiming that he wants a role with freedom associated with it. The angel silences him with the assertion that "the fruit of freedom is one: to do right." Rieder had considered some of the beggar's remarks blasphemous, and Hofmannsthal obliged by cutting a few of them.[15]

Many of the *Welttheater's* reviewers seized on the character of the beggar as the nucleus of the drama and its significance. The Social-Democratic *Salzburger Wacht* asserted in a front-page article on 14 August that the beggar equaled the proletariat, which in turn equaled Austria itself. Josef Gregor, in the *Salzburger Volksblatt* article cited above, echoed that national association. The beggar, he wrote, symbolizes the "return to the natural, and hence to redemption, salvation." These were not, however, the views of Raoul Auernheimer, who echoed his own negative 1920 reception of *Jedermann* in another *Neue Freie Presse* feuilleton article which concentrated on the issue of the beggar. Hofmannsthal's beggar, he wrote, is not to be viewed favorably as Calderón's had been. Hofmannsthal hadn't read Calderón carefully: "Calderón's beggar begs; Hofmannsthal's begs no more." Hofmannsthal's beggar was therefore to be seen in a negative light. His true identity:

14. *London Mercury* 7 (November 1922): 85–86; *Theater Arts* 7 (January 1923): 17–20.

15. Hofmannsthal, *Das Salzburger grosse Welttheater* (Frankfurt, 1977), pp. 23–24. Cynthia Walk, in her study of the play and its development, argues that Hofmannsthal made too many cuts and weakened the play (p. 67).

Anna Bahr-Mildenburg as World and Otto Pflanzl as Impertinence in *Das Salzburger grosse Welttheater*, 1922. Courtesy of the Max Reinhardt Archive, State University of New York, Binghamton, New York.

Bolshevism. He is the force that threatens a conservative, stable society: in the context of the drama, the "satisfied society," in Auernheimer's formulation, of king and peasant.

Cynthia Walk has at least tentatively supported Auernheimer's interpretation with the hypothesis that the later scene in which the beggar threatens to kill Wisdom with an ax reveals the political, revolutionary implications of his characterization.[16] The beggar is defeated, and sublimated into a passive religiosity. Walk corroborates this argument with the fact that after Hofmannsthal's death, the *Welttheater* became an increasingly significant political allegory for Reinhardt, with the revolutionary beggar perceived as a social threat. The beggar came to represent for Reinhardt the historical forces that tied together 1789 and 1933.[17] In 1937 Reinhardt went so far as to sketch a potential Hollywood production of the play, set in France in 1789, with the beggar cast as Danton, death as St. Just, the nay-sayer as Robespierre and Marat, the rich man as Robespierre, and of course the king and queen as Louis XVI and Marie Antoinette. Walk writes that Reinhardt's antirevolutionary stance was not attractive to potential American underwriters.[18]

The twelve performances of the *Welttheater* in the summer of 1922 rekindled the controversy over the high ticket prices, the problem referred to by Karl Kraus as "Ehre sei Gott in der Höhe der Preise"— "Praised be God up on high prices."[19] Tickets were priced at 60,000 kronen and were sold at up to 500,000 for premieres. The day of the *Welttheater* premiere, the Salzburg provincial government published a plea in the *Salzburger Chronik* under the heading "Festspiele und Volksnot"—"The Festival and the People's Distress"— decrying the shut-out of the local population from the festival. It stated: "That the local population can hardly attend the performances because of the difficult economic situation stands in dubious contradiction to the idea of a festival of the people."[20] As some measure of appeasement, public rehearsals of the *Welttheater* were given, for which tickets were sold for between 2,000 and 10,000

16. Walk, p. 129.
17. Reinhardt, letter to Graf Ledebour, July 1940, quoted in ibid., p. 141.
18. Ibid., pp. 146, 150–51.
19. Kraus, "Vom grossen Welttheaterschwindel," p. 5.
20. *Salzburger Chronik*, 12 August 1922, quoted in Walk, p. 117.

kronen. Finally, an additional performance was added for the local population only on 25 August.[21] Festival tickets were, however, not the only commodities selling at inflated prices; restaurant and hotel prices had also been raised, and the local press objected to this as well.[22]

At the height of the 1922 inflation, the Austrian krone was reduced to one fifteen-thousandth of its gold value. The currency was stabilized by the Geneva Protocols of October 1922, in which Chancellor Seipel negotiated a League of Nations credit of 650 million gold kronen. The schilling was introduced at this point, with a value of 10,000 old kronen. Yet although this long-term stabilization was crucial for the survival of the Salzburg Festival, it was not sufficient to prevent its short-term collapse.

III

The first full festival after that of 1922 was held in 1925, which became the year of the morality play. The season opened with a new staging of the *Welttheater*, performed this time in the festival hall, not in the Kollegienkirche. For very different reasons, this shift was a victory both for the Salzburg Catholic conservatives who objected to its performance at an altar and for Hofmannsthal himself, who had originally opted for the Felsenreitschule. There were two more morality plays performed that season: Karl Vollmöller's pantomime *Das Mirakel* and Max Mell's *Das Apostelspiel* (*Play of the Apostles*). Vollmöller's play, originally scheduled for 1924, was another vehicle for Reinhardt's religion-cloaked theatricality. Reinhardt had first staged it in London in 1911, the same year he had premiered Hofmannsthal's *Jedermann* in Berlin. In 1923 he took it on tour to New York, where its success stemmed from a coup brought off by Reinhardt and his assistant Rudolf Kommer: the engagement of the British actress and socialite Lady Diana Manners (Diana Cooper) for the role of the Madonna. Cooper re-

---

21. The rehearsals and the additional performance were announced in the *Salzburger Wacht* on 2 August and 23 August 1922, respectively.

22. "Die Festspielpreistreiberei," *Salzburger Wacht*, 11 August 1922.

peated the role—and assured the production's success—in Salzburg as well.

Although she gave no evidence of any personal religious connection with the drama in which she participated—or with the general religious ambience of the Salzburg morality plays—Diana Cooper's presence in Salzburg provided a catalyst for the strengthening of ties between the festival and the British conservative aristocracy, and hence for the reinforcement of Salzburg's conservative ideology. As the wife of Conservative party Home Secretary Duff Cooper, she belonged to a political and social circle that proved ultimately (unlike many British conservatives in the mid-1930s) anti-Nazi, though consistently anti-Semitic. In 1923, while the negotiations for the New York tour of *The Miracle* were going on, she wrote two effusive letters about the matter to "my dear Herr von Hofmannsthal"; when she first met him, in Salzburg in 1925, she wrote to her husband that he was "a perfect English scholar, a Jew I suppose."[23]

Max Mell was more of a major figure in his own right. A self-described Catholic conservative, he had been in fairly constant contact with Hofmannsthal since 1907 and had participated in the Österreichische Bibliothek project.[24] Like Hofmannsthal's, Mell's Catholic drama attempted to merge high baroque tradition with popular contemporary theater. His results have been compared to Hofmannsthal's in terms of the "mannerism that bedevils modern attempts to revive a 'popular' culture."[25] His participation in the 1925 festival transcended his own play; he objected to the transferral of the *Welttheater* to the festival hall, which he thought lacked the intimate and festive character of the original church setting.[26]

The reopening of the Salzburg Festival in 1925 with this string of plays made it clear enough that as a genre the morality play was

23. Diana Cooper, two letters to Hofmannsthal, unpublished, Frankfurt, Freies Deutsches Hochstift; letter to Duff Cooper, in *A Durable Fire: Letters of Duff and Diana Cooper*, ed. Artemis Cooper (New York, 1984), p. 196.

24. Their correspondence has been recently published: Hugo von Hofmannsthal and Max Mell, *Briefwechsel 1907–1929*, ed. Margret Dietrich and Heinz Kindermann (Heidelberg, 1982).

25. C. E. Williams, *The Broken Eagle* (New York, 1974), p. 10.

26. Quoted in Kindermann, Introduction to Hofmannsthal and Mell, *Briefwechsel*, p. 40.

and would remain at the center of the festival's dramatic repertory. Although this trend was just as much the result of Reinhardt's old-fashioned theatrical hocus-pocus as it was the result of conservative religious pretensions, it must also be remembered that Reinhardt was kept on—or, rather, tolerated—for his flattery of those pretensions and their alliance with conservative political ideology. As C. E. Williams has written about the antirevolutionary thrust of the *Welttheater:* "The festival audience in the early twenties would have comprised dignitaries of the Church, Catholic intellectuals, leading members of the main Government party, the Christian Socialists, visitors from the surrounding country areas of Salzburg, Upper Austria and Bavaria, and American and European tourists. A largely conservative audience witnessed the reiteration of a conservative social doctrine in the guise of religious edification."[27] The only thing wrong with this argument is the fact that in the Austrian political context of the 1920s, Catholicism and conservatism were clear companions, and furthermore that conservative social doctrine emerged through the ideology of the Catholic baroque, which in as well as beyond the morality plays operated in conjunction with religious culture but not solely as a function of it.

The tradition of the Salzburg morality play, with its union of conservative theatricality and religious conservatism, reached its height in Reinhardt's 1933 production of Goethe's *Faust, Part I.* There is no question that *Faust* differs in major respects from the dramas that preceded it. Beyond the obvious differences lies the essential incongruity (and arrogance) of including *Faust* in a trio of Catholic morality plays. The others had been conceived as morality plays; *Faust* was received, interpreted as one. The transformation of *Faust* from the poetic apogee of German Protestant romanticism to that of Austrian Catholic conservatism is one of the most interesting ideological processes of the Salzburg Festival enterprise.

Hofmannsthal paved the way for the inclusion of *Faust* among the Salzburg morality plays by already having infused *Jedermann* and infusing the *Welttheater* with numerous allusions to and leitmotivs from *Faust. Jedermann* is written in a Goethean tetrameter. It opens with a scenario and cast of characters that conflate the two

27. Williams, p. 28.

The Walpurgisnacht scene from Reinhardt's 1933 production of *Faust*.
Courtesy of the Max Reinhardt Archive, State University of New York,
Binghamton, New York.

property of every German schoolchild. Reinhardt thus realized the
ambition that Hofmannsthal had expressed sixteen years earlier
in his first projections for the Salzburg Festival and its repertory:
the rediscovery of *Faust* as moral entertainment for the *Volk*. In
Hans Conrad Fischer's terms, Reinhardt's *Faust* was a *Volksstück*—
a play for the people—with an emphasis on "soul" rather than on

"thought."[31] Complete disregard of Part II (which, it must be said, was the tradition in nineteenth-century Germany theatrical as well as pedagogical practice) allowed the end of Part I to be seen as the end of the drama: the final Christian redemption of Faust through the love of Gretchen (a sort of *Flying Dutchman* scenario), rather than a temporary moratorium on the perils of Faust the relentless striver.

Reinhardt's *Faust*, the reappropriation for the *Volk* of Germany's greatest drama, proved an ironic event. On 28 May, reacting to the Austrian Christian Social hostility to the Austrian Nazis, Hitler had imposed a 1,000 mark tax on all Germans crossing the Austrian border. The intended victim was Austrian tourism in general, but the Salzburg Festival, whose largest foreign constituent group had been its Bavarian neighbors, was hardest hit. The *Neue Freie Presse* calculated that there were 20 to 25 percent fewer festival visitors than there had been the year before. It also asserted that there was no noticeable percentage increase in French, English, Italian, or Czech visitors.[32] Nevertheless, a day before the premiere of *Faust*, the Vienna-based *Neue Freie Presse* ran an article that carried a hint of *Schadenfreude;* entitled "Salzburg as a Foreign City," it commented on the roster of foreign tourists there: "England dominates, then comes the 'F' [the license plate marking] of the French and the 'CS' of the Czechs, but also the noble signs of the Italians, Belgians, Swiss, Dutch, and Hungarians."[33]

IV

The performance of the first Mozart of any kind at the Salzburg Festival, an orchestra concert on 2 August 1921 conducted by Bernhard Paumgartner, had earned a review in the *Neue Freie Presse* (4 August) which noted the concert's international audience of "Germans and French, Americans and Japanese, British and Chi-

31. Fischer, p. 196.
32. "Steigender Besuch in der Festspielstadt Salzburg," *Neue Freie Presse,* 11 August 1933.
33. "Salzburg als Fremdenstadt," *Neue Freie Presse,* 16 August 1933.

nese, all united in adoration of the spirit of Mozart." The same paper's review of the Mozart operas the following year concluded with a similar thought, expressed in more explicit language: "The purpose of building in Salzburg a shrine to Austrian, German art is politically highly significant. It is a way for an impoverished Austria to prove that it is still rich in artistic impulses, artistic values, which it can give to the world. It proves that even the war was unable to destroy our idealistic efforts, that we are firmly committed at least in this aspect to hang on to our celebrated traditions and hence to document in this penetrating way the unshakable union of Austria and its old musical culture. . . . [These] performances signify in fact the fulfillment of this important program" (17 August 1922). Mozart had thus been successfully recruited as the kingpin of Salzburg's nationalist cosmopolitanism: the sharing of German culture with the outside world.

Of all the texts to be included in the Salzburg Festival repertory, the one that was intended, at least by Hofmannsthal, to be the most "overdetermined" was Mozart's *Don Giovanni*. It was possibly the greatest opera of Salzburg's greatest hero, and it was efficiently interpretable as a morality play. Mozart's consistent allowance of interpretive dramatic freedom perhaps reached its peak in *Don Giovanni*; every production of the opera faces the choice of interpreting the character of the Don as hero or antihero, as a metasocial animal who is the envy of all the lesser, more conventional characters who surround him or as a devil who learns his lesson in his ultimate and inevitable demise. Mozart and Da Ponte did provide an epilogue in which the six surviving characters speak to the audience about the moral implications of the drama just ended, but there is no indication that this fairly formal and restricted sextet speaks with Mozart's (or Da Ponte's) own moral voice. That is the decision of the individual production.

Don Giovanni as antihero (redeemed or unredeemed) is easily placed in the company of Jedermann and Faust. His roots in the Spanish baroque provide a tie (if one is sought) with that of Calderón's *Gran teatro del mundo*, the ultimate source—via Grillparzer—of the *Welttheater*. Yet the realization of Hofmannsthal's agenda for *Don Giovanni* would have required a new production, indigenous to Salzburg. There were no funds for this; the opera, sung in German and arbitrarily billed as *Don Juan* to differentiate it from the Italian-sung *Don Giovanni*, opened a series of four Mozart operas on 14 August 1922, all in productions of the Vienna State Opera, all directed by Hans Breuer, with scenery by Alfred Roller. This production had been done in Salzburg before, in a series of performances in 1906 commemorating the sesquicentennial of Mozart's birth, conducted by Gustav Mahler and staged by Lilli Lehmann, who at that time also sang the role of Donna Anna.

The remaining three operas, all sung in German, were *Così fan tutte*, *The Marriage of Figaro*, and *The Abduction from the Seraglio*. The last one, in a way a strange choice juxtaposed to the other "main" operas of Mozart in a group whose fourth member is *The Magic Flute*, is of particular significance. To a great extent a product of the "Turkomania" that controlled Viennese fashion in the eighteenth century (once the Turkish threat had evaporated), the *Abduction* is a comic evocation of the East-West problem. In that context its most interesting attribute is a surprise ending in which the Turkish pasha turns out to be an enlightened despot who is able to point to the barbarism of his former Western enemy (the father of the opera's romantic hero). Austria in 1922 had an Eastern problem: not the Turks but the Czechs and Hungarians. Performed in this climate, the *Abduction* offered a spirit of reconciliation similar to that of Hofmannsthal's *Arabella*, completed in 1928 (first performed in Salzburg in 1942).

Although the staging of Mozart in Salzburg did not alter much in the years before the Second World War, one significant change occurred when *Don Giovanni* and *The Marriage of Figaro* were performed in Italian, in 1934 and 1937, respectively. In the 1938 and 1939 seasons, as Hans Conrad Fischer has pointed out, this practice was kept up by the Nazi government as a gesture reinforcing the German-Italian alliance. During the war, *Figaro* was again performed in German; Italian versions of both operas returned in 1946. The reconciliatory gesture of the Nazis apparently did not extend into a period of war, when all nationalistic energy was recruited; the performance language of these operas was clearly a significant ideological issue.

The Salzburg Festival between 1938 and 1945 served Nazi ideology circumstantially as well as intentionally. Arturo Toscanini had conducted at the festival after refusing to return to Bayreuth in 1933; in 1936 and 1937 he conducted *Die Meistersinger von Nürnberg* in Salzburg. He did not return after the *Anschluss; Die Meistersinger,* conducted by Wilhelm Furtwängler, became the appropriately ideological operatic centerpiece of the 1938 festival. Yet it is a work from the Mozart canon, *The Magic Flute,* whose treatment in the war years says most about the path from baroque to National Socialist in the period after 1938 when the name Hofmannsthal could not be associated with the festival.

The Magic Flute was indeed Mozart's attempt to bridge the gap between high operatic culture and popular theater. As such, it is the only one of his late operas with a German text. Its basic plot—concerned with the rededication of a priestly order and the reassertion of good and calm over evil and chaos after a period of unexplained social and moral instability—proceeds less successfully than that of its twentieth-century heir, *Die Frau ohne Schatten.* Both operas juxtapose an aristocratic and an earthly romantic couple, but *The Magic Flute* does not bring them together in a shared moral dynamic and ultimately abandons the earthly couple when the aristocratic hero is inducted as the new leader of the social as well as the priestly order. Its ceremonious depiction of the priests, their leader Sarastro, and his successor Tamino can be said to conjure more the world of Monsalvat, Gurnemanz, and Parsifal than that of the Enlightenment.

The Magic Flute was thus a natural common denominator for Salzburg's Mozart and baroque cults and Third Reich *völkisch* ideology. It was mounted for the 1941 festival in commemoration of the sesquicentennial of Mozart's death. Around this enterprise an aesthetic and ideological dispute developed between two reigning Salzburg conductors, Clemens Krauss and Karl Böhm. Each had conducted a much publicized new production of *The Magic Flute* in 1940—Krauss in Munich and Böhm in Dresden. In the winter of 1941, a Berlin production of the work, conducted by Herbert von Karajan and staged by Gustav Gründgens and Traugott Müller, had attempted to modernize the opera through the use of stylized sets and costumes. The production traveled to Vienna and was to be used in Salzburg, until Karl Böhm vehemently protested this modernizing trend, especially in the context of a commemorative production. Böhm invited his own directors—the conservative Heinz Arnold and Ludwig Sievert. Clemens Krauss sympathized with Gründgens. The result: two successive Salzburg productions, despite the cost and trouble, the first one in 1941, conducted by Böhm, staged by Arnold with sets by Sievert, the second in 1943, conducted and directed (in the general style of Gründgens) by Krauss.[34]

The Böhm/Arnold/Sievert production attempted to rediscover the fairy-tale innocence of the text and score and jettisoned all the Egyptian and masonic elements, which had the potential for too obvious political referentiality. Krauss, on the other hand, tried as Gründgens had to emphasize the opera's roots in popular folk theater and hence stressed the artificiality of theatrical techniques: visible scene changes, thunder machines, and so on. Yet, interestingly enough, by the time Krauss's *Magic Flute* got to Salzburg in 1943, it had changed so much from the 1940 Munich production that it no longer appeared drastically different from Böhm's. Sarastro, the priest of Isis and enlightened despot, was once again portrayed in the conventional manner as a wise old man. In 1940, in a production that staged the entire opera as a solar myth about the formation of a new race, Krauss had portrayed Sarastro as the leader of a cult of Apollo, young, beardless, heroic, carrying a spear and a shield.[35]

Two points can be drawn, I think, from this series of episodes. First, Mozart can become and has become a potential source for ideological interpretation and dispute, a fate usually associated with Wagner. That the Mozart operas are no doubt more distant than those of Wagner from the tenets preached by ideologically minded interpreters did not prevent those interpreters from finding in those operas exactly what they were looking for. The claim of *The Magic Flute* is the harmonization of high and low music and culture into a vision of Enlightenment utopia, a claim that accrues added reso-

---

34. Gudrun Letz, "Die Mozart-Inszenierungen bei den Salzburger Festspielen" (diss., University of Vienna, 1963), pp. 133–48; Hans Jaklitsch, "Verzeichnis der Werke und der Künstler des Theaters und der Musik bei den Salzburger Festspielen 1920–1982," in Josef Kaut, *Die Salzburger Festspiele*, pp. 241–499.

35. Letz, pp. 143, 146.

nance in the context of its date—1791, just after the death of Joseph II, the most enlightened Habsburg despot and Mozart's patron.[36] But the problems of enlightened despotism notwithstanding, the Enlightenment principle of the overcoming of social difference is different from the ideological principle of the denial of social difference. As my comments on the plot of *The Magic Flute* suggest, which of these principles is the more applicable to this work is a matter of contestation. Even if *The Magic Flute* is defended as a genuine paean to an Enlightenment ideal of the overcoming of social difference, nineteenth-century *völkisch* ideology, which is grounded precisely in the denial of social difference (the assertion of the category of the *Volk* over that of the masses), easily absorbs and appropriates the opera's ideological message. The Salzburg Festival ideology had from the beginning relied on the assertion of a cohesive social body—although its principle of cohesion was baroque and not *völkisch*—and in the context of the wartime, Nazi-controlled festival, *The Magic Flute* became an ideal text with which to assert the convergence of Austria and Germany through the assertion of the harmony of baroque and *völkisch* social ideologies. The passage from baroque to *völkisch* totalities is a fluid one.

It follows, then, that either of the choices of a representational style for *The Magic Flute* and its ideology, whether the *völkisch*

36. The character of the High Priest Sarastro can be described as an enlightened despot and thus as a personification of the problems and contradictions of some Enlightenment political thinking. See Isaiah Berlin's essay "Two Concepts of Liberty": Section V, "The Temple of Sarastro," in *Four Essays on Liberty* (Oxford, 1969), pp. 145–54. Perhaps the best known example of a modern critical acceptance of *The Magic Flute* as a celebration of the Enlightenment is Theodor Adorno's comment in his essay "On the Fetish Character in Music and the Regression of Listening": "*The Magic Flute*, in which the utopia of the Enlightenment and the pleasure of a light comic opera song precisely coincide, is a moment by itself. After *The Magic Flute* it was never again possible to force serious and light music together." See Andrew Arato and Eike Gebhardt, eds., *The Essential Frankfurt School Reader* (New York, 1982), pp. 270–99; p. 273. But Adorno's passing remarks on *The Magic Flute* are themselves compromised by his general argument that high culture ("serious music") is morally superior to low culture ("light music") for its insistence on the listener's perception of the aesthetic whole rather than fetishistic enjoyment of the individual moment. In addition to ignoring the issue of the commodification of "serious music," Adorno seems to ignore the political implications of this aesthetic ideology of totality, implications that speak precisely to the problems of *The Magic Flute* and its political as well as musical engagement of the Enlightenment.

militarism of Gründgens and Krauss or the Burgtheater innocence
of Sievert and Böhm, would have served—and ultimately did
serve—the relevant ideological agenda. Although Clemens Krauss,
who had grafted onto his 1940 Munich *Magic Flute* a Stefan
Georgean warrior aesthetic—strictly compatible with the aesthetic
inclinations of the Third Reich—considerably toned down his conception for the Salzburg production of 1943, the resulting transformation of Sarastro from warrior-king to wise old counsel is less
significant that it might appear. Perhaps the change was inspired
by Salzburg's aura of sacred innocence, to which Krauss, who as
well as being an early-declared Nazi was an illegitimate member of
the Habsburg line, was especially sensitive.[37] Nonetheless, func-
tionally his 1943 Salzburg *Magic Flute* played the same role as its
opposing alternatives in the final descent of the Salzburg Festival
and official German and Austrian culture into kitsch.[38]

37. Krauss had been called to the Berlin Opera by Göring in 1935 to replace the
retiring Wilhelm Furtwängler. This was in part a political move, as Krauss's Nazi
affiliations were illegal in Austria and thus exposed him to danger. When he left
Vienna in November 1935 his Vienna apartment was searched by police. For more
on this and an excellent general account of musical life in the Third Reich, see Fred
K. Prieberg, *Musik im NS-Staat* (Frankfurt, 1982), p. 68.

38. The concept of kitsch as a mode of representation that is to be condemned
on intersecting criteria of aesthetic inferiority and ethical as well as political evil was
developed most profoundly by Hermann Broch. See "Einige Bemerkungen zum
Problem des Kitsches," in *Schriften zur Literatur 2*, ed. P. M. Lützeler (Frankfurt,
1975), pp. 158–73; also, *Hugo von Hofmannsthal and His Time*, passim.

CONCLUSION

Transformations of
the Baroque

THE history of the Salzburg Festival and of its meaning shows the simultaneity of cultural and representational intricacy with the reductive power of ideology. The presentation of that simultaneity has been the aim of the preceding seven chapters. As a paradigm for the paths of ideology and representation in Austria in the disjointed, unsuccessful, and therefore crucial First Republic—the period whose prime significance will remain that of transition from empire to "Austrofascism" and then Nazism—the festival also bears witness to the victory of ideology and brutal simplicity over critical culture and representational intricacy. I do not mean to suggest that after 1938 no Austrian resistance—political or cultural—to Nazism existed, or that culture in the Nazi period was devoid of conflict and contestation. But official Nazi culture was devoid of these things; the Salzburg Festival, existing in the space of official culture, passed into the service of Nazi ideology.

The modern history of the censorship of cultural contestation, intricacy, and diversity ends in the history of barbarism. In such a context there is only limited room for the identification of ambiguity. Thus even though cultural barbarism itself involves precisely the denial of ambiguity, such barbarism must be identified with clear strokes; the destruction of cultural ambiguity cannot be seen as an ambiguous process. The year 1938 marks for Austria a point of transition into an era in which the identification of absolutes is necessary, and even if the categories of evil and good remain elusive to the analytical observer, the categories of complicity and noncomplicity must be insisted upon if historical meaning is to be preserved at all. It is therefore obscene to rationalize evil in terms of a putative cultural or national Austrian exceptionalism, itself dependent on an assertion of cultural, national, or indeed ethical ambiguity.

As a paradigm, then, the Salzburg Festival shows the simultaneity of ideology and representation but also that of the simplification and brutalization both of ideology and of aesthetic production *within* an increasingly complicated and overdetermined process of cultural representation. As we have seen, the festival, as well as its cultural, intellectual, and political contexts, was both cosmopolitan and nationalistic, of the enlightenment and against it, both baroque and, ultimately, *völkisch*, both Catholic and Jewish. But the resulting picture is not one of cultural richness that was then destroyed from without in 1938, but instead, one in which intricacy and ambiguity were undermined from the inside and from the beginning by the drive to ideology. It is perhaps the most delicate figure of Austrian letters who bears the most responsibility for this process of cultural simplification. Hofmannsthal deliberately fashioned himself into an ideologue, and as a result his own thinking and work suffered first. If his intellectual biography indeed proceeds according to a paradigmatic conflict between critical modernism and ideological conservatism, between the aesthetic modes of symbolic indeterminacy and allegorical rigidity, his post-1914 commitments generated the equally paradigmatic defeat of the various forms of modernism he had explored.

Hofmannsthal therefore helped produce the ideological climate that ultimately interpreted his own genealogical ambiguity as a prime example of the kind of cultural ambiguity ("decadence," in the Nazi vocabulary) that was to be destroyed. Austrian Catholic conservatism is not Nazism, and Hofmannsthal, had he not died in 1929, would almost certainly have proved, like his fellow Catholic conservative Franz Rehrl, to be horrified at the *Anschluss*. Moreover, that speculation implies no necessary reference to his Jewish heritage. Whether he would have forced himself to rethink his Austrian ideology remains quite another matter. Max Reinhardt, who lived to be persecuted and exiled by the Austrian Nazis (he died in New York in 1943), shows no evidence of having forced himself to do so. His miracle plays—including those he staged in the United States well into his exile—show an unshattered faith in theatricality and totality. The drive to cultural totality and the resistance to fragmentation and ambiguity which Hofmannsthal and Reinhardt, despite their enormous differences, both pursued so naively emerges as the common denominator between the baroque and the fascist, between the Salzburg great world theater (the text and the historical process) and the political theater of the Nuremberg Rally of September 1934.

The opposition between a victorious politicized aesthetic ideology and a submerged critical modernism indeed substantiates Walter Benjamin's renowned distinction between the aestheticization of the political and the politicization of the aesthetic. When the first gained control, the second became the principle of critical confrontation with it and must remain the principle of a critical historiography that seeks to understand the interplay of political and aesthetic ideology. The exile of ambiguity and critical modernism from Austria entailed the literal exile of many surviving intellectuals. Hermann Broch and Arnold Schönberg, to name only two whose critical modernisms emerged in intimate confrontation with the modern Austrian baroque, died in American exile. During their exile, both continued to advance their critical and aesthetic programs in the spirit of a continuing ethical obsession with European political reality. In both these cases a sensitivity to the problem of the ideology of totality and the implications in that direction of an ideology of aestheticism produced a massive self-consciousness about the very possibility of valid aesthetic representation. Broch reacted to this dilemma by trying repeatedly to abandon aesthetic production in favor of rationalistic social science; Schönberg by the repeated engagement of Old Testament themes.

Yet perhaps the most profound continuing critical engagement with the combined problematics and ideologies of the baroque, of totality, and of political aestheticism was that of Walter Benjamin himself in the years between 1924 and his death in 1940. I shall therefore conclude with a short consideration of some of Benjamin's specifically relevant analytical and historiographical principles for an indication, literally, of a way out of the ideology of the baroque.

In 1924 the cultural statesman Hugo von Hofmannsthal extended his patronage to the unknown Benjamin, publishing the latter's analytical essay on Goethe's novel *Elective Affinities* in two issues (April 1924 and January 1925) of the literary journal he controlled, *Neue deutsche Beiträge*. This gesture is recognized by Benjamin's biographers as a crucial show of support for the thirty-two-year-old floundering intellectual who was still financially dependent on his parents.[1] But an additional perspective is necessary; we need to explore the intellectual importance of Hofmannsthal's journal and its ideology, and hence of Hofmannsthal's own engagement with the baroque, for the emerging critical work of Benjamin, in particular his *Ursprung des deutschen Trauerspiels*, written between May 1924 and April 1925.[2]

Hofmannsthal's journal, the first issue of which appeared in 1922, carried the same ideological agenda as the Salzburg Festival and other contemporaneous literary enterprises, such as the Österreichische Bibliothek. Hofmannsthal described the agenda himself in two editorial notes; the first referred to the "spiritual possession of the nation" (*zum geistigen Besitz der Nation*), the second to the desired condition where "in the loneliest hour of the spirit the power of oppressive events subsides and a loving and hoping knowledge spreads over our consciousness."[3] This "loving and hoping knowledge" was to be that of a reconstituted aestheticism, which for Hofmannsthal implied the conservative program he later adumbrated in the 1927 address "Writing as the Spiritual Space of the Nation." The form that such aestheticism usually took was the affirmation of the Austrian baroque, and the majority of the pieces published in the *Neue deutsche Beiträge* supported this position explicitly. Thus in the first number Hofmannsthal explicitly juxtaposed the text of his brand new *Salzburger grosses Welttheater* with

1. See Gershom Scholem, *Walter Benjamin: Die Geschichte einer Freundschaft* (Frankfurt, 1975), pp. 183–85; Werner Fuld, *Walter Benjamin: Zwischen den Stühlen* (Frankfurt, 1981), pp. 148–64; Bernd Witte, *Walter Benjamin—Der Intellektuelle als Kritiker: Untersuchungen zu seinem Frühwerk* (Stuttgart, 1976), pp. 99–106.

2. *The Origin of German Tragic Drama*, trans. John Osborne (London, 1977). The rendering of "Trauerspiel" as "Tragic Drama" is sensible but problematic, as will be discussed below.

3. Foreword (Vorwort), *Neue deutsche Beiträge*, 1, no. 1 (July 1922): 4; Editorial Note (Anmerkung des Herausgebers), *Neue deutsche Beiträge* 1, no. 3 (July 1923): 123.

an essay by the critic Florens Christian Rang on the "northern German Protestant spirit" (Hofmannsthal's phrase) of Goethe's *Selige Sehnsucht*. The second number included the first two acts of Hofmannsthal's Calderón *Tower* as well as an essay by Rudolf Kassner, "The Community of God and the Individual." A later volume printed the text of Max Mell's *Play of the Apostles*.[4]

Hofmannsthal presumably read Benjamin's *Elective Affinities* essay as sharing his own aestheticist agenda. Bernd Witte has in fact suggested that such a reading was legitimate, as Benjamin did indeed propose a model of literary criticism as an instrument for the social and the political reengagement of the German *Bildungsbürgertum*.[5] Benjamin opened his essay by distinguishing between the enterprise of philology as the search for factual content (*Sachgehalt*) and his own enterprise of criticism as the search for truth content (*Wahrheitsgehalt*).[6] Such a position can be read—as Hofmannsthal probably read it—to imply a conservative cultural program, but it does not.

Although Benjamin was deeply grateful to Hofmannsthal and to the *Neue deutsche Beiträge* for publishing his essay, he nonetheless reacted critically to the journal's ongoing celebration of and rededication to baroque culture and ideology. The critical treatment of baroque theatricality that he developed at this time and published as *Ursprung des deutschen Trauerspiels* must be seen to have emerged in critical confrontation with the baroque ideology of Hofmannsthal and his intellectual circle.

The term "Trauerspiel" is most literally translated as "play of mourning." For Benjamin, this baroque genre distinguishes itself from tragedy by adhering to a historical rather than a mythical cosmology. The element of mourning for the past implied by this baroque discourse is thus seen to refer to history as an ongoing process of dissipation. This vision of baroque culture thus implies historical dissipation rather than mythical (or mythhistorical) totality. Furthermore, unlike tragedy, which for Benjamin is a system of representation that does not require an audience, *Trauer*, as

4. See Witte, pp. 102, 213.
5. Ibid., p. 101.
6. Benjamin, "Goethes Wahlverwandtschaften," in *Gesammelte Schriften*, ed. Rolf Tiedemann and Hermann Schweppenhäuser (Frankfurt, 1980), I:1, p. 125.

George Steiner has suggested, "signifies sorrow, lament, the ceremonies and memorabilia of grief. Lament and ceremonial demand
audience."[7] The ritual, ceremonial context of *Trauerspiel* is that of
the court. For Benjamin, the process of allegorization in which
baroque drama engages the cosmos takes place within a public,
communicative appropriation of a divine model of representation—
the world theater imitates the world—through which the earthly
dissipation of that very model is represented and commemorated.
Baroque drama for Benjamin implies the recognition of historical
reality as the dissipation of imagined models. It is important to note
that the actual plays he analyzes are northern German, Protestant
works that emerged in a context entirely different from the affirma-
tive world of the Austrian Catholic baroque.

Despite his clear recognition of the cultural and representational
differences between Protestant and Catholic baroque, Benjamin
saw the tradition of *Trauerspiel* as a genre shared by both. Thus he
read and reviewed Hofmannsthal's "*Trauerspiel* in five acts," *The
Tower* (1925), as a modern invocation of the same genre he had
studied. Before doing so, however, he wrote to Gershom Scholem,
"I haven't read the thing yet. My private judgment has remained
constant from the beginning."[8] Recent forays into the baroque by
Hofmannsthal and his colleagues, published in the *Neue deutsche
Beiträge*, had apparently led Benjamin to expect to dislike the work;
yet his review, which appeared in the journal *Literarische Welt* in
April 1926, suggests a change of opinion. It recognizes the drama
that had resulted from Hofmannsthal's most tortuous creative process as a legitimate and powerful invocation of the *Trauerspiel* genre.

---

7. George Steiner, Introduction to Benjamin, *The Origin of German Tragic Drama*,
p. 17.

8. Scholem, p. 159. The letter from which Scholem quotes here is almost certainly
that of 6 April 1925. The version of that letter published in the edition of Benjamin's
letters edited by Scholem and Theodor Adorno mentions that "Hofmannsthal asked
for a private, personal statement of opinion on the *Tower*, a reworking of Calderón's
Life Is a Dream that he has produced; I plan to fulfill this task in a journalistic context.
[The publishing house] Rowohlt has come out with a new review for literary criticism
and requests my ongoing participation; I am thinking of sending them a review of
The Tower." At this point the edited text of Benjamin's letter shows an ellipsis; the
comment that Scholem reproduced was apparently omitted. See Benjamin, *Briefe*,
ed. Gershom Scholem and Theodor Adorno (Frankfurt, 1978), p. 377.

The review begins: "With his new *Trauerspiel The Tower* Hofmanns-thal harks back to the problematic of the baroque."[9] After a section in support of the legitimacy of modern adaptations of classical drama, Benjamin summarizes Calderón's oedipal problematic of the prince imprisoned in a tower after a prophecy of patricide/regicide. At the narrative and thematic center of Calderón's play is the dream in which the prince perceives heavenly will as the explaining and justi-fying power that controls his miserable earthly fate. By using the dream as a narrative totality that mediates between the world and God, Calderón infuses into his drama, writes Benjamin, "total, high-est baroque tension." Hofmannsthal's modern reworking of the play involves the revaluation of the meaning of dreams. Like the baroque in general, the dream in the modern world no longer mediates be-tween the world and the divine, but refers only to the world itself. Benjamin concludes: "The old *Trauerspiel* was grounded between creature (*Kreatur*) and Christ. The perfect prince exists at the latter's crowned heights. Where Calderón's Christian optimism placed him, the truthfulness of the new author's demise reveals itself. Sigismund [Hofmannsthal's prince] perishes. The demonic powers of the tower become his Lord. Dreams emerge from the earth and a Christian heaven has long forsaken them. . . . In the spirit of *Trauerspiel* the poet has stripped the romantic of its substance and we are thus con-fronted with the most severe tenets of German drama."

In *The Tower* Benjamin thus found a mirror of his own sense of baroque drama as a ritualistic commemoration of historical dissipa-tion. (In the review he called ritual the "pre-tragic" situation that "leaps over the polarity of deed and word.") Benjamin retained this idea of the baroque as he retained his pessimistic sense of history. Hofmannsthal, however, did not have the critical intransigence, the courage, or the historical pessimism to do either. The baroque engagement of *The Tower* dissipated into the ideology of *Jedermann*, *Das Salzburger grosse Welttheater*, and the Salzburg Festival itself. (Hofmannsthal reworked the 1925 version of *The Tower* at Max Reinhardt's encouragement, into the more streamlined and "play-

---

9. Benjamin, "Hugo von Hofmannsthal, *Der Turm. Ein Trauerspiel in fünf Aufzügen* (München: Verlag der Bremer Presse 1925)," *Gesammelte Werke III*, pp. 29–33. Of note is that Hofmannsthal used the term "Trauerspiel."

able" version of 1927.[10] Benjamin's pessimism, on the other hand, was clearly a high price to pay for critical vision. As Peter Szondi wrote, "A knowledge of ruin obstructed Benjamin's view into the future and allowed him to see future events only in those instances where they had already moved into the past. This ruin is the ruin of his age."[11]

Yet it is this very sense of history as a dissipatory and fragmented process that led Benjamin in and after the *Trauerspiel* study to work out a critique of totality and of aestheticism that slowly developed (more because of than in spite of its fragmentary character) into one of this century's most powerful and viable critical theories of the history of modernity. In his uncompleted and to a great extent unformed "Arcades Project" (*Das Passagen-Werk*), much of it compiled in exile in Paris, Benjamin turned to Second Empire France to discover the dynamics of the rise and constitution of modernity.[12] At the same time he maintained his engagement with the history of German aesthetic criticism and thus pursued the dual path of escaping German intellectual culture while at the same time rescuing its critical power.[13]

For example, the essay "The Work of Art in the Age of Its Technical Reproducibility" (1936) includes a critique of baroque ideology on two levels. Most generally, its argument for the desacralization of aesthetic experience can be read as a polemic against the ideology of aestheticism, in other words against the ideological application to social process of criteria of aesthetic form. This polemic is reinforced by the essay's renowned final passage: "Humanity, in the time of Homer an object of display for the Olympian Gods, has now become one for itself. Its self-alienation has reached the degree where it allows itself to experience its own destruction as the highest form of aesthetic pleasure. This is the condition of the aestheticization of

10. See Alfred Schwarz, Introduction to Hugo von Hofmannsthal, *Three Plays* (Detroit, 1966), p. 39.

11. Peter Szondi, "Hope in the Past: On Walter Benjamin," in *On Textual Understanding and Other Essays*, trans. Harvey Mendelsohn (Minneapolis, 1986), p. 155.

12. Walter Benjamin, *Das Passagen-Werk*, ed. Rolf Tiedemann (Frankfurt, 1982); subsequently published as volume 6 of a new edition of the *Gesammelte Schriften*.

13. I am planning an analysis of this critical, historical agenda in a future project currently entitled "Walter Benjamin's Paris: Toward a Negative Aesthetics of History."

politics, as practiced by fascism. Communism answers with the politicization of art."[14] More specifically, Benjamin may have shaped his argument in part as a response to Hofmannsthal. Werner Fuld has suggested that a 1921 essay of Hofmannsthal's on film culture may be a source for some of Benjamin's formulations in this essay. Hofmannsthal had argued in "The Ersatz for Dreams" that mass audiences flock to silent films to escape their own alienation, as the medium of the silent film offers a nonlinguistic aesthetic haven that transcends—and thereby helps the public to transcend—everyday life.[15] If Hofmannsthal's essay is a source, it is as a foil; his argument refers to (silent) film as the provider of what Benjamin later referred to in "The Work of Art" as the aura, that precise aspect of the sacralization of aesthetic experience which, for Benjamin, is productively undermined by technically reproduced art.

Thus a larger perspective on the work of Benjamin and Hofmannsthal emphasizes the widening polarity of the modernist historical critic and the conservative ideologue, but it does not diminish the importance for both thinkers of critical engagement with the baroque and its ideology of theatricality and totality that had provided their strongest communicative bond. Even after Hofmannsthal's death, Benjamin retained a profound sympathy for him, even as Hofmannsthal's problematic (and Benjamin's own of the 1920s) receded—dissipated—more and more into the past. Sympathy and distance appear together in a series of letters that Benjamin wrote from Paris to Theodor and Gretel Adorno in late 1939 and 1940, with reference to Adorno's intention to prepare an edition of the correspondence between Hofmannsthal and Stefan George. One of these letters includes a sentence that embodies the perspective of an exiled German critical modernism: "il paraît qu'un millésime nous sépare des temps où ces lettres (que je ne connais pas encore) ont été échangées."[16]

---

14. Benjamin, "Das Kunstwerk im Zeitalter seiner technischen Reproduzierbarkeit," *Gesammelte Werke* I:2, pp. 431–69; 471–508 (there are two versions; the cited passage is identical in both). The translations of the title and passage are my own.

15. Fuld, p. 273.

16. "It seems as though a millennium separates us from the time those letters (which I do not yet know) were written." The entire letter is in French. Benjamin, *Briefe*, p. 837.

Salzburg Festival
Repertory, 1920–1944

1920

Hofmannsthal, *Jedermann*

1921

Hofmannsthal, *Jedermann*
Mozart, *Bastien und Bastienne*

1922

Hofmannsthal, *Das Salzburger grosse
Welttheater*
Mozart, *Don Juan* (in German)
Mozart, *Così fan tutte*
Mozart, *Die Hochzeit des Figaro*
Mozart, *Die Entführung aus dem Serail*

1923

Molière, *Der eingebildete Kranke*

1924

(No festival)

1925

Hofmannsthal, *Das Salzburger grosse
Welttheater*

Vollmöller, *Das Mirakel*
Mell, *Das Apostelspiel*
Mozart, *Don Juan* (in German)
Mozart, *Die Hochzeit des Figaro*
Donizetti, *Don Pasquale*
Muffat, *Das Leben hängt an einem Faden*
(marionette show)
Hofmannsthal, *Die grüne Flöte* (ballet-
pantomime to music of Mozart)

1926

Hofmannsthal, *Jedermann*
Goldoni, *Der Diener zweier Herren*
Gozzi/Vollmöller, *Turandot*
Mozart, *Die Entführung aus dem Serail*
Mozart, *Don Juan* (in German)
J. Strauss, *Die Fledermaus*
R. Strauss, *Ariadne auf Naxos*
Gluck, *Don Juan*
Pergolesi, *La serva padrona*
Mozart, *Les petits riens*

1927

Hofmannsthal, *Jedermann*
Shakespeare, *Ein Sommernachtstraum*
Schiller, *Kabale und Liebe*
Mozart, *Die Hochzeit des Figaro*

Taken from Hans Jaklitsch, "Verzeichnis der Werke und der Künstler des Theaters und der Musik bei den Salzburger Festspielen, 1920–1981," in Josef Kaut, *Die Salzburger Festspiele* (Salzburg, 1982), pp. 241–469. Included here are opera and theater performances; excluded are orchestral and chamber concerts, and recitals.

Mozart, *Don Juan* (in German)
Beethoven, *Fidelio*

1928

Hofmannsthal, *Jedermann*
Goethe, *Iphigenie auf Tauris*
Schiller, *Die Räuber*
Billinger, *Das Perchtenspiel*
Mozart, *Così fan tutte*
Mozart, *Die Zauberflöte*
Beethoven, *Fidelio*

1929

Hofmannsthal, *Jedermann*
Mozart, *Don Juan* (in German)
Beethoven, *Fidelio*
R. Strauss, *Der Rosenkavalier*

1930

Hofmannsthal, *Jedermann*
Schiller, *Kabale und Liebe*
Goldoni, *Der Diener zweier Herren*
Maugham, *Victoria*
R. Strauss, *Der Rosenkavalier*
Mozart, *Don Juan* (in German)
Mozart, *Die Hochzeit des Figaro*
Beethoven, *Fidelio*
Donizetti, *Don Pasquale*
Gluck, *Iphigenie in Aulis*

1931

Hofmannsthal, *Jedermann*
Goldoni, *Der Diener zweier Herren*
Hofmannsthal, *Der Schwierige*
Goethe, *Stella*
R. Strauss, *Der Rosenkavalier*
Mozart, *Don Juan* (in German)
Mozart, *Die Hochzeit des Figaro*
Mozart, *Die Zauberflöte*
Mozart, *Die Entführung aus dem Serail*
Mozart, *Così fan tutte*
Gluck, *Orpheus und Eurydike*
Beethoven, *Fidelio*
Rossini, *Il barbiere di Siviglia*
Donizetti, *Don Pasquale*

Cimarosa, *Il matrimonio segreto*

1932

Hofmannsthal, *Jedermann*
R. Strauss, *Der Rosenkavalier*
Mozart, *Die Entführung aus dem Serail*
Gluck, *Orpheus und Eurydike*
Mozart, *Così fan tutte*
Mozart, *Die Zauberflöte*
Weber, *Oberon*
Mozart, *Die Hochzeit des Figaro*
R. Strauss, *Die Frau ohne Schatten*
Beethoven, *Fidelio*

1933

Hofmannsthal, *Jedermann*
Goethe, *Faust* (Part I)
Beethoven, *Fidelio*
Gluck, *Orpheus und Eurydike*
R. Strauss, *Der Rosenkavalier*
Mozart, *Die Hochzeit des Figaro*
Wagner, *Tristan und Isolde*
Mozart, *Così fan tutte*
Weber, *Oberon*
Mozart, *Die Zauberflöte*
R. Strauss, *Die ägyptische Helena*
R. Strauss, *Die Frau ohne Schatten*

1934

Hofmannsthal, *Jedermann*
Goethe, *Faust* (Part I)
Beethoven, *Fidelio*
Wagner, *Tristan und Isolde*
R. Strauss, *Der Rosenkavalier*
Mozart, *Die Hochzeit des Figaro*
Mozart, *Don Giovanni* (in Italian)
R. Strauss, *Die ägyptische Helena*
Weber, *Oberon*
R. Strauss, *Elektra*
Mozart, *Così fan tutte*

1935

Hofmannsthal, *Jedermann*
Goethe, *Faust* (Part I)
Wagner, *Tristan und Isolde*

Verdi, *Falstaff*
R. Strauss, *Der Rosenkavalier*
Mozart, *Don Giovanni* (in Italian)
Mozart, *Così fan tutte*
Beethoven, *Fidelio*
Mozart, *Die Entführung aus dem Serail*
Mozart, *Die Hochzeit des Figaro*

1936

Hofmannsthal, *Jedermann*
Goethe, *Faust* (Part I)
Beethoven, *Fidelio*
Mozart, *Die Hochzeit des Figaro*
Mozart, *Don Giovanni* (in Italian)
Mozart, *Così fan tutte*
Verdi, *Falstaff*
Gluck, *Orpheus und Eurydike*
Wagner, *Die Meistersinger von Nürnberg*
Wolf, *Der Corregidor*
Wagner, *Tristan und Isolde*

1937

Hofmannsthal, *Jedermann*
Goethe, *Faust* (Part I)
Beethoven, *Fidelio*
Verdi, *Falstaff*
R. Strauss, *Der Rosenkavalier*
Mozart, *Die Zauberflöte*
Gluck, *Orpheus und Eurydike*
Mozart, *Don Giovanni* (in Italian)
Wagner, *Die Meistersinger von Nürnberg*
R. Strauss, *Elektra*
Mozart, *Le nozze di Figaro* (in Italian)
Weber, *Euryanthe*

1938

Kleist, *Amphitryon*
Goethe, *Egmont*
Wagner, *Die Meistersinger von Nürnberg*
Mozart, *Don Giovanni* (in Italian)
R. Strauss, *Der Rosenkavalier*
Wagner, *Tannhäuser*
Beethoven, *Fidelio*
Mozart, *Le nozze di Figaro* (in Italian)
Verdi, *Falstaff*

1939

Shakespeare, *Viel Lärm um nichts*
Molière, *Der Bürger als Edelmann*
R. Strauss, *Der Rosenkavalier*
Weber, *Der Freischütz*
Verdi, *Falstaff*
Mozart, *Die Entführung aus dem Serail*
Mozart, *Don Giovanni* (in Italian)
Mozart, *Le nozze di Figaro* (in Italian)
Rossini, *Il barbiere di Siviglia*

1940

Ten orchestral and chamber concerts

1941

Shakespeare, *Viel Lärm um nichts*
Mozart, *Die Zauberflöte*
R. Strauss, *Der Rosenkavalier*
Mozart, *Die Hochzeit des Figaro*
Mozart, *Don Juan* (in German)

1942

Goethe, *Iphigenie auf Tauris*
Nestroy, *Einen Jux will er sich machen*
Mozart, *Die Hochzeit des Figaro*
R. Strauss, *Arabella*

1943

Goethe, *Iphigenie auf Tauris*
Anzengruber, *Der G'wissenswurm*
Anzengruber, *Der Meineidbauer*
Mozart, *Die Zauberflöte*
R. Strauss, *Arabella*

1944

(planned season, canceled by
Goebbels)
Lessing, *Emilia Galotti*
Nestroy, *Lumpazivagabundis*
Mozart, *Così fan tutte*
Mozart, *Die Zauberflöte*
R. Strauss, *Die Liebe der Danae*

Bibliography

Archival Sources

Archiv des Musikvereins, Vienna
Deutsches Literaturarchiv, Marbach
    Hofmannsthal Nachlass
    Hofmannsthal-Pannwitz letters
Festspielhausarchiv, Salzburg
Freies Deutsches Hochstift, Frankfurt
    Hofmannsthal Archiv
Konsistorialarchiv, Salzburg
Landesarchiv, Salzburg
Theatersammlung, Österreichische Nationalbibliothek,
    Vienna
    Hermann Bahr Nachlass

Books and Articles

Adler, Gusti. *Aber vergessen Sie nicht die chinesischen Nachtigallen: Erinnerungen an Max Reinhardt*. Munich: Albert Langen, 1980.
Althaus, Horst. *Zwischen Monarchie und Republik*. Munich: Wilhelm Fink, 1976.
Anstett, Jean-Jacques. "Les idées sociales de Hugo von Hofmannsthal." *Revue germanique* 8, no. 22 (1931): 15–24.
Ara, Angelo, and Claudio Magris. *Trieste: Un identità di frontiera*. Turin: Einaudi, 1982.
Aspetsberger, Friedbert. "Hofmannsthal und D'Annunzio: Formen des späten Historismus." *Hofmannsthal Forschungen* 1 (1971): 5–15.
——, ed. *Staat und Gesellschaft in der modernen österreichischen Literatur*. Vienna: Österreichischer Bundesverlag, 1977.

Ausstellung: Salzburg im Vierjahresplan. Kultur und Wirtschaftsschau vom 27. Mai bis 4. Juni 1939. Salzburg: NS-Gauverlag, 1939.

Auswirkung der Salzburger Festspiele auf Wirtschaft und Arbeitsmarkt. Salzburg: Presse und Informationszentrum des Landes Salzburg, 1981.

Bäck, Helga. "Entwicklungsgeschichte des Salzburger Freilichttheaters. Diss., University of Vienna, 1964.

Baernreither, Josef. *Fragments of a Political Diary*. Josef Redlich, ed. London: Macmillan, 1930.

Bauer, Roger. "Hofmannsthals Konzeption der Salzburger Festspiele." *Hofmannsthal Forschungen* 2 (1972): 131–39.

Bauer, Rudolf, ed. *Entwicklung der altkatholischen Kirche in Salzburg*. Salzburg: n.p., 1923.

Baumgartner, Eduard. *Die Arbeit der Sozialdemokraten im Salzburger Landtag*. Salzburg: n.p., 1932.

——. *Die Arbeit der Sozialdemokraten in den Gemeinden Salzburgs und die Hemmnisse dieser Arbeit*. Salzburg: n.p., 1931.

Beneš, Eduard. *Das Problem Mitteleuropas und die Lösung der österreichischen Frage*. Prague: Orbis, 1932.

Benz, Richard. *Ein Kulturprogramm: Die Notwendigkeit einer geistigen Verfassung*. Jena: Diederichs, 1920.

Bergsträsser, Arnold. *Hofmannsthal und der europäische Gedanke*. Kiel: Kieler Universitätsreden, 1951.

——. "The Holy Beggar: Religion and Society in Hugo von Hofmannsthal's *Great World Theater of Salzburg*." *Germanic Review* 20, No. 4 (1945): 261–86.

Bernhard, Thomas. *Der Atem*. Salzburg: Residenz, 1976.

——. *Der Keller*. Salzburg: Residenz, 1978.

——. *Die Ursache*. Salzburg: Residenz, 1976.

Bertram, Ernst. *Nietzsche: Versuch einer Mythologie*. Berlin: G. Bondi, 1918.

——. *Über Hugo von Hofmannsthal*. Dortmund: Ruhfus, 1907.

Binder-Johnson, Hildegard. *Die Haltung der Salzburger in Georgia zur Sklaverei (1734–1750)*. Salzburg: Gesellschaft für Salzburger Landeskünde, 1939.

Blaukopf, Kurt. *Gustav Mahler oder der Zeitgenosse der Zukunft*. Vienna: Fritz Molden, 1969.

Boberski, Heinrich. *Das Theater der Benediktiner an der alten Universität Salzburg*. Vienna: Verlag der österreichischen Akademie der Wissenschaften, 1978.

Borkenau, Franz. *Austria and After*. London: Faber & Faber, 1938.

Bottomore, Tom, and Patrick Goode, eds. *Austro-Marxism*. Oxford: Oxford University Press, 1978.

Boyer, John W. *Political Radicalism in Late Imperial Vienna*. Chicago: University of Chicago Press, 1981.

Brantley, R. L. "The Salzburgers in Georgia." *Georgia Historical Quarterly* 14 (1930): 214–24.

Brecht, Bertolt. "Salzburg Dance of Death." Eric Bentley, trans. *Encore* 11, no. 5 (1964): 26–30.

Broch, Hermann. *Hugo von Hofmannsthal and His Time: The European Imagination, 1860–1920*. Michael P. Steinberg, ed. and trans. Chicago: University of Chicago Press, 1984.

Brockhausen, Carl. *Deutschösterreich: Kulturpolitik, Wirtschaft*. Maria L. Klausberger, ed. Halberstadt: H. Meyer, 1927.

Bullock, Alan. *Hitler: A Study in Tyranny.* New York: Harper & Row, 1964.

Bunzl, John, and Bernd Marin. *Antisemitismus in Österreich: Sozialhistorische and soziologische Studien.* Innsbruck: Inn-Verlag, 1983.

Bury, J. B. *History of the Papacy in the Nineteenth Century.* London: Macmillan, 1930.

Butler, E. M. "Hofmannsthal's *Elektra*: A Graeco-Freudian Myth." *Journal of the Warburg Institute* 2 (1938): 164–75.

Canetti, Elias. *Die Fackel im Ohr.* Munich: Carl Hanser, 1980.

Carsten, F. L. *Fascist Movements in Austria: From Schönerer to Hitler.* London: Sage, 1977.

Coghlan, Brian. *Hofmannsthal's Festival Dramas.* Melbourne: Melbourne University Press, 1964.

Cooper, Artemis, ed. *A Durable Fire: Letters of Duff and Diana Cooper.* New York: Watts, 1984.

Damisch, Heinrich. "Zur Geschichte der Salzburger Festspiele." *Neueste Musiknachrichten,* 22 July 1933.

Diamant, Alfred. *Austrian Catholics and the First Republic.* Princeton: Princeton University Press, 1960.

———. *Austrian Catholics and the Social Question, 1918–1933.* Gainesville: University of Florida Press, 1959.

Doblhoff-Dier, Joseph Freiherr von. *Zur Erhebung des Fremdenverkehres in Salzburg.* Munich: n.p., 1888.

Doswald, Herman K. "The Reception of *Jedermann* in Salzburg, 1920–1966." *German Quarterly* 40 (1967): 212–25.

Dowden, Stephen, ed. *Hermann Broch: Language, Philosophy, Politics: The Yale Broch Symposium, 1986.* Columbia, S.C.: Camden House, 1988.

Ehalt, Hubert, Gernot Heiss, and Hannes Stekl, eds. *Glücklich Ist, Wer Vergisst . . . ? Das Andere Wien um 1900.* Vienna: Böhlau, 1986.

Fellner, Fritz, ed. *Dichter und Gelehrter: Hermann Bahr und Josef Redlich in ihren Briefen, 1896–1934.* Salzburg: Wolfgang Neugebauer, 1980.

———. "Österreich und die deutsche Frage im 19. und 20. Jahrhundert." In *Wiener Beiträge zur Geschichte der Neuzeit IX.* Vienna: Verlag für Geschichte und Politik, 1982.

Fellner, Günter. *Antisemitismus in Salzburg, 1918–1938.* Vienna: Geyer, 1979.

Festführer zum dritten Verbandsturnfest der Christlich Deutschen Turnerschaft Österreichs, Salzburg, 10.–13.Juli 1930. Salzburg: Turnerschaft Österreichs, 1930.

Fick, Richard. *Auslandsdeutschtum und Kulturpolitik.* Neumünster: n.p., 1920.

Fiedler, Leonhard. "Drama und Regie im gemeinsamen Werk von Hugo von Hofmannsthal und Max Reinhardt." *Modern Austrian Literature,* 7 (1974): 183–208.

———. *Festschrift für Rolf Badernhausen.* Munich: n.p., 1977.

Fischer, Hans Conrad. "Die Idee der Salzburger Festspiele und ihre Verwirklichung." Diss., University of Munich, 1954.

Fraenkel, Josef, ed. *The Jews of Austria: Essays on Their Life, History, and Destruction.* London: Vallentine & Mitchell, 1967.

Franckenstein, Georg von. *Facts and Features of My Life.* London: Cassell, 1939.

Fuchs, Albert. "L'idée nationale, l'européanisme, et l'entente planétaire chez Hofmannsthal." *Hommages strasbourgeois à Hofmannsthal.* Strasbourg: n.p., 1959.

Fuhrich-Leisler, Edda. *Hugo von Hofmannsthal auf dem Theater seiner Zeit.* Salzburg: Max Reinhardt Forschungs- und Gedenkstätte, 1974.

——. *Jedermann in Europa*. Salzburg: Max Reinhardt Forschungs- und Gedenkstätte, 1978.

——. *Max Reinhardt in Europa und Amerika*. Salzburg: Max Reinhardt Forschungs- und Gedenkstätte, 1976.

——. *Max Reinhardt: Regisseur und seine Schauspieler*. Salzburg: Max Reinhardt Forschungs- und Gedenkstätte, 1973.

——. *Die Reinhardt-Bühnen*. Salzburg: Max Reinhardt Forschungs- und Gedenkstätte, 1971.

Gallup, Stephen. *A History of the Salzburg Festival*. London: Weidenfeld & Nicolson, 1987.

Gebert, Erich. *Die wirtschaftlichen Auswirkungen des Fremdenverkehrs für Salzburg*. Salzburg: n.p., 1923.

Geissler, Klaus. *Zur Literatur und Literaturgesellschaft Österreichs um die Jahrhundertwende*. Weimarer Beiträge XX, 1974.

Gerlach, Hans Hartmut. *Politik und Gesellschaft im Essaywerk Hugo von Hofmannsthals*. Ann Arbor: University Microfilms, 1967.

Gregor, Josef. *Meister und Meisterbriefe um Hermann Bahr*. Vienna: Bauer, 1947.

——. *Theater des Volkes*. Vienna: Deutscher Verlag für Jugend und Volk, 1943.

Griffiths, Richard. *Fellow Travellers of the Right: British Enthusiasts for Nazi Germany, 1933–1939*. Oxford: Oxford University Press, 1983.

Gutman, Robert W. *Richard Wagner: The Man, His Mind, and His Music*. New York: Harvest, 1968.

Haas, Willy. *Die literarische Welt*. Munich: List, 1958.

Hadamovsky, Franz. *Ausstellung: Hugo von Hofmannsthal*. Salzburg: Amt der Salzburger Landesregierung, 1959.

——. *Richard Strauss und Salzburg*. Salzburg: Residenz, 1964.

Hamburger, Michael. *Hofmannsthal: Three Essays*. Princeton: Princeton University Press, 1972.

Hanisch, Ernst. *Die Ideologie des politischen Katholizismus in Österreich, 1918–1938*. Vienna: Geyer, 1977.

——. *Nationalsozialistische Herrschaft in der Provinz Salzburg im Dritten Reich*. Salzburg: Schriftenreihe des Landespressebüros, 1983.

——. "Provinz und Metropole: Gesellschaftsgeschichtliche Perspektiven der Beziehungen des Bundeslandes Salzburg zu Wien (1918–1938)." *Beiträge zur Föderalismusdiskussion*. Alfred Edelmayer, ed. Salzburg: Salzburg Dokumentationen Nr. 59, 1981.

——. "Die sozialdemokratische Fraktion im Salzburger Landtag, 1918–1934." *Bewegung und Klasse*, ed. G. Botz. Vienna: Europa, 1978, pp. 247–68.

——. "Zur Frühgeschichte des Nationalsozialismus in Salzburg (1913–1925)." *Mitteilungen der Gesellschaft für Salzburger Landeskunde* 117 (1977): 371–410.

Hanisch, Ernst, and Ulrike Fleischer. *Im Schatten berühmter Zeiten: Salzburg in den Jahren Georg Trakls (1887–1914)*. Salzburg: Otto Müller, 1986.

Haupt, Jürgen. *Konstellationen Hugo von Hofmannsthals: Harry Graf Kessler, Ernst Stadler, Bertolt Brecht*. Salzburg: Residenz, 1970.

Heer, Friedrich. *Gottes erste Liebe: Die Juden im Spannungsfeld der Geschichte*. Esslingen: Bechtle, 1967.

——. *Der Kampf um die österreichische Identität*. Vienna: Hermann Böhlau, 1981.

Hess, Konrad. *Von Nietzsche zu Pannwitz*. Langnau: Buchdruckerei Emmenthaler Blatt, 1963.

Heuss, Theodor. *Hugo von Hofmannsthal: Eine Rede.* Tübingen: Wunderlich, 1954.

Heyworth, Peter. *Otto Klemperer: His Life and Times,* vol. I. Cambridge: Cambridge University Press, 1983.

Hofmannsthal, Hugo von. *Deutsche Epigramme.* Munich: Bremer Presse, 1923.

——. *Gesammelte Werke in Einzelausgaben.* Herbert Steiner, ed. Frankfurt am Main: S. Fischer, 1945–1955.

——. "Vienna Letter." *The Dial,* February 1923, pp. 281–88.

——. *Wert und Ehre der deutschen Sprache.* Munich: Bremer Presse, 1927.

Hofmannsthal, Hugo von, and Leopold von Andrian. *Briefwechsel.* Walter H. Perl, ed. Frankfurt am Main: S. Fischer, 1968.

——, and Max Mell. *Briefwechsel, 1907–1929.* Margret Dietrich and Heinz Kindermann, eds. Heidelberg: Lampert Schneider, 1982.

——, and Helene von Nostitz. *Briefwechsel.* Oswald von Nostitz, ed. Frankfurt am Main: S. Fischer, 1965.

——, and Josef Redlich. *Briefwechsel.* Helga Fussgänger, ed. Frankfurt am Main: S. Fischer, 1971.

——, and Paul Zifferer, *Briefwechsel.* Hilde Burger, ed. Vienna: Verlag der Österreichischen Staatsdruckerei, 1984.

Hugo von Hofmannsthal in der österreichischen Nationalbibliothek: Katalog der Ausstellung. Vienna: Österreichischer Nationalbibliothek, 1971.

The Hofmannsthal Collection in the Houghton Library. Heidelberg: Lothar Stiehm, 1974.

Holl, Oskar. "Dokumente zur Entstehung der Salzburger Festspiele: Unveröffentlichtes aus der Korrespondenz der Gründer." *Maske und Kothurn* 13 (1967): 148–80.

Holzer, Rudolf. *Das Salzburger Festspielhaus.* Salzburg: Verlag der Salzburger Festspielhausgemeinde, 1926.

Hoppe, Manfred. "Hofmannsthals 'Ruinen von Athen': Das Festspiel als 'konservative Revolution.' " *Jahrbuch der deutschen Schillergesellschaft* 26 (1982): 325–56.

——. *Literatentum, Magie und Mystik im Frühwerk Hugo von Hofmannsthals.* Berlin: Walter de Gruyter, 1968.

Hubalek, Elisabeth. "Hermann Bahr im Kreise Hofmannsthals und Reinhardts." Diss., University of Vienna, 1953.

Huber, Gerlinde. "Hugo von Hofmannsthal der Österreicher in den Lesebüchern der Ersten und Zweiten Republik." Diplomenarbeit, University of Klagenfurt, 1970.

Huber, Wolfgang, ed. *Franz Rehrl, Landeshauptmann von Salzburg, 1922–1938.* Salzburg: SN-Verlag, 1975.

Hurdes, Felix. *Österreichische Kulturpolitik.* Vienna: Österreichischer, 1948.

Innes, C. D. *Modern German Drama: A Study in Form.* Cambridge: Cambridge University Press, 1979.

Jakob, Waltraut. *Salzburger Zeitungsgeschichte.* Salzburg: Salzburg Dokumentationen, 1979.

Janik, Allan, and Stephen Toulmin. *Wittgenstein's Vienna.* New York: Simon & Schuster, 1973.

Jászi, Oscar. *The Dissolution of the Habsburg Monarchy.* Chicago: University of Chicago Press, 1929 (reprinted 1971).

Jelavich, Peter. *Munich and Theatrical Modernism: Politics, Playwriting, and Performance, 1890–1914.* Cambridge: Harvard University Press, 1985.

Johnston, William. *The Austrian Mind.* Berkeley: University of California Press, 1972.

Jones, Ernest. *The Life and Work of Sigmund Freud*. New York: Basic, 1953.

Kahofer, Gertrude. "Hugo von Hofmannsthals Beziehungen zu den Vorlagen seiner Dramen 'Jedermann,' 'Das Salzburger Grosse Welttheater,' 'Der Turm.' " Diss., University of Vienna, 1950.

Kaindl-Hönig, Max, ed. *Resonanz: Fünfzig Jahre der Salzburger Festspiele*. Salzburg: SN-Verlag, 1971.

Karbach, Oscar. "Die politischen Grundlagen des deutsch-österreichischen Antisemitismus." *Zeitschrift für die Geschichte der Juden* I (1964): 1–178.

Die katholische Universität in Salzburg. Bericht über den akademischen Festakt vom 15. August mit der Ansprache des Bundespräsidenten Wilhelm Miklas und der Festrede des Univ. Prof. Wilhelm Schmidt S.V.D. Salzburg: Katholischer Universitäts-Verein, 1934.

Kaut, Josef. *Die Salzburger Festspiele, 1920–1981*. Salzburg: Residenz, 1982.

——. *Der steinige Weg: Geschichte der Sozialistischen Arbeiterbewegung im Lande Salzburg*. Salzburg: Graphia Druck- und Verlaganstalt, 1982.

Kerber, Erwin, ed. *Ewiges Theater: Salzburg und seine Festspiele*. Munich: Piper, 1935.

Kerekes, Lajos. "Zur Aussenpolitik Otto Bauers 1918/19: Die 'Alternative' zwischen Anschlusspolitik und Donaukonfederation." *Vierteljahrschrift für Zeitgeschichte* 22 (1947): 18–45.

Kern, Peter Christoph. *Zur Gedankenwelt des späten Hofmannsthal*. Heidelberg: Carl Winter, 1969.

Kindermann, Heinz. *Die deutsche Gegenwartsdichtung in der Aufbau der Nation*. Berlin: Junge Generation, 1936.

——. *Die europäische Sendung des deutschen Theaters*. Vienna: Verlag der Ringbuchhandlung, 1944.

——. *Der grossdeutsche Gedanke in der Dichtung*. Münster: Coppenrath-Verlag, 1941.

——. *Heimkehr ins Reich: Grossdeutsche Dichtung aus Ostmark und Sudetenland, 1866–1938*. Leipzig: P. Reclam jun., 1939.

——. *Hugo von Hofmannsthal und die Schauspielkunst*. Vienna: Böhlau, 1969.

——. *Max Reinhardts Weltwirkung: Ursachen, Erscheinungsformen und Grenzen*. Vienna: Böhlau, 1969.

——. *Rufe über Grenzen der Dichtung und Lebenskampf der Deutschen im Ausland*. Berlin: Junge Generation, 1938.

——, ed. *Des deutschen Dichters Sendung in der Gegenwart*. Leipzig: P. Reclam jun., 1933.

Kitchen, Martin. *The Coming of Austrian Fascism*. London: Croom Helm, 1980.

Klaus, Josef. *Salzburgs Kulturausgabe*. Salzburg: n.p., 1950.

Klemperer, Klemens von. *Ignaz Seipel: Christian Statesman in a Time of Crisis*. Princeton: Princeton University Press, 1972.

Kohn, Hans. *Karl Kraus, Arthur Schnitzler, Otto Weininger: Aus dem jüdischen Wien der Jahrhundertwende*. Tübingen: J. C. B. Mohr, 1962.

Kolakowski, Leszek. "Der Mythos der menschlichen Einheit." In *Der Mensch ohne Alternative*. Munich: Piper, 1976.

Kopal, Pawel. *Das Slawentum und der deutsche Geist*. Jena: Eugen Diederichs, 1914.

Kraus, Jakob. *Hofmannsthals Wege zur Oper "Die Frau ohne Schatten": Rücksichten und Einflüsse auf die Musik*. Berlin: Walter de Gruyter, 1971.

Kraus, Karl. *Auswahl aus dem Werk*. Munich: Kösel-Verlag, 1957.

——. *Die letzten Tage der Menschheit*. Vienna: Die Fackel, 1926.

——, ed. *Die Fackel VIII* (1919–1922). Munich: Kösel-Verlag, 1968–76.

Kunisch, Hermann. "Hofmannsthals 'Politisches Vermächtnis.' " *Jahrbuch der Grill-parzer Gesellschaft* (1976), pp. 97–124.

Kutscher, Artur. *Vom Salzburger Barocktheater zu den Salzburger Festspielen.* Düsseldorf: Pflugschar, 1939.

Lach, Robert. "Die grossdeutsche Kultureinheit in der Musik." *Die Anschlussfrage.* Kleinwächter, Paller, eds. Vienna: Braumüller, 1930.

Lamprecht, Carl. *Über auswärtige Kulturpolitik.* Stuttgart: W. Kohlhammer, 1913.

Leichter, Otto. *Otto Bauer: Tragödie oder Triumph.* Vienna: Europa, 1970.

Lendl, Egon. *Salzburgs Stellung im österreichischen Raum: Inaugurationsrede vom 14. November 1964.* Salzburg: Salzburger Festreden, 1966.

Letz, Gudrun. "Die Mozart-Inszenierungen bei den Salzburger Festspielen." Diss., University of Vienna, 1963.

Loewenberg, Peter. "Austrian Portraits." In *Decoding the Past.* Berkeley: University of California Press, 1982.

Loos, Adolf. *Ins Leere Gesprochen.* Zurich, 1921 (reprinted in Vienna: Georg Prachner, 1981).

——. *Die potemkinsche Stadt.* Vienna: Georg Prachner, 1983.

——. *Trotzdem.* Innsbruck, 1921 (reprinted in Vienna: Georg Prachner, 1982).

Low, Alfred D. *The Anschluss Movement, 1918–1919 and the Paris Peace Conference.* Philadelphia: American Philosophical Society, 1974.

Luft, David S. *Robert Musil and the Crisis of European Culture.* Berkeley: University of California Press, 1980.

Lunzer, Heinz. *Hofmannsthals politische Tätigkeit in den Jahren 1914–1917.* Frankfurt am Main: Peter D. Lang, 1981.

Lützeler, Paul Michael, and Michael Kessler, eds. *Brochs theoretisches Werk.* Frankfurt am Main: Suhrkamp, 1988.

Luza, Radomir. *Österreich und die grossdeutsche Idee in der NS-Zeit.* Vienna: Böhlau, 1977.

——. *The Resistance in Austria: 1938–1945.* Minneapolis: University of Minnesota Press, 1984.

McGrath, William J. *Dionysian Art and Populist Politics in Austria.* New Haven: Yale University Press, 1974.

Magris, Claudio. *Lontano da dove: Joseph Roth e la tradizione ebraico-orientale.* Turin: Einaudi, 1971.

——. *Il mito absburgico nella letteratura austriaca moderna.* Turin: Einaudi, 1963.

Mann, Heinrich. *Ein Zeitalter wird besichtigt.* Berlin and Weimar: Aufbau, 1982.

Mann, Thomas. "Sufferings and Greatness of Richard Wagner." In *Essays by Thomas Mann.* New York: Vintage, 1957.

Mannheim, Karl. *Ideology and Utopia.* Edward Shils and Louis Wirth, trans. New York: Harcourt Brace, 1936.

——. *Man and Society in an Age of Reconstruction.* Edward Shils, trans. London: Routledge, 1940.

Maravall, José Antonio. *The Culture of the Baroque.* Terry Cochran, trans., Minneapolis: University of Minnesota Press, 1986.

Marin, Louis. *Portrait of the King.* Martha M. Houle, trans. Minneapolis: University of Minnesota Press, 1988.

Matejka, Viktor. *Grundlinien der Kulturpolitik in Österreich.* Vienna: Typographische Anstalt, 1938.

Mauelshagen, Carl. *The Salzburg Lutheran Expulsion and Its Impact.* New York: Vantage, 1962.

Mauser, Wolfgang. *Hugo von Hofmannsthal: Kritische Information.* Munich: Wilhelm Fink, 1977.

Mayer, Hans. "Die Frau ohne Schatten." In *Versuche über die Oper.* Frankfurt am Main: Suhrkamp, 1981.

———. *Outsiders: A Study in Life and Letters.* Denis M. Sweet, trans. Cambridge: MIT Press, 1982.

Mayrhuber, Alois. *Hugo von Hofmannsthal und die Kultur im steirischen Salzkammergut.* Frankfurt am Main: Freies Deutsches Hochstift, 1979.

Meister, Richard. *Salzburg, sein Boden, seine Geschichte und Kultur; Festgabe der 57. Versammlung deutscher Philologen und Schulmänner in Salzburg vom 25. bis 29. September.* Baden: Rohrer, 1929.

Meyer-Wendt, H. Jürgen. *Der frühe Hofmannsthal und die Gedankenwelt Nietzsches.* Heidelberg: Quelle & Meyer, 1973.

Mika, Emil. "Hugo von Hofmannsthal und die österreichische Idee." *Die Furche: Jahrbuch,* 1947, pp. 277–81.

Mis, Léon. "De Nietzsche (Naissance de la tragédie) à Hofmannsthal (Electre)." *Revue germanique* 29 (1938): 337–61.

Mommsen, Hans. *Die Sozialdemokratie und die Nationalitätenfrage im Habsburgischen Vielvölkerstaat.* Vienna: Europa, 1963.

Nadler, Josef. "Hermann Bahr und das katholische Österreich." *Neue Rundschau* 34 (1923): 490–502.

Naef, Karl J. "Das Salzburger grosse Welttheater." *Zeitschrift für deutsche Geistesgeschichte* 2 (1936): 251–59.

Nasko, Siegfried, ed. *Karl Renner in Dokumenten und Erinnerungen.* Vienna: Österreichischer Bundesverlag, 1982.

Neuwirth, Rudolfine. *Hermann Bahr und Österreich.* Diss., University of Vienna, 1946.

Newman, Karl J. *European Democracy between the Wars.* London: George Allen & Unwin, 1970.

Nikisch, Martin. "Richard Beer-Hofmann und Hugo von Hofmannsthal. Zu Beer-Hofmanns Sonderstellung im 'Wiener Kreis.' " Diss., University of Munich, 1980.

Ott, Brigitte. *Die Kulturpolitik der Gemeinde Wien, 1919–1934.* Diss., University of Vienna, 1968.

Oxaal, Ivar, Michael Pollak, and Gerhard Botz, eds. *Jews, Antisemitism, and Culture in Vienna.* London: Routledge & Kegan Paul, 1987.

Pannwitz, Rudolf. *Die deutsche Lehre.* Nuremberg: Hans Carl, 1919.

———. *Die Krisis der europäischen Kultur.* Munich: Hans Carl, 1917.

Pantle, Sherrill Hahn. *Die Frau ohne Schatten: An Analysis of Text, Music, and Their Relationship.* Bern: Peter Lang, 1978.

Pauley, Bruce F. *Hitler and the Forgotten Nazis: A History of Austrian National Socialism.* Chapel Hill: University of North Carolina Press, 1981.

Pawlowsky, Peter. "Die Idee Österreichs bei Hugo von Hofmannsthal." Diss., University of Vienna, 1960.

Pfabigan, Alfred, ed. *Ornament und Askese im Zeitgeist des Wien der Jahrhundertwende.* Vienna: Christian Brandstätter, 1985.

Pirker, Max. *Die Salzburger Festspiele.* Zurich: Amalthea, 1922.

Piscator, Erwin. *Das Politische Theater.* Reinbek bei Hamburg: Rowohlt, 1979 [1929].

Pogatschnigg, Gustav Adolf. *Salzburgs Leistung und Aufbau.* Salzburg: n.p., 1939.

Praxmarer, Konrad. *Revolution der Kulturpolitik.* Vienna: Zeitschriftenverlag Ployer, 1957.

———. *Salzburg und der deutsche Festspielgedanke.* Vienna: Braumüller, 1937.

Prieberg, Fred K. *Musik im NS-Staat.* Frankfurt am Main: S. Fischer, 1982.

Prossnitz, Gisela. *Das Salzburger Theater von 1892 bis 1944.* Diss., University of Vienna, 1965.

Pulzer, Peter G. J. *Die Entstehung des politischen Antisemitismus in Deutschland und Österreich, 1867–1914.* Gütersloh: Moehn, 1966.

Rabinbach, Anson. *The Crisis of Austrian Socialism: From Red Vienna to Civil War, 1927–1934.* Chicago: University of Chicago Press, 1983.

Read, Herbert. *The Politics of the Unpolitical.* London: Routledge, 1946.

Reich, Willi. *Arnold Schönberg oder der konservative Revolutionär.* Vienna: Fritz Molden, 1968.

Reinhardt, Gottfried. *Der Liebhaber: Erinnerungen an Max Reinhardt.* Munich: Knaur, 1973.

Reinhardt, Max, and Arthur Schnitzler. *Briefwechsel.* Renate Wagner, ed. Salzburg: O. Müller, 1971.

Rieber, Arnulf. *Vom Positivismus zum Universalismus: Untersuchungen z. Entwicklung und Kritik d. Ganzheitsbegriffs von Othmar Spann.* Berlin: Duncker & Humblot, 1971.

Ritter, Frederick. *Hugo von Hofmannsthal und Österreich.* Heidelberg: Lothar Stiehm, 1967.

Rozenblit, Marsha L. *The Jews of Vienna, 1867–1914: Assimilation and Identity.* Albany: State University of New York Press, 1983.

Rudolph, Hermann. *Kulturkritik und konservative Revolution. Zum kulturell-politischen Denken Hofmannsthals und seinem problemgeschichtlichen Kontext.* Tübingen: Max Niemeyer, 1971.

Die Salzburger Festspiele 1842–1960: Ihre Vorgeschichte und Entwicklung. Salzburg: Internationale Stiftung Mozarteum, 1960.

Sayler, Oliver Martin, ed. *Max Reinhardt and His Theatre.* New York: Brentano's, 1924.

Schaefer, Rudolph Heinrich. *Hugo von Hofmannsthal's "Arabella."* Bern: Peter Lang, 1967.

Schlereth, Thomas J. *The Cosmopolitan Ideal in Enlightenment Thought.* Notre Dame: University of Notre Dame Press, 1977.

Schönberg, Arnold. "Brahms the Progressive." In *Style and Idea.* Berkeley: University of California Press, 1984 [1951].

Schorske, Carl E. *Fin-de-siècle Vienna: Politics and Culture.* New York: Alfred A. Knopf, 1980.

———. "Mahler and Klimt: Social Experience and Artistic Revolution." *Daedalus* 3, no. 3 (1982): 29–49.

Schüler, Winfried. *Der Bayreuther Kreis von seiner Entstehung bis zum Ausgang der Wilhelminischen Ära: Wagnerkult und Kulturreform im Geiste völkischer Weltanschauung.* Münster: Aschendorff, 1971.

Schumann, Detlev W. "Gedanken zu Hofmannsthals Begriff der 'konservativen Revolution.' " *PMLA* 54 (1939): 853–99.

Schuschnigg, Kurt. *My Austria.* New York: Alfred A. Knopf, 1938.

Schwarz, Egon. *Hofmannsthal and Calderón.* Cambridge: Harvard University Press, 1962.

Siegfried, Klaus-Jörg. *Universalismus und Faschismus. Das Gesellschaftsbild Othmar*

Spanns. Zur politischen Funktion seiner Gesellschaftslehre und Ständestaatskonzeption.
Vienna: Europa, 1974.

Sofer, Johann. *Die Welttheater Hugo von Hofmannsthals und ihre Voraussetzung bei Heraklit und Calderón.* Vienna: Mayer, 1934.

Spann, Othmar. *Der Wahre Staat.* Leipzig: Quelle & Meyer, 1921.

Spenlé, Jean-Edouard. "La magie d'Elektra." *Revue d'Allemagne* 8 (1929): 948–56.

Srbik, Heinrich von. *Deutsche Einheit: Idee und Wirklichkeit vom Heiligen Reich bis Königgrätz.* Munich: F. Bruckmann, 1935.

Steiner, Herbert. "Erinnerungen an Hofmannsthal." In *Deutsche Beiträge.* Chicago: University of Chicago Press, 1947.

Stendel, Wolfgang. *Hofmannsthal und Grillparzer: Die Beziehungen im Weltgefühl und im Gestalten.* Würzburg: Konrad Triltsch, 1935.

Stuckenschmidt, H. H. *Schoenberg: His Life, World, and Work.* Humphrey Searle, trans. New York: Schirmer, 1977.

Styan, J. L. *Max Reinhardt.* Cambridge: Cambridge University Press, 1982.

Suval, Stanley. *The Anschluss Question in the Weimar Era; A Study of Nationalism in Germany and Austria, 1918–1932.* Baltimore: Johns Hopkins University Press, 1974.

Talmon, Jacob L. *The Myth of the Nation and the Vision of Revolution.* London: Secker & Warburg, 1981.

Tenschert, Roland. *Salzburg und seine Festspiele.* Vienna: Österreichischer Bundesverlag, 1947.

Thür, Hans. *Salzburg und seine Festspiele.* Munich: Wilhelm Andermann, 1961.

Timms, Edward. *Karl Kraus, Apocalyptic Satirist: Culture and Catastrophe in Habsburg Vienna.* New Haven: Yale University Press, 1986.

Timms, Edward, and Naomi Segal, eds. *Freud in Exile: Psychoanalysis and Its Vicissitudes.* New Haven: Yale University Press, 1988.

Tünkl, Heinz. "Goethe und Salzburg unter besonderer Berücksichtigung des Theaters und der Festspiele." Diss., University of Vienna, 1953.

Vielmetti, Nikolaus, et al. *Das österreichische Judentum: Voraussetzungen und Geschichte.* Vienna: Jugend & Volk, 1974.

Waitz, Sigismund. *Zur Sache der katholischen Universität in Salzburg.* Salzburg: n.p., 1935.

Walk, Cynthia. *Hofmannsthals "Grosses Welttheater": Drama und Theater.* Heidelberg: Carl Winter Universitätsverlag, 1980.

Walter, Bruno. *Briefe, 1894–1962,* Frankfurt am Main: S. Fischer, 1969.

Warmuth, Margerita. *Hofmannsthals kulturpolitisches Engagement. Das Trauerspiel 'Der Turm'.* Diplomenarbeit, University of Klagenfurt, 1978.

Weber, Max. "A Catholic University in Salzburg." In *Max Weber on Universities: The Power of the State and the Dignity of the Academic Calling in Imperial Germany.* Edward Shils, ed. Chicago: University of Chicago Press, 1976.

Weinzierl, Erika, and Kurt Skalnik, eds. *Österreich: 1918–1938.* Graz: Styria, 1983.

Weiss, Walter. "Salzburger Mythos? Hofmannsthals und Reinhardts Welttheater." *Zeitgeschichte* 2 (February 1975): 109–19.

Williams, C. E. *The Broken Eagle: The Politics of Austrian Literature from Empire to Anschluss.* New York: Harper & Row, 1974.

Zabrsa, Erika. "Die Opern von Richard Strauss bei den Salzburger Festspielen." Diss., University of Vienna, 1963.

Zaisberger, Friedrich, and Franz Heffeter. "Schriften zur Geschichte des Landes Salzburg 1960–1980." *Mitteilungen des Instituts für österreichische Geschichtsforschung.* Vienna: Hermann Böhlau, 1982.

Ziegler, Philip, *Diana Cooper.* London: Penguin, 1983.

Zuckmayer, Carl. *Über die musische Bestimmung des Menschen: Rede zur Eröffnung der Salzburger Festspiele 1970.* Salzburg: Salzburger Festreden, 1970.

Index

247

Index 249

Library of Congress Cataloging-in-Publication Data

Steinberg, Michael P.
   The meaning of the Salzburg Festival: Austria as theater and
ideology, 1890–1938 / Michael P. Steinberg.
      p.   cm.
   Bibliography: p.
   Includes index.
   ISBN 0-8014-2362-7 (alk. paper)
   1. Salzburger Festspiele. I. Title.
M246.8.S2F435   1990
780'.79'4363—dc20   89-42881